TPI® NEXT

Business Driven Test Process Improvement

TPI® NEXT

Business Driven Test Process Improvement

UTN Publishers　　　　　　　　　　's-Hertogenbosch 2009

Trademarks
TMap, TMap NEXT and TPI are registered trademarks of Sogeti Nederland B.V.
CMMI is a registered trademark of Carnegie Mellon University.
DSDM, Dynamic System Development Methodology is a registered brand of DSDM Corporation.
ISTQB is a trademark of the International Software Testing Qualifications Board.
Prince2 is a registered trademark of the Office of Government Commerce.
RUP and Rational Unified Process are registered trademarks of IBM.

Second run 2010

© 2009, Sogeti Nederland B.V.
All rights reserved. No part of this book may be reproduced or transmitted in any form or by any means, electronic, mechanical, photocopying, recording, or otherwise, without the prior written permission of the publisher. For information contact:
UTN Publishers
Willem van Oranjelaan 5
5211 CN 's-Hertogenbosch
The Netherlands
www.utn.nl

ISBN 9789072194978

Contents

Part 1 Introduction — 21

1 The next step in test process improvement — 23

2 Positioning testing and TPI NEXT — 27

- 2.1 The scope and value of testing — 28
  - 2.1.1 Testing and other quality measures — 28
  - 2.1.2 Product risks — 29
  - 2.1.3 Test levels within the Software Development Life Cycle — 30
- 2.2 The scope and value of test process improvement — 31
  - 2.2.1 Test process improvement enables you to align your test investment with business drivers — 32
  - 2.2.2 There are advantages to structuring the test process — 33
  - 2.2.3 Test process improvement integrates closely with software process improvement — 34
- 2.3 A reference model is needed to support test process improvement — 35
  - 2.3.1 The model has specific properties to ensure its quality and relevance — 36
  - 2.3.2 The Business Driven TPI model is an improvement of the original TPI model — 37

Part 2 The Business Driven TPI model — 39

3 The model — 41

- 3.1 The Business Driven TPI model provides insight into the quality of the test process — 41
- 3.2 Key areas break down the test process into different aspects — 43
- 3.3 Maturity levels provide a scale from Initial through to Optimizing — 47
- 3.4 Checkpoints measure the maturity of each Key area in an objective way — 49
- 3.5 The Test maturity matrix provides a visual overview — 50
- 3.6 For a specific test process the current situation is drawn in the Test maturity matrix — 51
- 3.7 Clusters of Checkpoints make Business Driven TPI a continuous model — 52

3.8	The current and target situation are drawn in the Test maturity matrix	53
3.9	Improvement suggestions indicate how Checkpoints can be met	54
3.10	Enablers relate the test process to other SDLC processes	55

4 Key areas — 57

4.1	Stakeholder commitment	58
4.2	Degree of involvement	63
4.3	Test strategy	67
4.4	Test organization	72
4.5	Communication	78
4.6	Reporting	83
4.7	Test process management	87
4.8	Estimating and planning	92
4.9	Metrics	96
4.10	Defect management	103
4.11	Testware management	108
4.12	Methodology practice	113
4.13	Tester professionalism	117
4.14	Test case design	121
4.15	Test tools	127
4.16	Test environment	132

Part 3 Improving Test Process Maturity — 137

5 BDTPI follows the steps of a generic change process — 139

5.1	(Generate) awareness	140
5.2	Determine goal, scope and approach	141
	5.2.1 Setting the goals	141
	5.2.2 Determining the scope	142
	5.2.3 Define the approach	144
5.3	Assess current situation	145
	5.3.1 Gathering information	146
	5.3.2 Analyzing the information	148
	5.3.3 Describe the strengths, weaknesses, opportunities and threats	150
5.4	Define improvements	151

5.5	Make a plan of action	153
5.6	Implement actions	155
5.7	Evaluate and redirect	155

Part 4 Business Driven Improvement — 157

6 Business Driven Test Process Improvement — 159

6.1	BDTPI aims at a specific result	159
6.2	The BDTPI model used in a business driven manner	160
6.3	Business drivers affect the use of the model	163
	6.3.1 BDTPI used to make sure that IT services are reliable and secure	164
	6.3.2 BDTPI used to support Effective automated solutions	166
	6.3.3 BDTPI used to Shorten the Time to market	168
	6.3.4 BDTPI used to Improve cost efficiency of IT	172
	6.3.5 BDTPI used to Improve transparency and understanding of IT	176
6.4	Cost and Benefit of Test Process Improvement	180
	6.4.1 Introduction	180
	6.4.2 Value for money	180
	6.4.3 Cost	181
	6.4.4 Benefits	182

7 The BDTPI Model can be used in any situation — 187

7.1	BDTPI can be used in iterative development methods	187
	7.1.1 Iterative development and testing	188
	7.1.2 Iterative development and test process improvement	189
7.2	BDTPI can be used in agile development methods	191
	7.2.1 Agile development and testing	191
	7.2.2 Agile development and test process improvement	193
7.3	BDTPI can help with multiple test processes	201
	7.3.1 Multiple test processes and testing	201
	7.3.2 Multiple test processes and test process improvement	201
7.4	BDTPI can be used to set up the test process from scratch	203
	7.4.1 Testing from scratch	203
	7.4.2 Test process improvement from scratch	204
7.5	BDTPI can be used in software maintenance	205
	7.5.1 Functional maintenance and testing	205
	7.5.2 Functional maintenance and test process improvement	206
7.6	BDTPI can be used within software process improvement	207
	7.6.1 SPI and testing	208

	7.6.2 SPI and test process improvement	211
	7.6.3 Maximizing ROI when combining Business Driven TPI and CMMI	214
7.7	**BDTPI can be used with outsourcing and offshoring**	**217**
	7.7.1 Outsourcing and testing	218
	7.7.2 Outsourcing and test process improvement	218
7.8	**BDTPI can be used with managed test services**	**220**
	7.8.1 Managed test service	220
	7.8.2 Managed test services and test process improvement	221
7.9	**BDTPI can be used in development testing**	**223**
	7.9.1 Development testing	224
	7.9.2 Development testing and test process improvement	226
7.10	**BDTPI can be used for evaluation**	**227**
	7.10.1 Evaluation and static testing	227
	7.10.2 Evaluation and test process improvement	229
7.11	**BDTPI can be used for integration**	**230**
	7.11.1 Integration and testing	232
	7.11.2 Integration and test process improvement	233

8 The BDTPI Model has proven its value in practice — 235

8.1	Generate awareness	235
8.2	Determine goals, scope and approach	235
8.3	Assess the current situation	237
	8.3.1 Interviews and document study provide the information needed about the test process	237
	8.3.2 The results are shown in the Test maturity matrix	240
8.4	Define improvements	243
8.5	Make a plan of action	244
8.6	Implement actions	246
8.7	Evaluate and redirect	247

Appendices — 249

A Appendix: Maturity of the use of test tools — 251

A.1	Maturity in the use of test tools	251
	A.1.1 Tool-specific maturity stages	251
	A.1.2 Application of the tool-specific maturity stages	252
	A.1.3 Types of tools	253
A.2	Test management tools	253
	A.2.1 Test management tools at a tool-focused maturity stage	255

	A.2.2 Test management tools at a process-focused maturity stage	255
	A.2.3 Test management tools at a goal-focused maturity stage	255
A.3	Automated test execution tools	256
	A.3.1 Automated test execution tools at a tool-focused maturity stage	257
	A.3.2 Automated test execution tools at a process-focused maturity stage	257
	A.3.3 Automated test execution tools at a goal-focused maturity stage	258
A.4	Performance test tools	258
	A.4.1 Performance test tools at a tool-focused maturity stage	259
	A.4.2 Performance test tools at a process-focused maturity stage	259
	A.4.3 Performance test tools at a goal-focused maturity stage	260

B Appendix: Creating new Clusters — 261

B.1 Introduction — 261

B.2 Cost reduction as an example — 261

B.3 Re-clustering — 262
  B.3.1 Categorized Key areas — 263
  B.3.2 Shift Checkpoints to new Clusters. — 263
  B.3.3 Taking dependencies into account — 264
  B.3.4 Balancing the Clusters — 266

C Appendix: Backwards compatibility — 269

C.1 Introduction — 269

C.2 Transform assessment information to the BDTPI model — 269

C.3 Transform the original TPI matrix into the Business Driven TPI matrix — 269
  C.3.1 Groups of Key areas — 269
  C.3.2 Two examples of TPI maturity — 270
  C.3.3 Working with the conversion table — 272
  C.3.4 After conversion — 273

Glossary — 275

Bibliography — 287

About Sogeti — 289

Index — 291

Foreword by Paul Hermelin, CEO Capgemini S.A.

Over the past decade, the structured testing of software has grown to be an acknowledged discipline and profession in its own right. The complexity of integrated software from multiple sources, both bespoke and packaged, and over multiple platforms, requires rigorous and exacting standards of testing to minimize the potential business risks of IT systems failure. Sogeti's Test Process Improvement (TPI®) methodology, developed in 1998, has been instrumental in helping many organizations improve their overall test processes, an essential initiative to ensuring the quality of information systems and critical business processes. Providing insight into the maturity of the test process, TPI has offered logical and practical steps to enhance test efficiency and effectiveness, and moreover to instill a belief in achieving a permanent improvement cycle. As in most things in life, there is always room for improvement.

I am therefore delighted to introduce you to TPI® NEXT, another step forward in raising the standards of test process improvement. This completely revised version has been a truly collaborative initiative. Firstly, it is a measure of the trust that our worldwide customers have placed in the effectiveness of the original TPI model that they have been actively involved in providing us with 'live' examples of the enhancements they wanted made. Secondly, our own TPI specialists' hands-on experience of implementing TPI in organizations, public and private, all over the world, has been considerable.

Combining this valuable feedback, a team of Sogeti professionals, supported by their Capgemini colleagues, has developed a significantly revised model that takes the business drivers of the organization as its starting point. This is an essential difference. IT strategy is generally now much more overtly aligned to business strategy. This alignment therefore filters down to individual systems and processes, so enhancing the test process must be considered in this context.

Since business drivers change over time and from entity to entity, this model is flexible and adaptable, and works in synch with Sogeti's other world-leading test methodology, TMap®. Also, input from renowned industry experts such as Professor Winter, has enabled us to take care that TPI NEXT also aligns perfectly with ISTQB-based testing and other software quality methods.

I am convinced that this new business-driven approach will not only help your organization improve the quality of its software testing and therefore its overall IT development process, but also at a pace that enables you to stay at the forefront of and competitive in your market.

Foreword by Paul Hermelin, CEO Capgemini S.A.

My thanks go to everyone who has worked to create this improved TPI model and I am sure that it will continue to make a significant contribution to the testing profession over the coming decade.

Paul Hermelin
CEO Capgemini S.A.

Foreword by Professor Mario Winter

Needless to say, software is one of the key assets of today's organizations. Needless to say too, that the rate of change of today's life is rapidly increasing. So what is one of the key business values of software? Software should add flexibility (or should I have said agility?) to its operating organization! Flexibility of software is needed on all scales: On a micro scale, where single features of the software have to follow changes of individual functional requirements, for example due to changes of law or other regulations; on a meso scale, where single modules or applications have to follow changes of non-functional requirements for example due to changed platforms or COTS software; and on a macro scale, where whole systems or application landscapes have to follow organizational or market changes due to mergers or technological advances.
Flexibility is one of several quality requirements for software, all of which have to be assured by constructive and analytical quality assurance measures. Since testing is one of the key analytical quality assurance measures, it plays a key role in achieving business value of software. The International Software Testing Qualifications Board (ISTQB®) affirms in its Certified Tester® Foundation Level syllabus that, besides finding and preventing defects (before the customer finds them), the main business value of testing is to gain confidence in the level of quality and to provide information for decision making. All in all, in order to gain quality and business value, a well structured testing process is essential.
Unfortunately, many of today's IT departments are a long way from owning such a well structured test process, which is well aligned with the whole software development lifecycle process. Thus the assessment and improvement of testing processes is extremely important. For you and me, as software quality or testing professionals, Sogeti's Test Process Improvement (TPI®) is one of the most prominent models or methods to this end. First published in 1998, TPI® was aligned to Sogeti's TMap® approach of software testing and, since then, it has been approved by many evaluations as being practical and timely.
But as well as testing, also the improvement of the testing process is not an end, but only a means to an end - an end, which may differ from organization to organization! My own experiences using TPI® in different organizations have been twofold. On the one hand, due to the key areas and checkpoints of TPI®, there was a clear way to assess and visualize the current state of a testing process via the TPI® matrix. But on the other hand, the way to improve the testing process in the context of the organization and the improvement of the whole software development lifecycle process was not so clear. So most of all I needed some flexibility (or should I have said tailorability?) of the TPI® model with regard to the different software development processes and process improvement models.

Foreword by Professor Mario Winter

Sogeti's answer to this need now lies in front of you: TPI® NEXT, the Business Driven Test Process Improvement model (BDTPI)! In addition to many other updates and clarifications, the main enhancement of TPI® NEXT is its built-in flexibility on all scales: On a micro scale, where checkpoints and improvement suggestions are now stated very generally and allow for adaption to methods, techniques, and tools already used in your testing department; on a meso scale, where the new concept of Enablers link Key areas of the testing process to methods, techniques and tools already used in your software development lifecycle process; last, but not least, on a macro scale, where the new concept of clusters allows the improvement path to be tailored to the business goals and needs of your organization.

If you have not started improving your testing process, now it is the time to begin, and, with the TPI® NEXT book at hand, it is now even easier to do so and to convince all of your stakeholders of its business value. But also, if you are already on the way to improving your testing process, a close look at Business Driven TPI will help you focus even more on the goal of improving your testing process, namely bringing business value to your organization!

Mario Winter

Prof. Dr. Mario Winter is currently the speaker for the SIG on Testing, Analysis and Verification (TAV) of the German Gesellschaft für Informatik e.V. (GI). He is a founding member of the German Testing Board e.V. (GTB) and authored respectively co-authored many publications on software quality, among them Software Testing Practice: Test Management.

Preface

Our society has become totally dependent on IT systems. Nowadays, it is simply one of the necessities of life. If an IT system fails, people not only lose time (waiting for it to be repaired), or money (purchasing a replacement system), but even our lives can be at stake (through malfunction of medical equipment).
Therefore all organizations that create or implement IT systems know that testing is a 'must'. Modern IT is totally integrated and thus complex, and complex systems will always contain faults and flaws. The testing profession mitigates the risks that are related to these imperfections, by both measuring quality and reporting on the risks that were determined by relevant stakeholders, and by taking measures so that the greatest risks are covered first and most comprehensively. This, in itself, is a challenging process and, in an ever-changing world, there is a constant need for improving the test process.
Sogeti's Test Process Improvement model (TPI®) was developed in the second half of the nineties when organizations were experiencing the negative outcomes of faulty systems and had become aware of the increasing need to improve their test processes. The original TPI book, first published in 1998, has grown to be an enormous success, having been translated into various languages and sold all over the world. Moreover, the model has been used by thousands of professional testers and has demonstrated its value in many situations, in industries ranging from finance to automotive.
As you can imagine, in over a decade of use, our customers, colleagues and ourselves gathered a huge amount of experience and best practices. So ten years after the original book was published, Sogeti's division Software Control in the Netherlands initiated an international project to bring this valuable learning together and create a revised version of TPI.
Along the way, we did more than just update the model. We used the accumulative experience to add new features (such as Enablers and Clusters) to the model, and to rearrange the Key areas. Actually we ourselves were surprised that so many elements of such a robust and successful model could still be improved!
Nowadays, business drivers are much more important within IT than they were ten years ago and, to ensure alignment with those business drivers, we have created the concept of Clusters. This is a major improvement because it enables you to align the improvement process to the specific business situation. But the model can also still be used as it is, using the base Clusters. And we have taken care of 'backwards compatibility' so that you can still compare the outcomes of an assessment with the new model to your historical data.

Preface

This book contains the knowledge and experience of many people from all over the world without whom we would not have been able to achieve this result. Therefore we would like to express our thanks to the following contributors:
First we would like to thank Cecile Davis and Marco Jansen van Doorn of Sogeti Netherlands for creating the sections on Agile testing and Tooling respectively.
Initially, we discussed what to improve and how to improve it; Debby de Laet of Sogeti Belgium must be mentioned for her contribution at this stage.
In subsequent discussions, many colleagues joined the team and helped us review the various drafts. This book is a truly international endeavor. Sogeti and Capgemini colleagues from nine countries reviewed and contributed to the book's content.

In no particular order we would like to thank: Markus Adam, Marc Barnscheidt and Hubert Beckmann of Sogeti Germany; Göran Fransson, Björn Ömnan and Gudrun Wettermark of Sogeti Sweden; Fran O'Hara and Stephen Hyland of Sogeti Ireland; Geert Vanhove of Sogeti Belgium; Trude Rosendal and Gro Rognstad of Sogeti Norway; Ole Christian Hansen of Sogeti Denmark; Dan Hannigan and Joy Thiele of Sogeti USA; Anand Padhye and Ajay Walgude of Capgemini India; Julian Bensaid, Maurice Siteur and John van Veen of Capgemini Netherlands; and last, but not least, Leo van der Aalst, Rob Baarda, Dré Robben, Monique Bax, Harm de Vries, Frank Geerts, Gert Stad, Marc Roekens, Niek Fraanje, Pepijn Paap, Andréas Prins, Thomas Veltman, Ewald Roodenrijs, Rob Kuijt, Maarten Strootman, Richard Ammerlaan, Joop van der Veen, Tom Hoppenbrouwer, Philip Boerse, Martin van den Berg, Jeroen van Berkel, Gina Utama, Robin Mackaij and Dimitri Fioole of Sogeti Netherlands.

As we mentioned, this book also includes first-hand feedback from many of our customers and other experts in the testing world. We would especially like to thank the following for their input and reviews:
Dennis van Velzen and Wilco Rakhorst of AFAS in the Netherlands;
Birdie Maobifei of Huawei in China;
Paul Jansen of KLM in the Netherlands;
Bonney Joseph of Wipro Ltd. in India;
Dr. Jürgen Eckstein and Matthias Wenzel of the Bundesagentur für Arbeit in Germany;
Ingrid van Andel of ASN Bank in the Netherlands.

As with any new product TPI NEXT had to be tested prior to release. We organized a field test within almost a dozen organizations, involving over twenty people from both business departments and test centers. From this field test, we gained very valuable feedback, which we used to enhance the model and make the checkpoints even more comprehensible and logical.

Preface

The field test was an invaluable source of information regarding the practical application of the Business Driven TPI model and we are grateful to the following clients and colleagues for their willingness to evaluate the revised model and to try it out in a 'real world' environment:
Ken Graham of Storebrand in Norway;
Gro Rognstad and Trude Britt Rosendal of Sogeti Norway;
Rune Andersson and Pia Mehra of Sogeti Sweden;
Björn Kemmelmeier of Telefónica o2 in Germany;
Jean Vaessen of Vodafone Group Services in Germany;
Dr. Matthias Hamburg and Markus Niehammer of Sogeti Germany;
Ine Lutterman and Thomas de Graaf of Equens in the Netherlands;
Thomas Som, Gerwin van Eersel, Reinder Otter and Ralf van der Ven of Capgemini in the Netherlands;
Gert Stad, Jille Berends, Dennis van den Bosch and Thomas Veltman of Sogeti in the Netherlands.

Two people reviewed our entire manuscript and we very much appreciate their help, input, sharp comments and support.
Thank you Mario Winter for your feedback, support and 'to the point' Foreword.
Thank you Martin Pol for your ideas, comments and 'food for thought', based on your vast TPI experience, that helped us balance the book's contents for the diverse audience.

Apart from input and help with knowledge on testing and its improvement, we also could not have made this book without help on practical matters. Clare Argent was of invaluable help in improving the language since none of the authors were native English speakers. Jan Tigchelaar undertook to get all the documents into a standard format, and Mathijs Jonker created one look and feel for the figures. Andréas Prins did a great job in designing the cover. Ralf van der Ven did a thorough comparison of CMMI goals and practices with BDTPI Checkpoints to create the specific CMMI clusters.

Thanks to all of you!

We remain very grateful for the ground-breaking work of Tim Koomen and Martin Pol who not only wrote the original TPI book but also taught us and many many others how to use the model and implement improvements.

We could never have done this work without support of our managers. Many thanks go to Nijs Blokland, Maarten Galesloot, Anders Hedensjö, Göran Fransson and Marc Valkier for enabling us to carry out this work even when economic circumstances made it difficult to maintain the

Preface

investment. They have shown that continual improvement is important, even (or maybe we should say especially) in difficult times.
Although it is a long list of 'thank yous', we realize we may have forgotten someone. If so, please accept our apologies for our fallibility.

We hope this book will inspire you to make further improvements to your own organization's test process. Please look at www.tpinext.com and keep sending us your feedback, comments and suggestions, so that in another ten years or so we can make another updated version of TPI®.

The central team of authors from Germany, Sweden and the Netherlands:
Alexander van Ewijk
Bert Linker
Marcel van Oosterwijk
Ben Visser
Gerrit de Vries
Loek Wilhelmus
Rik Marselis (project leader).

Diemen, October 2009

Recommendations

"The Business Driven TPI assessment supported us with a detailed analysis of our as-is state and produced new ideas to increase our quality of service, professionalism and efficiency."
Björn Kemmelmeier
Team leader Test & Validation
Telefónica o2
Germany

"Storebrand is focused on having a solid test process and we find it satisfying to have a well-known framework to investigate whether the process is good enough or not. With the release of TPI NEXT Storebrand looks forward to find improvements and required solutions based upon the business drivers. The opportunity to focus on different improvement areas with a business perspective is completely unique! Storebrand welcomes the Business Driven TPI model and looks forward to using BDTPI on a broader scale!"
Ken Graham
Head of Test Centre
Storebrand
Norway

"BDTPI is our compass towards improvement. It's a small step for testers but a giant leap in improving our test process."
Ine Lutterman
Testspecialist Testcentrum Cards Processing
Equens SE
The Netherlands

"Reflecting on our internal processes using Sogeti's Business Driven TPI has clearly shown the weaker areas and gave a clear guidance where we need to focus to improve the quality, cost and time to market components of our products by test process optimization."
Jean Vaessen
Head of Terminal Verification Management
Terminals Products & Technology
Vodafone Group Services GmbH
Germany

"TPI Next introduces business drivers into the TPI model that help aligning testing to support the organization's needs even better. Testing has already made the transition, along with other IT disciplines, from an "IT department" to an integral part of the business. During a field test at a

Recommendations

Dutch public organization, responsible for Employee Benefits and reintegration, we discovered that the introduction of business drivers took our TPI-discussions with our stakeholders to another level, discussing both testing ànd business issues. The new model also helped both the stakeholders and us to control and steer the improvement process by making the reporting easier and more accessible for non IT readers. After the field test our overall conclusion is that TPI Next is a valuable revision of TPI, which will help to further enlarge the added value of Testing."
Thomas Som
Managing Consultant Testing
Team lead TPI team Capgemini
The Netherlands

Part 1
Introduction

1 The next step in test process improvement

Over the past ten years, TPI® has proved to be the leading method to assess the maturity of an organization's or project's test process. This is a success we, at Sogeti, are very proud of. But this success by no means implies that we are 'done' and can rest on our laurels.

Much has changed over these ten years: instead of delivering vast, monolithic applications, a multitude of mainly web-based services, accessible through an 'Enterprise Service Bus' and used by numerous and sometimes unknown parties are developed. This development takes place both onsite and offsite and even offshore - at the other side of the world and with different parties in the demand and supply chain. This evolution had its impact on the related testing activities and the improvement of the testing process.

Also we now have extensive experience in applying TPI in the field of outsourcing, Agile development, integration and in every other new way of working that has emerged in recent years. Finally, management attention has shifted from being process-driven to business-driven. Obviously, how things are done matters, but what they deliver matters even more. To quote the Agile manifesto: "while there is value in the how, we value the what more!"

All this has led to the decision to update the original TPI model [16] with the experience of hundreds of assessments and improvement projects all over the world. The key here is 'update', not 're-invent'! The strengths of the model have been kept and some have been made even stronger. These strengths are:

- *The model itself:* the division of the test process into Key areas and, per Key area, Maturity levels, Checkpoints and Improvement suggestions.
  - We tightened the scope of the Key areas, making them more self-contained and removing some overlap. For instance, monitoring the progress of the test process and initiating corrective measures are now concentrated in Test process management, whereas in the original model Checkpoints to this effect were positioned in the Key area that described the demands on the deliverables.
    Also some new Key areas have been introduced and some of the original ones removed.
  - Instead of the non-descriptive Maturity levels A, B, C and D, we have introduced the well described Maturity levels: Initial, Controlled, Efficient and Optimizing for both the test process and the Key areas.
  - Checkpoints have all been considered, redefined and, where possible, made even more unambiguous than they already were. The Maturity

matrix in which all Checkpoints are positioned continues to be the means to benchmark your own maturity to your peers in the market.
- The Improvement suggestions, which have played such an important part in the practical use of the model, are enriched with ten years' of best practice.
- *Stepwise improvement:* one of the cornerstones of TPI's success. The new model is still focused on identifying improvement actions, both in the short term as well as in the long term. The TPI NEXT model has become more adaptive; it is now possible to adjust the steps to the specific needs of your organization, making this an even greater strength of the model (See also the section below about Clusters).
- *Independent:* TPI NEXT can easily be used in conjunction with Sogeti's world-renowned Test Management Approach - TMap®, but it is not restricted to TMap. No matter what test method is used, the business-driven TPI approach can be applied under any circumstance.
- *Improvement suggestions:* TPI NEXT provides more than just a means to assess the maturity of your test process or test organization. It also offers a wide range of hints and tips on *how* to actually improve them. These Improvement suggestions focus on how to meet Checkpoints. This might imply that these suggestions fit certain business objectives, development methods or organizational structures better than others. There is no 'one solution fits all' way to achieving Checkpoints. The Checkpoints of TPI NEXT implicitly guide you to possible improvement measures.

So what are the improvements that make the new model business-driven?
- *Clusters:* a Cluster is a set of coherent Checkpoints from various Key areas. The book provides a base Cluster arrangement that can be applied when there is no predominant business driver. Also, when TPI NEXT is applied within the context of an overall software process improvement initiative, the base Clusters are the logical choice. In general, one could say that in all the situations original TPI sufficed, TPI NEXT's base Clusters also suffice. But more importantly, when test process improvement is aimed at a specific result - whether it be test cost reduction, improved time to market, or any other business driver - the Clusters can be rearranged, ensuring that the most effective improvement measures end up at the top of the list.
This makes TPI NEXT very versatile: in a balanced, more or less standard situation, the base Clusters can be applied, in situations that require a fine-tuned approach, Clusters can be rearranged to reflect any specific business need or goal. Please note that, in the latter case, assessors, experienced in IT in general and TPI in particular, are required if the full potential of TPI NEXT is to be exploited!
- *Enablers:* testing is an integral part of software development, which both influences and is influenced by a wide variety of adjacent processes. This interaction between 'testing', 'developing' and 'production' is made

explicit by introducing the concept of Enablers: processes, practices or disciplines that closely interact with testing, and if executed well, positively influence testing maturity and vice versa. Conversely, if executed poorly, they negatively influence testing maturity and vice versa. Enablers play an important role in recognizing possible quick wins and ensuring a close alignment to overall software process improvement models such as CMMI or SPICE.

TPI NEXT can only be truly business-driven when the business itself actively participates. As a first step, business drivers such as 'good return on investment' or 'improved business continuity' need to be recognized. But just as important is a second step: prioritizing the Key areas jointly by all relevant stakeholders including the business. Leaving prioritization of the Key areas to the TPI NEXT consultants or IT staff constitutes a missed opportunity for the business to really steer improvement initiatives in the desired direction. There is no one single recipe for delivering a 'good return on investment'; that recipe must always be shaped by, and attuned to your own organization. But no matter what, TPI NEXT can always provide the recipe!

2 Positioning testing and TPI NEXT

Testing is a part of the software development life cycle (SDLC). Testing should be a structured and controllable process, detecting the 'right' defects and giving satisfactory advice within an acceptable amount of time and costs. Testing should be ready for future challenges such as new technologies, increasing complexity of information systems, shorter time to market, etc. In fact, testing should be in line with business goals.
However, test processes are not always this controlled and well arranged. Testing is often being criticized (testing is too expensive, testing doesn't find the most important defects, etc.) and this criticism can often be justified. But, since each organization is unique, its testing issues are also unique, requiring a customized solution. This book will help you to find the right solution for the testing challenges that you face now or in the future.
This TPI NEXT book describes a controlled and gradual improvement of testing. The Business Driven TPI model is a powerful tool that can be tailored to specific situations or needs and which takes into account the business drivers of an organization.

> **Definition - Business driver**
> A business driver is a management directive, usually a direct derivative of the organization's vision and/or business strategy, which desires specific outcomes of the organization at an operational level. A business driver is a reason, motivator or challenge for test process improvement, commonly indicated as (a combination of) result, risk, cost and time.

This new Business Driven TPI model, is an enhancement of the original TPI model [16], that has been used for more than ten years by many companies around the world with much success. The original has proven its value over the years, but now we recommend using the new model, Business Driven TPI, because it makes it easier to focus on business drivers and describes the application of BDTPI in any situation. Moreover, this model has been developed leveraging the practical real-life experience of users and consultants around the world, built up over the last decade.
The new Business Driven TPI model is - like the original model - based on best practices and has proven to be a very creditable and powerful model in extensive field tests.

The book is structured as follows:
- Part 1 'Introduction' comprises an introduction providing an overview of testing and business driven test process improvement.
- Part 2 'The Business Driven TPI model' describes the model itself, first the aspects of the model are described, followed by detailed descriptions of the Key areas.

2 Positioning testing and TPI NEXT

- Part 3 'Improving Test Process Maturity' elaborates the steps that are followed within Business Driven Test Process Improvement, from doing an assessment to implementing improvement actions.
- Part 4 'Business Driven Improvement' shows how the model can be applied in following a business-driven approach. This part also describes how to use the model in various situations, in support of diverse business goals, and different types of software development. Part 4 concludes with a case of how the Business Driven TPI model has been used in practice and the value it can generate.
- The book also contains appendices on the stages in the use of test tools, an algorithm for creating your own clusters and backwards compatibility with the original TPI model.

2.1 The scope and value of testing

The purpose of this section is to give an understanding of the context in which this book is written. Definitions and background information is provided on a number of test concepts and test terms, although it's not intended to describe a (new) test method nor to give a summary of an (existing) method. For practical reasons, TMap NEXT® [17] test terminology is used as reference, but if you are used to another frame of reference like ISTQB [11] you will not find much difficulty in the terms used. The next sections give a very brief introduction on testing. More information about testing can be found in existing literature.

2.1.1 Testing and other quality measures

Many definitions of testing exist. In essence, testing gives insight into the difference between the actual and the required behavior of an object. The test team needs a test object and a frame of reference to which that object should comply: a test basis.

> **Definition - Testing**
> Testing is a process that provides insight into, and advice on, quality and the related risks.

Often testing is described as finding defects, but this is actually a *means* to obtain insight into the quality of the software or process, not the *aim* of testing. Indeed, the number of defects found is not a 'pure' indication of the thoroughness of testing. A client does not want to be surprised by critical errors (previously undiscovered) that appear once the system is in use. But finding a lot of defects can still mean that other critical defects have not yet been found. Furthermore, finding 'only' a few defects can mean

2.1 The scope and value of testing

that the most critical have been overlooked, but also that the test object no longer contains any critical errors.
Delivering faultless and flawless products is still a challenge for most IT departments. Testing is not the sole solution for delivering quality products; testing is just one instrument that contributes to the overall quality enhancement of IT systems.

There are three kinds of quality measures:
- Preventive measures - that aim to *prevent* insufficient quality; for example documentation norms, implementation of methods, techniques, etc.
- Detective measures - that aim to *discover* insufficient quality; for example conducting reviews, walk-throughs and, of course, (dynamic) testing.
- Corrective measures - that aim to *remedy* insufficient quality, such as correcting defects discovered by testing.

Testing is not the cheapest quality measure since it is situated later in the development process and the costs of correction increase exponentially as demonstrated by Boehm [5]. Structural quality enhancement should start from the top down. Quality must be built, not tested, into a system! One of the building blocks of quality thinking is that prevention is better than cure, and that prevention is cheaper!

2.1.2 Product risks

One of the difficulties of testing is that it is practically impossible to test everything, because of time and cost constraints. But at the same time executed tests need to give sufficient certainty. Management has to decide how much time and money they want to spend on resolving uncertainty. The level of testing effort is dependent on the level of risks in bringing the IT system into operation.

> **Definition - Product risk**
> Product risk is the chance that a product fails in relation to the expected damage if this occurs.

Based on the assigned requirements and on the product risks involved test teams try to find the most important errors as early as possible and in the most efficient way. By mitigating possible damage to the business, testing preserves business value. Business value includes all forms of value that determine the health and well-being of the firm in the long-run. As such, testing can also be considered as an insurance against product risks.
Like a commercial insurance, it is extremely hard to calculate the product risks and the associated test costs. The principal stakeholder will take the lead in deciding the amount of insurance premium he or she wants to pay. But the role of the principal stakeholder stretches beyond providing

resources: strong, clear commissioning up front, including commitment from stakeholders, helps the test process to run smoothly. Testing should not be regarded as a process that only begins at the moment at which the object to be tested is delivered. A test process requires good planning and preparation before the actual 'measurement' can be done. Therefore testing should be involved early in the software development life cycle.

Of course these activities require a certain effort. Testing therefore costs money. But how much should testing cost? Or rather, when should you stop testing? The 'insurance premium' one has to pay depends on the coverage or extent of the insurance. The amount of costs allocated to testing should depend on the product risks. When a product is critical to an organization, society or the health/life of individuals then a test process should reflect that.

2.1.3 Test levels within the Software Development Life Cycle

The traditional V-model is a clear and concise way to explain how and when testing is involved in the software development life cycle; see Figure 2.1 below.

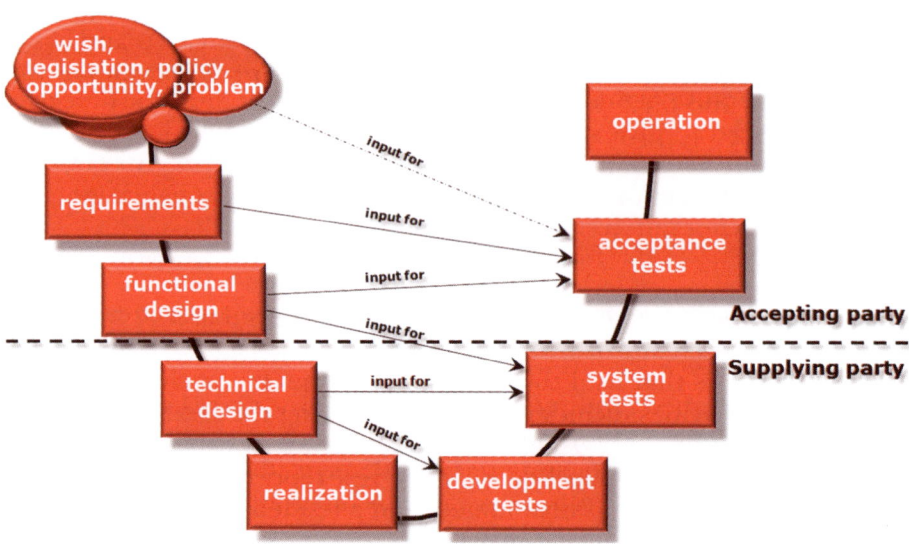

Figure 2.1: The process of software development and testing, known as the V-model.

On the left side of the model are the phases when the system is built or extended, starting with the business requirement for the solution, whether it is driven by external factors such as legal and regulation changes, or internal such as commercial ambitions. On the right side is the testing. To organize tests in an efficient way, different test levels are used where each test level addresses a certain group of requirements or functional or technical specifications.

> **Definition - Test level**
> A test level is a group of test activities that are organized and executed collectively.

The dotted line shows the separation of responsibilities between client and supplier. For testing, it is especially important to determine the responsibilities; who commissions a test; who requires a quality report? Against each development phase, there is one or more test level.
The blocks of the V-model only represent the execution phases of the different test levels. Planning and preparation activities however take more than half of the total effort of such a test level.
At the end of the tests within a test level, a decision has to be made whether the test object is transferred to the next phase, being either the next test level or production, based on a release advice produced by the test team. The release advice should not actually contain information that comes as a surprise. Constant communication and reporting should give regular insight into the progress of the test and the quality of the test object. An overview of which test goals that have been covered by the tests and of the defects (in terms of severity, solved, unsolved, etc.) are important parts of both progress and final reports [1].

2.2 The scope and value of test process improvement

A process can be defined as a series of actions or steps that leads to a goal. Testing, no matter how it is done, should be considered as a process, a series of activities that lead to insight into the quality of the test object. Usually such activities include: planning, checking the quality of the test basis, design of test cases, execution of test cases, reporting of test results including defects found, and delivering a test report. In addition, a test environment is set up and maintained, and a test team is established.
Many organizations see the need for improving the test process. But because everyone has his own notion of test process improvement the next sections give a background on the reasons and advantages of test process improvement.

2.2.1 Test process improvement enables you to align your test investment with business drivers

Ideally a test is focused on and aligned with product risks which are - again ideally - based on business requirements. These requirements have a strong relationship with the business drivers that are triggers for test process improvement. After all, a business driver is a direct derivative of the business vision and strategy.

Some examples of business drivers are:
- Reduce the annual cost of operations.
- Decrease the time to market and increase the quality to market of products and services.
- Ensure compliance with external laws and regulations.

At the same time, most triggers for test process improvement come from the people who are closely involved in the test process. They have a feeling that "something is wrong" or at least that there is room for improvement in the test process. And frequently they simply want to get 'proof' that the test process is, or is not, mature enough.

In practice, both business drivers and other triggers for improvement often come down to one or a few specific issues that are experienced:
- Testing is too expensive.
- Testing does not have enough time and/or resources.
- Testing takes too much time.
- Testing does not provide the information and advice regarding product quality and risks that managers need before systems are put into operation.
- Test environments are either not available on time or the test data has integrity issues.
- Testing does not find the most important defects at the right time.
- Defects found are not being fixed on time, making accurate test planning very default.

The BDTPI model gives the client the means to address business drivers and/or triggers. This book will zoom in on the way you can apply the BDTPI model on business drivers in general and for some business drivers (and/or triggers) in specific.

But to what degree should the test process be improved? When will the costs of improvement be worth the gain of a more mature test process? Certainly, the improvement goals for a test process depend on the kinds of issues that need to be solved, but there will also be a need for a cost/benefit analysis that will set out the estimated return on investment for the actual improvement of the test process. This book will provide directions that help to find the answers to these questions.

2.2.2 There are advantages to structuring the test process

While the test approach is to a certain extent dependent on the development process, testing can be done in many ways from ad hoc to fully-structured. An ad hoc approach, for example, uses no quality criteria to neither determine and prioritize risks, nor test design techniques for creating test cases.

Some typical limitations of ad hoc testing include:
- Time pressures, as a result of the absence of:
  - A good test plan and estimation method.
  - Any kind of planning.
  - Solid agreements on terms and procedures for delivery and reworking of applications.
- No insight into, or ability to supply, advice on the quality of the system due to:
  - Absence of a risk analysis.
  - Absence of a test strategy.
  - No focus on test coverage.
  - Inadequate quality or even lack of test cases.
- Inefficiency and ineffectiveness due to:
  - Lack of co-ordination between various test parties.
  - Lack of agreement in the area of configuration, change and requirements management.
  - Incorrect or insufficient use of test tools although these are often available.
  - Lack of prioritization so that less important elements are tested before those that carry more risk.
  - Unclear agreements or contracts.

A structured approach has the following advantages:
- It can be used in any situation, regardless of the business, the organizational structure or the system development approach taken.
- It delivers insight into and advice on risks regarding the quality of the tested system.
- It finds important defects at an early stage, so that cost reduction occurs as the defects are fixed early in the development process.
- Through testability reviews it prevents defects in future development products.
- It prevents costs of damage whether material or immaterial.
- The test products (e.g. test cases) are reusable.
- Testing is on the critical path of the total development lifecycle for as short a time as possible, so that the total lead time of the development is reduced.
  - The test execution is the only phase of testing on the critical path of a development project.

- The test process is comprehensible and manageable.

In practice, testing is carried out somewhere between the extremes of ad hoc and highly-structured. But test processes often receive a lot of criticism, so in these situations, there is probably need for improvement.

2.2.3 Test process improvement integrates closely with software process improvement

If there are any issues in a software development process, the effects are visible primarily in testing. Since testing integrates tightly with the software development life cycle (SDLC), three different situations are possible with regard to test process improvement:
1. The maturity of the test process is ahead of the maturity of the SDLC.
2. The maturity of the test process is behind the maturity of the SDLC.
3. The maturity of the test process and the SDLC are aligned.

The first situation is evident when issues in the SDLC show up in testing. From this perspective, testing depends on other processes in the SDLC; the dependencies can be described as prerequisites. When those prerequisites are not met, testing cannot fulfill its goals as planned. The test process therefore has to be adjusted every time a prerequisite has not been fulfilled, which often results in a lower quality of testing. Because of these dependencies, improving the test process by itself has a limited effect. On the other hand if the test process has a high level of maturity it is easier to set prerequisites. It is best to improve the Software Development Life Cycle as a whole starting with the weakest part. BDTPI can be used to measure the test maturity and thus to determine whether the test process is a part of the SDLC that should be improved at this moment in time.

> **In more detail - Typical prerequisites for a test project**
> - *Quality of the test basis*
>   If the quality of the determined test basis does not allow proper design or execution of tests, the shortcomings must be reported to the design team immediately, in order to be rectified or completed.
> - *Quality of the development tests (in case of a system test)*
>   The development team performs the development tests in the agreed and proven manner and thoroughness.
> - *Change control of the test object*
>   The test team should be involved in the implementation of changes. For example, the test manager should participate in the Change Control Board in order to estimate the consequences of a change from the test point of view.
> - *Availability of the test environment*
>   The test team has the availability over a test environment that is representative for the production environment (conform the documented requirements) during the agreed time.

A common phenomenon, once test process improvement has started, is that the matured test process will define more prerequisites. These new prerequisites highlight the relationship with the other processes in the SDLC. Unfortunately in an immature organization these prerequisites are often regarded as obstructions to the ongoing process. But in fact the entire SDLC benefits once these prerequisites have been fulfilled, so test process improvement can drive the improvement of the end-to-end software development process and can be used as a lever for enhancing other parts of the SDLC.

If the test process is not as mature as the rest of the SDLC, then all prerequisites for testing have already been fulfilled. Improving the test process will be much easier, since the focus of attention will be just on the test process itself.

A special situation arises when the SDLC is being improved within the context of Software Process Improvement (SPI)[1]: The most common SPI models impose some general requirements on testing once the software process has reached higher maturity levels. Unfortunately, those models provide little support for actually improving the test process to fulfill these requirements. Business Driven TPI can be used to fulfill the requirements set for testing by SPI.

Section 7.6 in this book explains how test process improvement can be integrated with software process improvement.

2.3 A reference model is needed to support test process improvement

Practice has shown that process improvement is rarely carried out without a reference model. For software process improvement a few models exist, but their application to testing is limited. It is for this reason that Sogeti published the TPI® (Test Process Improvement) model for the first time in 1998.

The TPI model has been considered to be very successful in many situations, but there are good reasons to enhance the model:

- New IT developments, such as outsourcing, agile development and increasing complexity of IT systems and programs, have had an influence on the practical use of the TPI model;
- The focus of process improvement has shifted from process goals to business goals, so improving the test process is more likely to be seen in business terms;

---

[1] SPI models such as CMMI and SPICE address the total development process, from specifying the requirements to building, testing, etc..

2 Positioning testing and TPI NEXT

- Test process improvement needs to be put into a clearer context with software process improvement (especially CMMI and SPICE);
- More than ten years of extensive experience of using the TPI model needed to be integrated with the original practice-based model.

For these reasons, Sogeti developed the Business Driven TPI model as a new version of the original TPI model.

2.3.1 The model has specific properties to ensure its quality and relevance

The Business Driven TPI model was designed with the following properties in mind:
- *Specific, controlled improvement steps.* This is the most important requirement. Specific and controllable steps should be possible, to gradually implement improvements.
- *Based on best practices.* The model is practice-based and the range of choices offered means that it is appropriate for any real-life testing situation.
- *Objectivity.* The model must be sufficiently controllable to be able to determine as objectively as possible what the maturity of a test process is and if the required situation is achieved. Two different persons who analyze the same test process, should, within small margins, produce the same results.
- *Options and priorities.* Each test process is different. That is why each time different choices for improvement have to be made. The making of these choices should be supported. In addition, the book must provide suggestions, ideas and tips that are an important source to define tailor-made improvement actions.
- *Detailed.* To be able to make a good use of the model it should contain a high level of detail. It should not be too generic and must be applicable to test processes which are regarded as reasonably or even very "mature", but also to test processes which are still at an "initial" level.
- *Rapid insight into a current situation.* The model must offer support for a fast analysis of the current situation. This is an important benefit, both for determining the starting situation of an improvement process, as well as for performing intermediate measurements to determine if the improvement process is meeting (interim) goals.
- *Independent.* In order to be widely applicable the model must be independent of test methodologies or software development methodologies. Furthermore the model should be used regardless of the fact if an organization tries to improve the total software process or just the test process.

2.3 A reference model is needed to support test process improvement

- *Based on consideration of business drivers.* The model enables variable and specific prioritizations in order to meet specific business drivers or triggers.
- *Alignment with other SDLC processes.* Other SDLC processes can influence the quality of the test process and vice versa. The model must provide information on which aspects of the test process are related to other specific processes.

2.3.2 The Business Driven TPI model is an improvement of the original TPI model

Most of the properties above were already part of the original TPI model, but there are other aspects that are new and important enhancements. Some enhancements are intrinsic to the model itself, while others are guidelines, described in Part 2 of this book.

- More emphasis on the maturity categories. The initial maturity categories of the original TPI model - Controlled, Efficient and Optimizing - have become maturity levels. This means that the initial maturity levels A, B, C and D per Key area no longer exist.
- Each Key area possesses all three maturity levels. All three maturity levels, Controlled, Efficient and Optimizing, have been defined for each Key area.
- All checkpoints are shown in the Test Maturity Matrix. The Matrix shows clearly which checkpoints have been fulfilled, even if not all checkpoints at that maturity level have been completed.
- Dependencies and priorities between Key areas have been replaced by clusters. Clusters of checkpoints across Key areas provide an improvement path from Initial to Controlled, to Efficient and to Optimizing.
- The Key areas have been revised. Statements have been added which describe the main achievement of raising the maturity for this Key area. The checkpoints have been sharpened to amplify the focus of the Key area.
- Support for defining improvement goals. Depending on the business drivers, different clusters are used to build a suitable improvement path.
- 'Enablers' reduce the distinction between the test process and other SDLC processes. Enablers clarify how the test process and other processes within the SDLC can benefit from exchanging best practices and working more closely together.
- Support for testing in an iterative and agile development process. The book also describes how to apply the Business Driven TPI model for iterative and agile testing.

2 Positioning testing and TPI NEXT

The authors of this TPI NEXT book are convinced that the properties and the enhancements have resulted in a powerful *next* step in test process improvement.

Part 2
The Business Driven TPI model

3 The model

3.1 The Business Driven TPI model provides insight into the quality of the test process

The Business Driven TPI model ('the model') is used to analyze the current situation of a test process, showing its relative strengths and weaknesses. The model is also used to discuss and establish specific goals for improving the test process, as well as providing a roadmap for reaching these specific goals.

> **In more detail - Testing in project and maintenance activities**
> Test activities can be organized in test projects and can be part of permanent maintenance activities. In both situations the scope is defined and budget and time lines are agreed upon. When not explicitly stated otherwise in the model, speaking about a 'test project' will cover a maintenance situation too.
> The specifics of applying Business Driven TPI in a maintenance situation are elaborated in section 7.5.

This section explains the elements of the model and their relationships. The elements of the model are shown in Figure 3.1.

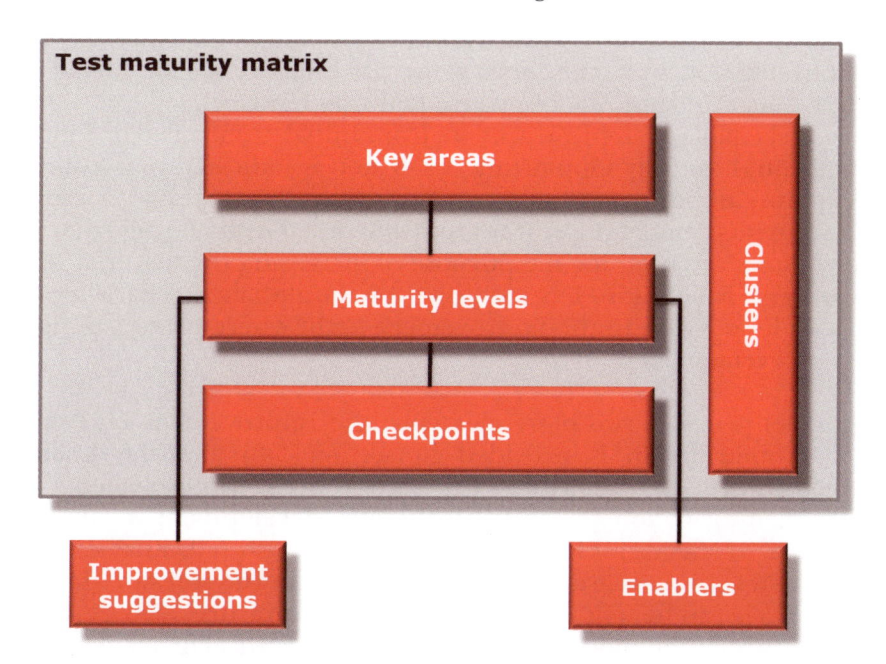

Figure 3.1: The elements of the Business Driven TPI model.

3 The model

Model overview

Each test process can be divided into a combination of coherent aspects called Key areas and the Business Driven TPI model categorizes 16 Key areas. Each Key area may have a different level of maturity and the combination of the Key areas defines the maturity of the test process as a whole.
Business Driven TPI has 4 Maturity levels which characterize the test maturity: Initial, Controlled, Efficient and Optimizing (detailed information is provided in section 3.3). A particular Maturity level can only be reached if the preceding Maturity level has also been reached.
The Initial level is the only Maturity level that does not contain any specific expectations and this Maturity level is automatically present in a test process.

For all other Maturity levels, expectations for the test process are defined through Checkpoints (detailed information is provided in section 3.4), which is the measuring unit of the model. A Checkpoint is phrased as a statement that can be confirmed with a 'yes' or a 'no'. Fulfilling a Checkpoint means that the answer for a specific test process is 'yes', with sufficient proof available to substantiate it. A Checkpoint always relates to one Key area and one Maturity level.
A Key area is at a certain Maturity level when all its related Checkpoints have been fulfilled.
The test process as a whole is at a certain Maturity level when all Key areas have reached that Maturity level. It is possible to state that the entire process is Controlled if all Key areas have at a very minimum a Maturity level of Controlled. Likewise, the entire process is Efficient or Optimizing if all Key areas have at least this respective Maturity level.
The model enables a stepwise growth, from Initial, Controlled or Efficient levels through to fully Optimizing. Each step is indicated by Clusters of Checkpoints as indicated in Figure 3.5 in section 3.7. A Cluster is a group of Checkpoints from multiple Key areas that function as one improvement step. Clusters are used for the purpose of increasing the maturity of the test process. Each Cluster is identified by an alphabetic character that identifies its position in the improvement path, where Cluster 'A' is the first improvement step.

The model provides two more elements: the Improvement suggestions (detailed information is provided in section 3.9) and the Enablers (detailed information is provided in section 3.10). Both elements give additional information to accelerate further development in maturity. Improvement suggestions focus on the test process itself. Enablers show where the test process and other processes within the software development lifecycle can benefit from each other's best practice.
The structure of the model is indicated in Figure 3.1. The elements Key areas, Maturity levels and Checkpoints are all brought together visually in the Test maturity matrix indicated in Figure 3.3 in section 3.5.

3.2 Key areas break down the test process into different aspects

The next sections describe each element of the model in more detail.

In order to measure and improve the test process in a more detailed way and step by step, the Business Driven TPI model consists of a set of 16 Key areas. For each Key area, the maturity can be measured separately. The Key areas together cover all aspects of the test process.
The Key areas are divided into three groups, being associated with Stakeholder Relations (SR), Test Management (TM) or Test Profession (TP). By grouping the Key areas in the Test maturity matrix it becomes easy to view the relative strength of each group, after the current situation of a specific test process has been assessed.

Table 3.1 describes each Key area.

#	Key area	Group	Significance
K01	Stakeholder commitment	SR	Committed and proactive stakeholders create good conditions for efficient communication and cooperation: The commitment of the persons involved in testing is an important condition for a smooth running test process. Stakeholders can be project management or line management, but also (end) users, internal accountancy and marketing. The principal stakeholder provides the necessary time, money and resources (quantitatively and qualitatively) to perform a good test.
K02	Degree of involvement	SR	Tight involvement of testing in the project helps to improve the product quality from the beginning, and helps to keep test activities off the project's critical path: Timely preparation and coordination between different tests can be done and the time that the test project is on the critical path of the project can be kept as short as possible. Early involvement of the test team in the software development lifecycle helps to find defects as soon and easy as possible and perhaps even to prevent errors. At an early stage the test team supports the analysis of project risks, the review of requirements and designs.

3 The model

#	Key area	Group	Significance
K03	Test strategy	SR	The test strategy guides the test process towards an optimal allocation of effort and resources: The test strategy defines the distribution of the test effort and the coverage over the parts to be tested or aspects of the test object. The test strategy aims at detecting the most important defects as early and cheaply as possible. The qualification 'most important' is driven by the test goals such as business processes, critical success factors or perceived product risks.
K04	Test organization	SR	A test organization meets the needs of projects for test resources, test products and test services: Testing is the work of human resources. Each participant will have their own skills, tasks, responsibilities, authorities, competences and interests and this needs to be clear to everyone involved. The test organization deals with all these aspects and relationships in order to have smooth running communication and processes.
K05	Communication	SR	Distinct communication ensures common understanding and alignment of expectations between all parties involved: In a test process, clear and effective communication between people involved is needed for creating the right conditions, coordinating the test strategy, tuning activities, negotiate priorities, etc. Communication takes place in different directions, from, towards and within the test team. Communication at its best encourages interactivity and feedback.
K06	Reporting	SR	Reporting provides stakeholders with insight to support the decision making process and test project accounting: Reporting, as a one-way communication, aims at providing substantiated advice and insight in the quality of both the test object and the test process. Reporting provides test project accounting and supports the decision making process. This makes reports one of the most important test products.
K07	Test process management	TM	Managing the test process maximizes the execution of the test assignment within the required time, costs, and results: Test process management is about keeping the resources, stakeholders, the infrastructure, the techniques and the cycle of planning, preparation, actions, checks in control and related to each other. Proper test management ensures an effective and efficient test process.
K08	Estimating and planning	TM	The proper use of appropriate estimating and planning techniques makes the test process planning and estimating predictable and reliable: Test estimating and -planning indicate which activities have to be carried out, what the necessary resources (people) are and when they are needed.

3.2 Key areas break down the test process into different aspects

#	Key area	Group	Significance
K09	Metrics	TM	Metrics provide objectivity by quantifying observations: Metrics are quantified and objective observations of the characteristics of a product or process. They are used to control the test process, to substantiate the test advices and to compare systems and/or processes. Specifically for improving the test process metrics are important to evaluate consequences of certain improvement actions, by comparing data before and after performing the improvement action.
K10	Defect management	TM	Defect management treats defects both at an individual level and at a group level where root causes are analyzed and guidelines are available: Although administrating and managing defects is in fact a matter of the entire software development project and not specifically for the test team, the testers are the most involved people. A good administration is able to monitor the life-cycle of a defect and provide various (statistical) overviews and reports such as the quality advice.
K11	Testware management	TM	Testware management ensures coherence between test artifacts, and between test artifacts and their related design documents: The input products (such as design, test object) as well as the output products of testing (such as test cases, scripts, test plans, reports) must be maintainable and reusable, so they must be managed. Furthermore, testware management ensures coherence between testing artifacts on the one hand and between testing artifacts and their related design documents on the other hand.
K12	Methodology practice	TP	A described method for testing directs and supports the test projects: For each test activity or test process a certain working method is used, comprising actions, procedures, regulations, techniques etc. This test method needs to be sufficiently generic to be applicable in every situation, but contains enough detail to direct and support daily test practice.
K13	Tester professionalism	TP	Tester professionalism includes the right mix of the various skills, competences, disciplines, functions and knowledge that are necessary to perform test activities to the levels expected: Testing requires a large set of skills: familiarity and understanding of the business and the organization, knowledge of the test object, general IT know-how and technical skills. In addition, testers need to have specific test skills, from expertise in methods through to the ability to communicate with stakeholders effectively (social competence). Tester professionalism refers to the right mix of these skills and competences that are necessary to perform test activities to the levels expected.

3 The model

#	Key area	Group	Significance
K14	Test case design	TP	Test case design directs test execution to search for defects according to the test strategy: Test cases are derived from source information (the test basis) in a standardized way. This approach provides insight into the coverage and depth of tests and makes the (re)design and the (re) execution of the test cases easier.
K15	Test tools	TP	Test tools enable or accelerate specific test activities: Test tools are automated or unattended aids for the test process. Test tools excel in systematically doing repetitive work, independent of complexity and volume, in situations where manual activities would take too much time, would be infeasible or error prone. Test tools enable or accelerate specific test activities, resulting in shorter lead time, more test depth, better motivation of testers etc.
K16	Test environment	TP	The test environment is explicitly designed, implemented and maintained with the goals of the test level in mind: The test environment mainly comprises the following components: - Client environment - Network - Storage - (Enterprise) Server - Middleware - Test data The test environment should be composed and set up in such a way that it reflects the test goals. The test environment has a large influence on the quality, lead time, and cost of the test process. Important aspects of the test environment are responsibilities, management, on-time and sufficient availability, representativeness, and flexibility.

Table 3.1: Description per Key area.

SR = Stakeholder Relations; TM = Test Management; TP = Test Profession.

3.3 Maturity levels provide a scale from Initial through to Optimizing

Each test process can be classified as having a certain level of maturity. Starting at an Initial level, a test process can develop from Controlled through Efficient towards Optimizing, each level being more mature than the preceding level, and adding more value to the business.

1. *Initial:* Ad hoc activities

   A test process at the Initial level consists of a variety of insufficiently documented test activities, carried out in a rather ad hoc way and focused on '(how) does it work?' rather than: 'does it work as requested and specified?' Such a test process offers insufficient or random insight into risks and the quality of the test object and insufficient insight into the quality of the test process itself. Test activities tend to be on the critical path of the project, frequently causing delays in the project particularly when defects are found late. Typically, the quality of the test process heavily depends on one or more key individuals ('heroes at work').

   Some typical limitations of ad hoc testing are described in section 2.2.2.

2. *Controlled:* Doing the right things

   The first major step towards a mature test process is to address what needs to be done. A test process at this Maturity level offers ways and means to control and steer the process, and gives sufficient insight into the quality of the test object. The test process is effective in such a way that it enables earlier and better insight into the quality, allowing for timely corrective measures and less chance of delays caused by insufficient product quality.

   The Checkpoints of the Business Driven TPI model for the Controlled level address the fact that activities are recognized as being important, rather than how such an activity is carried out (this is addressed at the Efficient level).

   > **In more detail - The Controlled level in practice**
   > Many organizations set the Controlled level as their target Maturity level, being 'in full control' of their test processes and establishing effective test processes. The Efficient and Optimizing levels are provided for test organizations to meet increasing expectations and ambition by further increasing their test process maturity.

3. *Efficient:* Doing things the right way

   Once the right activities are being done, the next step is to improve how they are done. The different elements and aspects of the test process can be controlled and steered in such a way that cost and benefit are optimized. The most critical defects (those that have the highest

3 The model

impact (risk) on the business) are being detected at the lowest cost and in a minimum of time.

A test process needs to be at the Controlled level before it can work efficiently. For example: in order to make efficient use of test techniques or tools, you must know how to use and control them. The focus also broadens to include the interaction with software development. In general this means additional demands regarding the way Key areas are performed. This depends on the environment in which the test process takes place. The requirements on planning in a true agile environment differ quite substantially from those in a more traditional approach. But in either situation, planning needs to contain a baseline of activities and milestones that will make it possible for the test manager in charge of the test process, to know if he or she is still on schedule or not.

4. *Optimizing:* Continuously adapting to ever-changing circumstances
When the right activities are done in the right way, the focus should shift towards making sure it stays that way in the future. This should lead to self-evaluation that can be depicted by Deming's Cycle[1] (see Figure 3.2 and see also [8]). At the Optimizing level this is done continuously. The Deming Cycle defines a process of improvement through the incremental steps of Plan, Do, Check and Act. Checkpoints in the Optimizing area reflect the necessary measurements to keep the quality of the process up to standard, especially in changing situations and circumstances. For instance, after the successful completion of a release, the test strategy of that release can serve as the starting point for the new release - always taking into account changes in stakeholders, or changes in what they consider to be acceptable risks.

> **In more detail - The Optimizing level in practice**
> Reaching the Optimizing level is always a great achievement, but not always the best approach for improving testing. A test process at the Optimizing level can probably not operate as efficiently as possible in a 'managed' software development process, equivalent to the maturity level 2 of CMMI [6]. Instead of pursuing the highest Maturity level possible for the test process, it is better to have the maturity of the test process and software development process both constantly improved and kept in balance.
> Enablers in the Business Driven TPI model connect Key areas with aspects of the software development process for this purpose.

---

1   The Deming Cycle: Developed by W. Edwards Deming in the 1950s, this proposed a continuous feedback loop so that managers could identify and change the parts of a process that needed improvement, commonly known as the PDCA cycle for Plan, Do, Check, Act.

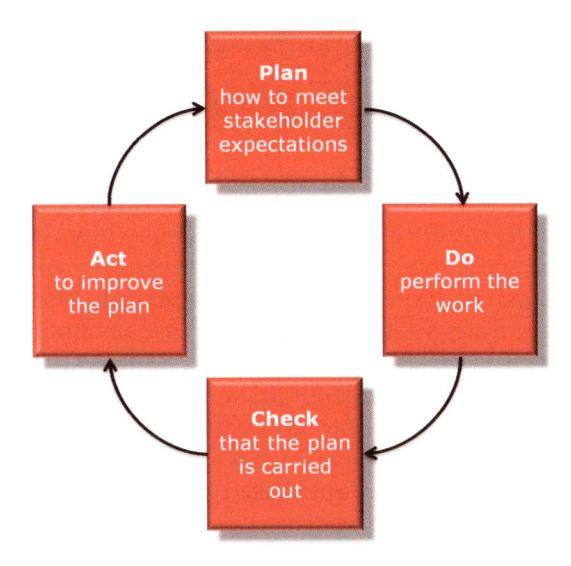

Figure 3.2: The Deming Cycle of continuous improvement.

Maturity levels per Key area
Within the test process, each Key area will have a certain level of maturity with significant aspects per Maturity level. These aspects are addressed in Chapter 4, where the different Key areas and their Maturity levels, the Checkpoints, the Enablers and Improvement measures are described.

3.4 Checkpoints measure the maturity of each Key area in an objective way

To determine the maturity of a Key area in an objective way, the Business Driven TPI model provides Checkpoints for each Key area to achieve the Controlled, Efficient or Optimizing levels. No Checkpoints are provided for the Initial level.
A level of maturity can only be reached if the preceding Maturity level has also been reached. A Key area must fulfill all the Checkpoints for Controlled to be considered as being at a Controlled level; the same applies to Efficient and Optimizing levels. It is not possible for a Key area to be Efficient if any of the Checkpoints for Controlled has not yet been fulfilled. A Key area cannot be Optimizing without first being Efficient.
The number of Checkpoints per Key area/Maturity level combination varies from 3 to 4 for Controlled and Efficient. For Optimizing, it varies between 2 and 3 Checkpoints. The Checkpoints address what needs to be achieved, rather than how it should be achieved. The Improvement suggestions give practical guidance on how to achieve a Maturity level for a Key area.

3.5 The Test maturity matrix provides a visual overview

The Test maturity matrix (see Figure 3.3) provides an overview of all Key areas, together with their respective maturities.
The Checkpoints in the Test maturity matrix are put into a fixed order. This can lead to 'gaps' in the Test maturity matrix when the fulfilled Checkpoints are marked and others are not (see the example in Figure 3.4).
The Test maturity matrix lists all 16 Key areas in the vertical rows, and the Maturity levels (Initial, Controlled, Efficient and Optimizing) in the columns. As described before, the Key areas are grouped and associated with respectively Stakeholder Relations, Test Management or Test Profession.
For each Key area/Maturity level combination, the related Checkpoints are shown in the Test maturity matrix.
As an example: Stakeholder commitment has 4 Checkpoints at the Controlled level, 3 Checkpoints at the Efficient level and 3 Checkpoints at the Optimizing level. These Checkpoints are numbered accordingly.

Key area	Initial	Controlled	Efficient	Optimizing
1 Stakeholder commitment		1 2 3 4	1 2 3	1 2 3
2 Degree of involvement		1 2 3 4	1 2 3	1 2
3 Test strategy		1 2 3 4	1 2 3	1 2
4 Test organization		1 2 3 4	1 2 3 4	1 2 3
5 Communication		1 2 3 4	1 2 3	1 2
6 Reporting		1 2 3	1 2 3	1 2
7 Test process management		1 2 3 4	1 2 3	1 2
8 Estimating and planning		1 2 3 4	1 2 3 4	1 2 3
9 Metrics		1 2 3	1 2 3 4	1 2
10 Defect management		1 2 3 4	1 2 3 4	1 2 3
11 Testware management		1 2 3 4	1 2 3	1 2 3
12 Methodology practice		1 2 3	1 2 3 4	1 2
13 Tester professionalism		1 2 3 4	1 2 3 4	1 2 3
14 Test case design		1 2 3	1 2 3 4	1 2 3
15 Test tools		1 2 3	1 2 3 4	1 2 3
16 Test environment		1 2 3 4	1 2 3 4	1 2 3

Figure 3.3: Test maturity matrix.

Note: *Figure 3.3 shows that the visualized width of Checkpoints in the Test maturity matrix vary. The number of Checkpoints per Key area/Maturity level determines the visualized width in the Test maturity matrix as the Checkpoints always fill up the column that represents a Maturity level. The visual size of a Checkpoint does therefore not express an indication on the complexity or importance of the Checkpoint.*

3.6 For a specific test process the current situation is drawn in the Test maturity matrix

The result of analyzing a specific test process by working through the Checkpoints can be plotted in the Test maturity matrix. This is done by marking the fulfilled Checkpoints with a color. In Figure 3.4 the color pink is used to mark the Checkpoints that are met indicating the current situation.

Two different Test maturity matrices containing the current situation of a previous and recent moment in time can be used to denote the progress of test process improvement of an organization. Moreover, the Test maturity matrices of two test processes of different projects, departments or organizations can be compared with each other as a comparative benchmark.

> **In more detail - Comparing two Test maturity matrices**
> Although the Test maturity matrix makes it easy to compare two current situations, this is not significant if the investigated scope and/or organizations are not comparable too. It is not useful to compare the current situation of a large test organization with the current situation of a single test level in a small test organization.

	Initial	Controlled				Efficient				Optimizing		
1 Stakeholder commitment	■	1	2	3	4	1	2	3		1	2	3
2 Degree of involvement	■	1	2	3	4	1	2	3		1	2	
3 Test strategy		1	2	3	4	1	2	3		1	2	
4 Test organization	■	1	2	3	4	1	2	3	4	1	2	3
5 Communication	■	1	2	3	4	1	2	3		1	2	
6 Reporting	■	1		2		3	1	2	3		1	2
7 Test process management		1	2	3	4	1	2	3		1	2	
8 Estimating and planning		1	2	3	4	1	2	3	4	1	2	3
9 Metrics	■	1		2		3	1	2	3	4	1	2
10 Defect management		1	2	3	4	1	2	3	4	1	2	3
11 Testware management		1	2	3	4	1	2	3		1	2	3
12 Methodology practice		1		2		3	1	2	3	4	1	2
13 Tester professionalism	■	1	2	3	4	1	2	3	4	1	2	3
14 Test case design	■	1		2		3	1	2	3	4	1	2	3
15 Test tools		1		2		3	1	2	3	4	1	2	3
16 Test environment	■	1	2	3	4	1	2	3	4	1	2	3

Figure 3.4: A current situation drawn in the Test maturity matrix.

This fictitious Test maturity matrix gives following information:
- Seven Key areas are at the Controlled level: Test strategy, Test process management, Estimating and planning, Defect management, Testware management, Methodology practice and Test tools.
- The Key area Metrics is at the Efficient level.
- The remaining eight Key areas are at the Initial level. Although all Checkpoints of the Communication Key area at the Efficient level are fulfilled, this Key area is at the Initial level only since 3 Checkpoints at the Controlled level are not met.

3 The model

- The Test Management group of Key areas (Key areas 7 - 11), as being at the Controlled level, is stronger developed than the Stakeholder Relationship group of Key areas (Key areas 1 - 6) and the Test Profession group of Key areas (Key areas 12 - 16).

3.7 Clusters of Checkpoints make Business Driven TPI a continuous model

Successful process improvement requires taking small steps and constantly celebrating each success, in order to not get overwhelmed by day-to-day business. To progress from the Initial process maturity to fully Controlled, it is necessary to invest considerable time and resources: the Checkpoints cannot be met overnight. The same pragmatism applies when striving to progress from Controlled to Efficient or from Efficient to Optimizing.

In order to take these small steps, Clusters are created. A Cluster is a group of Checkpoints from multiple Key areas that make up one small improvement step. Each Cluster is identified by an alphabetic letter and the Clusters, ordered in alphabetic sequence, create an improvement path with defined priorities. Each Checkpoint in the Test maturity matrix is marked with the alphabetic letter of the Cluster to which it is assigned.

The base Cluster arrangement, as detailed in Figure 3.5 is based on the assumption that the test process, in its entirety, must move to Controlled, Efficient or Optimizing levels.

Each Checkpoint is assigned to precisely one Cluster; each base Cluster contains between 10 and 14 Checkpoints. It is recommended that the Checkpoints of Cluster A are fulfilled first, then Checkpoints of Cluster B etc. Business Driven TPI provides a step-by-step implementation of

	Initial	Controlled			Efficient			Optimizing		
1 Stakeholder commitment		A	B	B	C	F	H	H	K	M	M
2 Degree of involvement		A	B	C	E	H	H	J	L		L
3 Test strategy		A	A	B	E	F	F	H	K		L
4 Test organization		A	D	D	E	I	I	J	J	K	L	L
5 Communication		B	C	C	D	F	F	J	M		M
6 Reporting		A		C		C	F	G	G	K		K
7 Test process management		A	A	B	B	G		H	J	K		M
8 Estimating and planning		B	B	C	C	G	H	I	I	K	L	L
9 Metrics		C		C		D	G	H	H	I	K		K
10 Defect management		A	A	B	D	F	F	H	J	K	L	L
11 Testware management		B	B	D	E	I		I	J	L	L	L
12 Methodology practice		C		D		E	F	H	J	J	M		M
13 Tester professionalism		D	D	E	E	G	G	I	I	K	K	M
14 Test case design		A		A		E	F	I	I	J	K	K	M
15 Test tools		E		E		E	F	G	G	I	L	M	M
16 Test environment		C	D	D	E	G	H	J	J	L	M	M

Figure 3.5: The view of base Clusters (A, B, C etc) in the Test maturity matrix.

improvements that is both recognizable and meaningful. The composition of the base Clusters is based on extensive experience in the field of testing.

Equally important to taking the next steps in improving the test process is to consolidate the achievements already made. Improvements are to be integrated in the (daily) test process to prevent that the test process maturity slowly decreases.

Base Clusters and business-driven Clusters
For the base Clusters no single business driver is relevant or leading: the improvement of the test process is regarded as a general improvement process. Each Key area is equally significant in supporting the growth towards higher maturity. However: the base Clusters do contain relationships between the different Key areas and/or Checkpoints.

In many situations, a different approach is preferred, in which the Clusters need to be adjusted to a specific business situation and to particular business drivers. The Clusters constitute the core of the business-driven aspects in Business Driven TPI. In a situation where cost reduction is the main driver for test process improvement, other priorities are required than a situation where the focus is on 'time-to-market'. By first acknowledging which Key areas are more or less relevant to the required bias (e.g. cost, time, quality as a business driver), and secondly by determining how this influences the distribution of the Checkpoints over the Clusters, it is possible to specify new Clusters attuned to specific business drivers. In this situation a Cluster can exceed the border of a Maturity level and contain Checkpoints of multiple Maturity levels. In Chapter 6 the influence of business drivers on the constellation of the Clusters is described. Appendix B presents a method to re-arrange the Checkpoints to new business-driven Clusters and an example of adjusted Clusters for cost reduction as business driver.

Note: Be aware that the use of business-driven Clusters doesn't change the position of individual Checkpoints in the Test maturity matrix as the position of Checkpoints is fixed.

3.8 The current and target situation are drawn in the Test maturity matrix

Figure 3.6 is created by projecting the current situation of Figure 3.4 in the base Clusters of Figure 3.5. In addition, a target situation is drawn in the Test maturity matrix consisting of two improvement steps for reaching the Controlled level for the test process as a whole.

3 The model

	Initial	Controlled			Efficient			Optimizing		
1 Stakeholder commitment	A	B	B	C	F	H	H	K	M	M
2 Degree of involvement	A	B	C	E	H	H	J	L		L
3 Test strategy	A	A	B	E	F	F	H	K		L
4 Test organization	A	D	D	E	I	I	J	J	K	L	L
5 Communication	B	C	C	D	F	F	J	M		M
6 Reporting	A		C	C	F	G	G	K		K
7 Test process management	A	A	B	B	G	H	J	K		M
8 Estimating and planning	B	B	C	C	G	H	I	I	K	L	L
9 Metrics	C		C	D	G	H	H	I	K		K
10 Defect management	A	A	B	D	F	F	H	J	K	L	L
11 Testware management	B	B	D	E	I		I	J	L	L	L
12 Methodology practice	C		D	E	F	H	J	J	M		M
13 Tester professionalism	D	D	E	E	G	G	I	I	K	K	M
14 Test case design	A	A		E	F	I	I	J	K	K	M
15 Test tools	E	E		E	F	G	G	I	L	M	M
16 Test environment	C	D	D	E	G	H	J	J	L	M	M

Figure 3.6: A target situation drawn in the Test maturity matrix with base Clusters and current situation.

This fictitious Test maturity matrix gives the following information:
- The Checkpoints in pink are the ones met (the current situation), taken from Figure 3.4.
- The Checkpoints in gray constitute the first improvement step that the test organization has defined towards reaching the Controlled level. The missing Checkpoints of Cluster A, B and C were chosen to be part of this improvement step.
- The Checkpoints in red constitute the second and last improvement step towards reaching the Controlled level. The missing Checkpoints of Cluster D and E were chosen to be part of this improvement step.

3.9 Improvement suggestions indicate how Checkpoints can be met

When the need for increasing the maturity of an individual Key area has been identified, the first thing to do is to look at the Checkpoints that have been missed for that required Maturity level. In addition, help is given in the Improvement suggestions, which are provided for each Maturity level.

While Checkpoints describe what is to be reached, the Improvement suggestions describe how this can be done. Improvement suggestions indicate how Checkpoints can be met, but also provide additional useful tips not directly related to the Checkpoints, but which are related to the Key area.

Improvement suggestions are practice-based and adaptable, as well as optional. These suggestions are meant as hints and tips and not compulsory steps to achieve that Maturity level. Furthermore, the list of suggestions is not meant to be exhaustive and the effectiveness of suggestions will vary from context to context when they are actually put into practice.

Information from several sources should be used, in addition to the Improvement suggestions. Examples are books on test methods and test techniques, for example 'TMap NEXT' [17].

3.10 Enablers relate the test process to other SDLC processes

The test process is closely related to other processes within the Software Development Life Cycle (SDLC). The element of Enablers clarifies how the test process and other processes within the SDLC can benefit from exchanging best practices and working closely together. On the one hand, an Enabler may strengthen and accelerate the improvement process for testing and, on the other hand, persuade the other SDLC process to adopt measures to improve their maturity.

For the SDLC process, the Enablers provide interesting points. For example, it is possible to implement a highly-efficient testware management process without proper configuration management for non-testing artifacts. But when an organization routinely enforces proper version control on development documentation, testware management becomes much easier. This issue is addressed in the Testware management Key area.

For more information about the interaction between the test process and other processes, please read the explanation on Business Driven TPI and models for Software Process Improvement (SPI) in section 7.6.

4 Key areas

This chapter describes in detail each of the Key areas in the Business Driven TPI model.
As a start a brief statement shows the focus of the Key area followed by an introduction.
For every Key area the 4 Maturity levels, Initial, Controlled, Efficient and Optimizing are elaborated. Per Maturity level a specific statement describes the main achievement of raising the maturity for this Key area.
Checkpoints describe how to measure if a specific Maturity level is reached.
Enablers show how the test maturity of this Key area can benefit from other IT disciplines and IT processes (and vice versa).
Improvement suggestions give instructions on how the related level can be achieved. An Improvement suggestion has no direct relation to any specific Checkpoint. The Improvement suggestions are generic for the Maturity level and must be tuned to your test method.

4.1 Stakeholder commitment

> Committed and proactive stakeholders create good conditions for efficient communication and cooperation.

Besides the test team, many other people are involved and have their interest in testing. There will be stakeholders like line management, project management or a steering committee. Their interests will be, among other things, to enforce conditions or restrictions to the process like time and budget. There are also stakeholders who interact with and work alongside testing, such as requirements management, architecture and development. The test process needs them for their valuable input like the test object and the test basis. Finally, there can be other parties, outside the test process, such as a marketing department, business units and Quality Assurance department. Their interest may be to check compliancy to rules and regulations.

> **In more detail - the principal stakeholder**
> For the test process there is always one *principal* stakeholder. This is the person who is responsible for the test assignment and the one that testing reports to directly. The principal stakeholder combines two interests: on the one hand he sets the (pre)conditions for testing, on the other hand he depends strongly on the results and outcome of the test process. This role can be played by many people: a project manager, a line manager, the chairman of a steering committee. Other names or terms for such a role are client, customer or sponsor.

Testing depends on the commitment of stakeholders because they are responsible for fulfilling the preconditions for testing: ensuring that test resources (both human and technical), as well as time and budget, are made available for testing.

In addition, testing needs to interact with (stakeholders from) other disciplines in or around the project, since they have an impact on each others' process.

Last, but not least, improvement of the test process may require extra demands on other disciplines. To make this effort successful, commitment from these stakeholders is necessary to ensure that they accept and take responsibility for such requirements.

Initial level

At an Initial level, commitment from stakeholders is rather low. There may not be a fixed budget to start with, test resources may not have been made available in time, or lack of communication from the project to testing has resulted in (often negative) surprises for testing. As a result, testing cannot do its job properly, despite the best intentions of the test team itself. Often testing is considered to be a necessary evil and has a low status within the development project and line organization. The quality of the test object before testing is overestimated and the defects found by testing are not regarded as being significant.

4.1.1 Stakeholder commitment at a Controlled level

> Stakeholders commit to and support the test process by granting and delivering negotiated resources.

At the Controlled level, testing and its results are taken seriously by the stakeholders. They are aware that testing needs resources such as human resources, test environments, test tools and, if available, test methods and reusable testware.

The resource requirements are negotiated between the test team and stakeholders and the latter commit to the delivery of agreed resources on time. This commitment also ensures a certain independency of the testing efforts from the ongoing business process, especially when testing activities are part-time.

The awareness of the value of testing is also reflected in the stakeholders' contribution to the Product Risk Analysis and the test strategy. The interests of the various stakeholders are taken into account in this strategy.

Checkpoints
1. The principal stakeholder is defined (not necessarily documented) and known to the testers.
2. Budget for test resources is granted by and negotiable with the principal stakeholder.
3. Stakeholders actually deliver the committed resources.
4. The principal stakeholder is responsible for a documented product risk analysis (the input for the test strategy).

Enablers
- Project Management Methodology: many project methods deal with stakeholder commitment and management.
- Quality Assurance in the line and project organization: requires the commitment of the same stakeholders as testing.

Improvement suggestions

The first step to a stronger commitment can be to find the person that gives the order for the test activities and/or is very much dependant on the test results.

Important for this Key area is awareness, such as understanding the consequences if testing is not done correctly. Research the effect of insufficient or inaccurate testing in production (such as quality problems and potential damage to the business), but also the effects on the project.

4 Key areas

Show stakeholders how testing can help avoid such problems. Be specific about which defects could have been found earlier, and how many problems could have been avoided.

Make clear what prerequisites for testing are required in order to avoid such problems. What could the stakeholders have done to avoid these specific issues and what can the stakeholders do now to avoid similar problems in the near future.

Stay down-to-earth with actual examples and focus on the short-term investment and short-term results.

4.1.2 Stakeholder commitment at an Efficient level

> Stakeholders anticipate the implications of changes, thus enabling the test process to respond adequately.

In practice, changes in projects and deviations from the original plans happen all the time. There can be delays in the project but also changes in the scope of the project. Testing is affected by both kinds of change.

At an Efficient level, stakeholders are (made) aware that these changes have consequences for testing. Therefore they keep testing informed. The testing consequences are discussed with the test team and changes in the test plan (planning or scope) are agreed.

Note that sometimes changes in the project and their consequences may look as if there is a lack of commitment to testing. When the time allocated to testing is reduced to an absolute minimum because of development delays, or testing is forced to accept a test object that has not been tested by developers, it may feel to the test team that testing is not being taken seriously. This may be the case. But it is also possible that other interests have a higher priority than product quality and testing. In such cases, stakeholders' commitment is evidenced in their willingness to have an open discussion with testing about the consequences.

> **Example - Scope change**
> During the project, requests for changes (RFC) can be filed and may lead to additional project effort, extra design, development and testing time. A committed Project Manager not only negotiates with his customer. Also testing is involved because the RFC may affect:
> - Risk analysis: new risks, other priorities?
> - Test strategy: different allocation of available resources to the test levels?
> - Resource planning: more resources, different skills?
> - Test planning: re-test of formerly tested objects?

Checkpoints
1. All relevant stakeholders are defined (not necessarily documented) and known to the testers.

2. Stakeholders actively acquire information on the quality of both the test process and the test object.
3. The stakeholders proactively take action on aspects that affect the test process. This includes changes in the delivery sequence of the test object and changes in the project scope.

Enablers
- Change management process. If a proper change management process is implemented and followed it helps the stakeholders to also support the test process.

Improvement suggestions

Make sure that testing is included in the change management process. This way when changes occur in the project scope, the test team itself can judge how testing is likely to be affected. Indicate the changes and their consequences to project management and steering committee as appropriate.

While demonstrating the consequences of change for testing, make suggestions as to how the consequences can be managed. Make this a transparent process indicating which suggestions can be handled by the test team itself, and making recommendations for project management.

Involve stakeholders in (test) project evaluation.

4.1.3 Stakeholder commitment at an Optimizing level

> Stakeholders recognize and stimulate process improvement as a shared responsibility.

When improving the test process, the effects are limited if other processes in the SDLC do not follow accordingly. Sooner or later, test process improvement will make demands on other processes such as requirements and configuration management. The owners of other SDLC processes will need to accept these demands and adjust their own processes. This will take time and may lead to reduced productivity. Stakeholder commitment is required to accept this temporary loss of productivity.

> **Example - Acquiring additional learning time**
> It might be decided to introduce a new test design technique in order to achieve a specific coverage type.
> Applying this new test design technique could mean:
> - Testing needs extra time for designing the test cases (the learning curve) or accepting less coverage.
> - Certain (additional) information in the test basis is required, such as decision points.
>
> The stakeholders must be willing to give both testing the time to go up the learning curve and give other processes the time to align their process to the improvement.

Checkpoints
1. Line management acknowledges that test process improvement comes with the need for increased learning time for which resources are provided.
2. Stakeholders are willing to adapt their way of working to suit the test process. This includes the software development and requirements management.
3. An adapted way of working by the stakeholder to suit demands of the test process is jointly evaluated by the test organization and the stakeholder.

Enablers
- Software Process Improvement projects and methods like CMMI or SPICE (ISO 15504).

Improvement suggestions
At this stage it is vital to show the costs and benefits of improvements. One way to do it is to gather statistics and metrics (e.g. from comparable circumstances and situations) to indicate that efforts pay off or have a positive Return On Investment.

4.2 Degree of involvement

> Tight involvement of testing in the project helps to improve the product quality from the beginning, and helps to keep test activities off the project's critical path.

This Key area describes the moment and the degree of involvement of the test process within the Software Development Life Cycle. The first aspect indicates the moment in which the test activities are planned and started. While test execution can only be started once the test object has been delivered by the developers, testing includes activities (in many cases more than 60% of the activities) that should be done earlier or rather: as soon as possible. Test planning, for example, should be done in parallel with project planning. Testing can help to improve the quality of the test basis by doing testability reviews. Test design can be started once the test basis is being created. Finalization activities like conserving testware for reuse, can be done in parallel with deployment of the product. While doing so test execution will be the only test activity that remains on the critical path of the project.

The second aspect, degree of involvement, relates to the actual involvement of test activities in the project or the development process. An example of such an approach is the contribution of test expertise to the analyses and mitigation measures of product and project risks by supporting project management and other stakeholders. Testing supports control on and improvement of product quality from the start. This prevents delays in the project itself that are caused by insufficient quality and too much rework.

Early and firm involvement of testing in development shows that testing has added value and is taken seriously. It enables clarification of roles and responsibilities between testers and stakeholders and of the test goals.

Initial level

At the Initial level, testing is involved in a rather late stage of development, for instance once the test object has been delivered. A characteristic of this level is the amount of rework due to late detection of defects, errors and unwanted and missing functionality. Despite an insufficient quality of testing itself (e.g. many defects are found late in the software process) the project suffers from delays due to the unexpected amount of rework to be done. Both developers and testers work under pressure and typically work overtime to minimize the delays in the project, while trying to raise the quality of the system to a reasonable level.

4.2.1 Degree of involvement at a Controlled level

> Test activities are started up early to enable systematic preparations.

4 Key areas

At a Controlled level, testing is involved in the project in time to make proper preparations: planning the tests, defining a test strategy and design test cases. One of the first activities for testing to do is to discuss the test assignment with the principal stakeholder: why is testing necessary, what needs to be tested, what is or is not in scope. If the test process is well involved from the start of a project it can be a great contribution to the mitigation of project and product risks. Also, there is time to arrange all required resources, both human and technical. All this means that the majority of the test activities is kept off the critical path of development.

Checkpoints
1. The test assignment, scope and approach are negotiated early with the principal stakeholder as one of the first test activities.
2. Test activities are started early, timely before test execution, with the goal of keeping the test activities off the project's critical path.
3. A tester is involved in project planning: dependencies between the test process and other processes are taken into account.
4. A tester is involved in the analysis and mitigation of overall project risks.

Enablers
- Project management methods: project methods describe many activities, roles, responsibilities and other aspects. This also helps to set up the test process. Vice versa, methods for testing help to perform better project management.

Improvement suggestions

Contact both line and project management to emphasize the necessity of (an early) involvement of testing.

Start as early as possible with planning the test activities, preferably at:

Project initiation, otherwise at:

Start of the requirements definition, otherwise at:

Start of the test basis, otherwise at:

Completion of the test basis.

Clarify the following aspects: stakeholders, roles and responsibilities (especially for testing), scope for testing, possible project risks, the goals and aim of the test process.

4.2.2 Degree of involvement at an Efficient level

> The involvement of testing enables reliable test process output and prevention of defects.

If testing is involved timely and to a serious degree, testing can prove its value by improving the quality of the test basis and with that the quality of development products. Tester feedback is taken into account before base lining the test basis. This can be achieved by having testers review the test basis. Moreover, testing offers support to the design team, helping them to create clear and unambiguous documents by challenging inconsistencies in e.g. the functional design. After all, an inconsistency in the functional design can lead to defects in any derived product, such as a detailed design, test object and/or a test case.

Design documents are derived from other documents, like the technical design is derived from the functional design. But all design documents have in common the fact that they are derived from one root document: the requirements. Therefore, at the Efficient level of the process, it is a good practice to not only review the specific design documents for the test level, but the requirements as well.

By their experience and knowledge of the product under test, the testers are well equipped to support the analysis of (the impact of) defects. This helps to analyze the seriousness of defects and by that the strategy for retests.

Checkpoints
1. Testers contribute to impact and risk analysis of change requests and changes to the test basis.
2. Testers contribute to the impact analysis of defects.
3. Testers are actively involved in optimizing the test basis (more than a testability review), in which the object under test is described.

Enablers
- Project management: decide which defects found in the test basis should be resolved and which can be postponed. This also helps to shorten the test process.
- Development of Requirements and Functional Design: testers participate in the review sessions for these documents and provide their knowledge to solve possible defects.

Improvement suggestions

Inform the authors of the test basis on what you will be watching for in your evaluation. Show them the checklists you will be using so they are informed.

The review team's shared success is, besides a better mutual understanding, the number and severity of the defects found. Report these statistics to the stakeholders that provided the resources for the evaluation.

Make clear that the test basis is subject of the review and not the author.

4 Key areas

Collect metrics or other experience based data, for instance on the carry-over effect of an early defect, in order to substantiate remarks and suggestions made.

Be involved in the low level tests. Helping the programmers and receiving help from them will assure a more efficient approach (and better quality) for the entire project.

Perform a post project analysis on all defects to distinguish requirement defects vs. development defects vs. test defects vs. production defects. It will help to demonstrate the benefit of early testing involvement. For instance your analysis may show that defects found in production could have been found in a much earlier stage or by a (better) review of the test basis.

4.2.3 Degree of involvement at an Optimizing level

> The involvement of testing in the project makes it possible to optimize both the project and the test process.

At the Optimizing level 'testing' is a fixed item on the (project) agenda and its early and tightly involvement enables all involved to optimize their contribution. For this it is necessary that testing shows its value and participates on different levels and stages of the SDLC.

Checkpoints
1. The test team is involved in the evaluation of the project. The lessons learned from the test process are valued and used for (the set up of) future projects.
2. The test team has an undisputed part in all relevant development activities, being accepted and valued.

Enablers
- Process Management at the organization level, where process areas focus on continuous process improvement and knowledge management.

Improvement suggestions

Gather examples of delays in testing or incidents in a production environment that could have been prevented with proper preparation.

Try to be involved in the Business Case definition phase of the project. During that phase, the value of a project is evaluated against the investments required. This will ensure that more (investment) activities are taken into consideration thus providing a SMART Business Case and a good start for the Test Strategy.

4.3 Test strategy

> The test strategy guides the test process towards an optimal allocation of effort and resources.

The test strategy helps to allocate the available test effort and resources in an optimal way across different kinds of tests and different parts of the system, as well as to choose to what extent each part of the system will be tested. This ensures that the most important defects are found as early as possible. This makes the test strategy the perfect means to make choices concerning time, money and quality and thus it is the ultimate key area for managing the test process.

The 'optimal allocation' of efforts and resources is related to the (product) risks for the organization when deploying the product or system under test. Such risks are based on the potential damage to the organization should defects occur when the system is in production.

> **In more detail - Product risks versus project risks**
> **Project risks**
> Project risks are those that can obstruct the execution of a project in accordance with the plan. Examples include:
> - The test basis is not frozen in time, for example due to changing demands from the customer.
> - The test environment is not ready in time, for instance due to understaffing of test environment managers.
>
> Such risks are identified in the test plan and managed within the test project. After the project has finished, these risks are no longer relevant.
>
> **Product risks**
> Product risks can obstruct the proper use or functioning of a product. Product risks (the actual basis for the test strategy) are those to which the client is exposed, when deploying the system (or bringing the product to market). Examples include:
> - The performance is too low, which means that potential customers may switch to a competitor's offering.
> - Hackers have access to confidential information, exposing the organization to potentially huge damage claims.
>
> These risks are directly related to defects that show up when the system is in production (or the product is on the market).

Input for the test strategy is a product risk analysis that indicates the risks for different characteristics and components of the product to be tested. Different ways of testing, with varying test depth and/or techniques, are derived from these risks.

A prerequisite for a meaningful product risk analysis and test strategy is co-operation between stakeholders and the test team. Stakeholders not only indicate potential risk factors (such as possible damage, chances of a fault occurring, etc.) but also take decisions regarding the required resources: time, money, material and people.

Initial level

At the initial level of a test process, the test strategy is often based on the individual testers' experience and knowledge of the system or the business. The test process is merely controlled by resources and time. Usually a simple test technique is used and only the functionality is tested. There is no co-ordination between different test levels as to how different product risks are covered.

4.3.1 Test strategy at a Controlled level

> The test strategy enables the distribution of the test efforts and resources among the test levels and test activities.

At a Controlled level, the prioritization and distribution of the test effort is based on the product risks of a test object, which are identified and prioritized by stakeholders. The principal stakeholder has the responsibility to determine the product risks. The test strategy indicates what, where, how much and how many times (retests after repair) is to be tested regarding these product risks. This is put into practice by spreading test activities over several test levels and test types, each with a test depth and coverage that follows from the decisions made. The number of test cases has a strong relationship with this strategy.

The way to minimize future product risks in the project is to find and repair the most important defects (those with the highest product risks). The test strategy aligns the test coverage with the associated product risks.

Checkpoints
1. The principal stakeholder agrees with the documented test strategy.
2. The test strategy is based on a product risk analysis.
3. There is a differentiation in test levels, test types, test coverage and test depth, depending on the analyzed risks.
4. For retests and regression testing a simple strategy determination takes place.

Enablers
- Risk management is an important part of the project but often related to project risks. When a risk analysis of the product is performed at an early stage in the project, the project has a steering instrument and testing has a sound basis for the test strategy.

Improvement suggestions

Involve the various stakeholders, such as the business customer, end user, systems manager, project manager, maintenance, (senior) developers in the product risk analysis and test strategy.

Create awareness by indicating the possible risks of the more vulnerable parts of the system, and the time that could be gained by not testing those parts that show little or no risk at all.

Convince project and line management to perform a product risk analysis, with people who have knowledge of the possible impact of a defect (such as business or sales line management), the chance of failure (such as engineers and architects) and the frequency of use (users).

Discuss the defects, found in the going or preceding project, with the stakeholders and set up a method to categorize the defects with the perceived risks. Based on these categories, define a retest strategy, considering per function or system a 'full' retest (test everything again), a 'thin' retest (only [a subset of] the fixed defects) or no retest at all..

Set up and maintain a regression test set, used to test new releases of the system for regression, often composed of existing test cases and suitable for automation.

Determine the test strategy using some or all of the following steps:
- *Determine the product risks:* Identify the chance of a failure and the likely damage if a defect occurs in production. Relate these to test goals, parts of the system and/or quality characteristics. Consult involving different stakeholders in this task: business stakeholders may identify possible damage; IT may identify the chance of failure.
- *Determine the relative importance of the test goals:* For each test goal, determine the relative importance for example in terms of high, medium or low risk. Note that the 'total system' may also be a test goal for a possible integral test.
- *Determine the test effort for each risk category/test goal:* The starting point for this could be that each test goal is equally time and effort consuming. Determine variations for the different categories; high, medium and low. Use the categories for planning activities: those parts with a higher risk should be tested first.
- *Determine the measuring techniques to be used:* As a final step within the test strategy, the measuring techniques and, in particular, test design techniques are selected, which are then applied to the selected test goals.

4.3.2 Test strategy at an Efficient level

> The test strategy is used to achieve the adequate balance between analyzed product risks, test coverage and available efforts and resources, involving all stakeholders.

To apply the Test strategy in an efficient way it is necessary that all stakeholders are involved in this process. Not only to deliver input on risk matters, but also to agree on the test approach. At this maturity level, the test strategy is an overall strategy, with derived strategies for test levels or test

4 Key areas

types. Mutual alignment of all the test activities in the overall test strategy prevents gaps and overlaps between tests. This also provides a greater possibility of performing the tests at the right moment; in other words when (with an equal test coverage) the costs of testing plus the costs of rework and retesting are at their lowest levels.

Defining the test strategy on each level follows a structured set of consecutively-executed steps. Development testing (often performed by the programmer) and system and acceptance testing (often performed by the business or users) are within the scope of the Test strategy. Also evaluations and reviews of the test basis, e.g. the functional or technical specifications are included.

Based on the chosen coverage or depth of testing one or more suitable test design techniques are applied. Next to required depth, the choice for a particular design technique may be based on aspects like the quality characteristics to be tested, the knowledge and experience of the testers and the test basis.

Checkpoints
1. All relevant stakeholders agree with the defined (and documented) test strategy.
2. The overlap or gaps in test coverage between test levels or test types are well considered.
3. The test strategy includes adequate test design techniques.

Enablers
- Integrated Project Management: close coordination and smooth integration with Project Management that will make testing also efficient.

Improvement suggestions

Investigate the test activities of different testers in test levels or test types and, if practiced, the evaluations. What do they do? How do they work? How do they approach the depth and completeness of the tests? Indicate the possible risks in the approach and emphasize the strong points. Discuss the possibilities and advantages of setting up an overall strategy.

Define and allocate the tasks of the coordination between test levels and continuously monitor this process. This role must be documented in the master test plan. This person reports to the project manager and other stakeholders. To prevent a conflict of interests, this person should have an independent relationship to the various test levels.

Perform an inspection on testware from previous test activities or reviews. The system test delivers a functionally-tested system, including test cases through to the acceptance test. The acceptance test evaluates these test cases (complete or spot-check) and, when in doubt, performs one or more test cases on the delivered software. Consequently its main effort can be directed towards testing the suitability and/or the usability of the system for the organization.

If there is a considerable overlap between test levels, a combined test (like combining the system test and acceptance test to an integrated test) may be an option. However, consider the suitability of the test environment, the different test tools and the know-how and skills of the (user) testers.

4.3.3 Test strategy at an Optimizing level

> The method of the test strategy is maintained well to ensure easy and valid application.

In the Optimizing situation, the test strategy is used in every project or test process as a basic rule. The strategy (the consecutive steps, the people involved, fine tuning, etc.) is evaluated and improved by using best practices and has become a crucial part of all SDLC management instruments within the organization. Where applicable, experiences from the production environment are used to substantiate and adjust the conclusions drawn.

Checkpoints
1. The process of creating the test strategy is evaluated regularly and, where necessary, adapted for future use.
2. The test strategy itself is evaluated against metrics on incidents that occur in production.

Enablers
- Process Management at an organizational level.
- Measurement and Analysis; Measurement objectives and activities are aligned with identified information needs and objectives.
- Measurement results, which address identified information needs and objectives, are provided.

Improvement suggestions
Define the role of a Test and Evaluation Coordinator (TEC), to co-ordinate and monitor all test and evaluation activities. The TEC reports to the business representatives. A point of interest is the independence of the TEC in relation to (on)going projects.

Make the test and evaluation plan an integral part of the project plan.

4.4 Test organization

> A test organization meets the needs of projects for test resources, test products and test services.

When speaking about a test organization we mean the organization as an entity. A test organization is the whole of test functions, facilities, procedures, activities, responsibilities and authorities including their relationships. A test organization utilizes means and activities to provide for test products and/or test services. As any organization it pursues collective goals, it controls its own performance and it is responsible for its own results.

In a test organization it's all about 'the right people expertise and experience at the right place', but most certainly also about the way people relate to each other, in terms of roles, tasks, responsibilities and authorities. One of the goals of a test organization is anchoring knowledge. Furthermore a test organization should be visible as an entity in an organization. This way testing can literally be found, being - let's say - a single point of information and making clear to others that testing earned its place and is regarded as important.

To be able to adjust quickly to changing circumstances the test organization needs to be set up to be flexible and needs to be aligned with the test process.

According to EFQM[1] organizations vary from activity-oriented (think of governmental organizations), to process-oriented, to system or even chain-oriented (e.g. Japanese car manufacturers). When organizations mature they have a tendency to develop in this order. This is an important reason to consider the position of the test organization within the Software Development Life Cycle (SDLC) organization. There are many different possibilities, for example:

- Within a project organization.
- As a staff organization (a supporting organization with limited responsibilities -advisory to the line function).
- As a line organization - a line organization is the classical organizational form: personnel are managed from above through the line; the organization has a pure operational focus.
- Externally.
- Partially line, partially externally.

---

[1] EFQM or European Foundation for Quality Management is a non-profit membership foundation that seeks to support organizations and their senior leaders in their need to implement strategies. The member enterprises work together to improve their capabilities in understanding and implementing what delivers higher performance.

4.4 Test organization

Ultimately a test organization is independent of other SDLC processes and completely accountable for its results. Nevertheless, there is no direct relation between the way a test organization is positioned and the maturity of a test organization. Within the SDLC for instance there may be no organization of distinct disciplines. When as an example functional application managers also have the role of designer and developer, is it efficient and effective to have your test organization designed as an independent test factory?

> **Example - Place of end-to-end testing in the organization [23]**
> End-to-end testing focuses on integrated processes. Chains can exceed projects, programs, departments and even organizations. Ideally the end-to-end test organization is placed within the end-to-end organization of the program or the line organization.

A test organization offers several products and services, e.g.:
- Equipped test resources with testing knowledge and specific expertise like business knowledge or test-specific knowledge:
  - Support the Product Risk Analysis.
  - Setting up a test approach for the overall project (master test plan).
  - Experience in test estimations.
  - Coordination of test projects.
  - Test automation.
- Test process description, templates and training materials for structured testing.
- Test tools, tool licenses and scripts.
- Communication and reporting structure.
- Overall procedures for defect management (this remains a project responsibility however).
- Test process improvement.

Many of the mentioned test products and test services are (to a certain extent) related to other Key areas. A test organization forms the glue between the different Key areas. That's why the actual place and set up of the test organization is to be considered a strategic choice.

Initial Level
At the Initial level of maturity people involved in testing are spread over the mostly business-oriented departments and often their roles concern specific child tasks (sub-tasks). Responsibilities are insufficiently clear and not well arranged. Often the testers have no common vision on quality and testing. Information is poorly shared and outputs of test activities are hardly compared (e.g. against a standard or amount of defects). There is no real organization of test, merely a random collection of (part time) individuals performing separate activities and showing individual initiatives.

4.4.1 Test organization at a Controlled level

> A test organization enables uniformity in test approach, test products and procedures, agreements and clear test results.

Within the Software Development Life Cycle different test activities with their own responsibilities can be identified. Most likely design, development and maintenance are somewhat organized and regarded as specific functions. In order to get the same effects test is also organized to a certain extent (within a project), depending largely on the maturity of the other processes in the SDLC and how they are organized.

At the Controlled level the test organization has identifiable people who are responsible for testing. They are recognized by the (rest of the) organization, both on the business and supplier side. It is clear what the 'testers' have to offer in terms of test products and test service. People know what to expect from test.

Checkpoints
1. People involved know where to find the persons (or department) responsible for test services.
2. There is a structure of control and accountability within the test organization.
3. Test tasks and responsibilities are defined (and documented) and are assigned to a person or organizational unit.
4. The products and services of the test organization are clear to its clients.

Enablers
- The organization needs to have a good knowledge management system in place which the test organization can leverage to consolidate the knowledge.

Improvement suggestions

In a small organization, make someone responsible for testing. This 'Mr. or Mrs. Test' should be approachable for any test related item.

In a larger organization or organizational unit, the best possible option for the (physical) test team location can be decided on, based on what kind of test organization is in place.

Enable exchange and sharing of knowledge, experiences and best practices between testers and/or people with test tasks e.g. by regular workshops or meetings.

Explain to stakeholders that it is necessary to distinguish roles and responsibilities for assigning the test tasks, acceptance and execution.

List possible products and/or services for a test organization. This could be something like 'performing a test level', 'drawing up a test plan' or 'provide test consultancy'.

Set up a marketing and communication plan: what are we selling?, for whom is this interesting?, at which price?, under which precondition?, etc.

4.4.2 Test organization at an Efficient level

> A test organization enables the right test expertise and experience at the right place.

Different persons from different departments can be involved in a form of testing. They may not be aware of other test activities being performed in other places of the organization. Their way of working may be completely different and templates, procedures and tools used may differ. The first step towards an efficient test organization may be an organic coordination of all these separate test activities.

In an efficient test organization, test resources are provided to projects in the form of a service that covers the following activities:
- Execution
- Support (coaching and training)
- Control (audit and review)
- Maintenance
- Research and development.

It is also possible that external parties provide test services, including delivering resources and support or, in case of outsourcing, taking full or partial responsibility for testing. When the needs of project resources change, reallocation of resources between different projects takes place.

Within the test organization there is a stronger focus on the actual needs of a client than at the controlled level, resulting in a shift from activities towards output. Related test activities are identified, structured and monitored.

In order to achieve a predictable output procedures are designed and (internal) training is provided for. Need for tools and other support is mutually investigated and made available.

The organization's vision on testing, being a high level collaborated view by senior management and the test organization, is described in a test policy. The test policy is owned by the senior management.

Checkpoints
1. Different persons or departments that provide test services reconcile the organizing of their test work.
2. The test organization provides the agreed test resources and services to the projects.

4 Key areas

3. A well considered choice has been made as where and how to position the test organization.
4. The test policy is followed.

Enablers
- Project support organization: one or more project support organization(s) that provides services around human resources, development environments and tools, and processes, can include services around test resources as well.

Improvement suggestions

Research the demand from different test projects. Categorize the demand in terms of types of resources and kinds of services per resource. Develop a service catalogue with types of resources and kinds of services and decide which services should be provided by a test organization, based on a simple business case.

Define a vision and growth path for the test organization.

4.4.3 Test organization at an Optimizing level

> A test organization leads to continuously improved results of test services.

Improvement and innovation are important as are relations with groups and people outside the test organization. The test organization is working for all levels and the most important processes.

In an optimizing process the attention for internal and external quality leads to better results. This includes the maintenance of the service catalogue which is maintained in the way that it reflects the need of supply to adjust to demand. The test organization will focus on providing the 'right people' with proper expertise and experience as required.

The test organization improves itself continuously by evaluating the internal processes and making changes. Comparisons with external parties are made and external parties are used for supply if they can provide a better service.

Checkpoints
1. The products and services of the test organization are regularly evaluated; new services are added when they are cost-effective.
2. The test organization is held accountable for success and failure of test assignments.
3. The test organization performance is regularly compared with external suppliers or similar test organizations.

Enablers
- A test organization can always perform better when the interrelated parts of the organization are at the same maturity level, and co-operate with and respond proactively towards each other.

Improvement suggestions

Monitor the demand of existing services and adjust services for which demand has changed.

Check periodically if demand emerges for new test services and make a decision about including those services in the service catalogue.

Keep track of costs for delivering services and compare with external parties, and/or test organizations in similar organizations (which are at a similar maturity level).

Review the internal processes of the test organization and see where optimizations can be done.

4.5 Communication

> Distinct communication ensures common understanding and alignment of expectations between all parties involved.

Communication can be (very) informal and can have no official status, meaning that possible agreements need not to be formalized. It can also be very structured: (official) meetings or reports. In more formal organizations decisions are being made solely on the basis of reporting. But in most situations any form of communication can lead to decision making, with the possibility to confirm this in the reporting. There are various means through which communication takes place, such as face-to-face, phone, email, conference calls, intranet pages, wikis, etc.

Clear communication is needed to create the right conditions for performing tests, co-ordinate the test strategy, tune activities, negotiate priorities, etc. Communication, at its best, encourages interactivity and feedback. Lack of communication can result in taking the wrong decisions (due to wrong, unverified or failing information) and in the end cause lack of motivation with testers and/or lack of commitment for the test activities by stakeholders.

All considered, communication within the test process doesn't really differ from communication in other processes. However, there are some aspects that need to be taken into consideration. Communication from and towards the test process addresses progress like all other processes. But in addition it focuses on product quality and pro-actively advising on risks and opportunities. The test team communicates these to the different stakeholders. In a test process, various stakeholders like developers, management and clients are involved. In turn stakeholders keep the test team informed. However, all too often the test team is left out from information or isn't consulted in certain project matters (possibly due to a lack of commitment or underestimation of the impact for the test project).

With the improvement of the test process come different demands on communication. More formal aspects are being introduced. More formal communication does not automatically mean more communication, but fixed composition of participants, frequency and agenda.

Initial level

At the Initial level communication takes place, but is rather ad hoc and incidental. In practice, ad hoc communication can be very effective. Nevertheless at this level there is just not sufficient information from and towards the test team to manage and control the test process adequately.

4.5.1 Communication at a Controlled level

> Communication of information to all involved makes it possible to take the appropriate decisions.

At the Controlled level, the test team receives ample information for managing their tests. Stakeholders get decision making information (apart from reports). There is sufficient transparency within the test team, as well as between testers and stakeholders.
The level of communication within the test team and between the test team and other parties ensures a good mutual relationship, motivation and common understanding. It also leads to early detection of (emerging) problems, so if measures are needed they can be taken in time.

4.5.2 Checkpoints

1. Every team member is aware of decisions being made and of internal progress.
2. The test team actively gathers relevant information from stakeholders.
3. It is possible to trace back points of action, agreements and decisions of the test team.
4. The test team deliberates with stakeholders about progress, product quality and risks and signals proactively potential delays as well.

Enablers
- Project management: (minutes from) project meetings form input for managing decisions within the test process.

Improvement suggestions

Set up a schedule of all types of information that are required for managing the test and who or which meeting can provide it. Choose the most appropriate communication means based on their relative advantages.

Get involved in meetings, as mentioned above.

Schedule and prepare test team meetings on a fixed time and day, while ensuring the space for ad hoc meetings. These meetings have a fixed agenda and have as its main focus progress (lead time and spent hours) and the quality of the object to be tested or under test. Meeting minutes are taken.

When it is not possible to gather the whole test team, have each team member participate periodically in the meeting. Or split up the team into smaller groups so everyone can have their say and can focus on, for example, one particular part of the test process.

Provide a consistent handling of the actions which arise from meetings.

4 Key areas

Particularly during the execution phase, it is wise to keep the test team constantly up-to-date and well informed on progress, for example with a short kick-off each day.

Arrange for project news to be announced in the test team meeting.

Ensure that test results are on the agenda of the project and steering group meetings.

Communicate about the progress of defects since they are important for the control of the test process.

4.5.3 Communication at an Efficient level

> Concise form and content of information for the target audience contributes to more productive work.

Like in any process there are different goals of communication within the test process. Depending on the goals and the audience the appropriate form and medium need to be used. For test projects but also for test organizations a communication plan (a reporting plan may be part of this) may be drawn up.

Different means of communications have been developed to overcome limitations. Very large teams cannot meet face-to-face all the time, especially if they are widely distributed geographically (beware of issues like time zone differences). Additionally, not everyone works from the same place all the time.

> **In more detail - New possibilities for communication**
> In the internet era, new means of communication are developed continuously. Possibilities for chatting, conference calls with voice and or video, sharing documents and presentations online improve while network capacities increase. New phenomena like social networking, blogs, wikis and other services appear and provide new possibilities for more effective and efficient communication.

Also, not all information will be relevant to all people. Depending on people's responsibilities, they may only need to be informed or consulted, without actually participating in the decision making. People who are responsible or accountable have different information needs. Still, sometimes it is necessary to have everyone involved in a meeting and to discuss or brainstorm possible solutions or decisions.

If meetings are held, the most appropriate way for the test team to share information is to participate in those meeting. Relevant meetings are project meetings, defects consultation, change control board, etc.

Be aware that efficient communication can actually mean more effort needs to be made by the sender (e.g. the test manager) since fine-tuning the content of communication to the needs of the receiver(s) requires more thought than simply providing all the data or information. Furthermore, besides more formal communication there is always space for ad hoc communication.

Checkpoints
1. The test team identifies which information needs to be shared with which stakeholder.
2. The test team participates in relevant meetings with other stakeholders.
3. The test team has the different (communication) means necessary to its disposal to communicate with its stakeholders using an appropriate form.

Enablers
- Stakeholder management: identifying different target groups with their respective information needs and authority levels will enable more effective communication.

Improvement suggestions

Get involved in project meetings for exchanging information about progress, meeting prerequisites, project changes, etc.

Invite other expertise to the test team meeting for obtaining mutual understanding and quick insight.

If for any reason it is not efficient to join a specific project meeting, communicate relevant test issues to the project manager and make sure they are on the agenda. Ensure that the project manager gives feedback on these issues to the test team.

Defects consultation is a periodic discussion about the progress of solving defects. Although the test team is not responsible for the progress of defects, it is very dependent on the progress. Make a set up and procedure for the periodic defect meeting.

Establish a list of available communication means which are to be used for a specific test project. Think especially about intranet or sharenet solutions.

Do not underestimate the power of face-to-face communication and personal interaction. Even in times of pressure, this kind of communication may be more effective than sending a SMS or email.

Encourage feedback, both inside and outside the test process, based on mutual respect. Ask each team member to regularly evaluate communication, what is going well and what could be improved.

4.5.4 Communication at an Optimizing level

> Communication is a means for team building.

In order to prevent possible future miscommunication, all of the communication is periodically being analyzed and best practices and lessons learned are collected for future use.

> **In more detail - Prepare for meetings**
> In order to achieve effective meetings, decision making documents and minutes from the previous meeting are being sent and read in advance. Every participant should prepare for the upcoming meeting.

Checkpoints
1. Best practices and lessons learned regarding communication and its efficiency are evaluated during and at the end of a test project for future purposes.
2. The organization investigates the use of new means of communication and defines policies.

Enablers
- None.

Improvement suggestions
Arrange for training and education in effective communication. Focus not only on presentations, reports and documentation, but also on face-to-face communication like meeting techniques.

The test team or test organization may come across means of communication that are theoretically available, but not in current use within the organization. Inform the rest of the organization about their potential benefits and how they can be used in the organization.

4.6 Reporting

> Reporting provides stakeholders with insight to support the decision making process and test project accounting.

Reporting is considered the most important output product of the test process. Its actual significance is based on the degree of formalism and test accounting, needed or expected within the project. The test process is about providing insight into the quality level of the product (test object) which is more than 'finding defects'. Therefore reporting should be focused on giving concrete evidence to the principal stakeholder concerning the product quality versus the risks of insufficient quality.

Reporting is written communication going one-way, from the test project to one (the principal) or more stakeholders. With reporting the test process provides insight into a number of aspects:

- *Progress:* People involved in testing need to know what the status and progress of the test activities is. Not only in terms of time (hours planned, spent and forecast) or money (budgeted and spent). The progress of the test process is also reported by figures on planned and executed test cases, the number of open and solved defects and last but not least: successes.
- *Product risks:* The quality of the test object can be indicated by the priority and severity of (solved and unsolved) defects. These defects have a strong relationship with the perceived and analyzed product risks: do the defects belong to a high or low risk category, do the solved defects require re-testing, etc. The report needs to indicate the status of these risks.
- *Project risks:* The test project reports about projects risks, bottlenecks and possible mitigation measures. An important project risk can be not meeting the deadline for the test object to move to production. Also for these risks the report must produce possible measures and recommendations. Such an advice can be a full re-test for high risk areas and a thin re-test or no re-test at all for the non-risky areas.
- *Release advice:* The test team does not take a decision for a product to 'go live'. The test team should provide sufficient information, to the principal and other stakeholders, to take this decision. When the next stage after testing is 'production' the report on the product quality is called a release advice and contains, next to product quality figures, information on the possible behavior of the product in production. A well defined product risk analysis and test strategy are vital for this advice.

Adequate reporting makes it possible for the stakeholders to take measures in time. Substantiating the advice with trend information provides stakeholders with arguments for taking the (often costly) measures.

4 Key areas

Initial level

At the Initial Level reporting is done ad hoc and the most important stakeholders consider the test reports to be insufficient for their decision making process.

4.6.1 Reporting at a Controlled level

> The test team and stakeholders agree on what is reported and how, thus preventing a lack of information or an information overload.

The approach for reporting is clear and preferably formalized, for instance in a (master) test plan or in a separate reporting plan. This approach for reporting includes the target groups for reporting, the frequency, means and content of reporting.

Checkpoints
1. The reporting contains aspects of time and/or costs, results and risks.
2. The reporting frequency and content matches the basic demands of stakeholders for the decision making process.
3. Reporting is done in writing.

Enablers
- Project management: the structure of reporting and metrics used can be exchanged between the test project and the project.

Improvement suggestions

Negotiate with stakeholders (at least with the principal stakeholder) how and how frequently they are informed and which information they want to have. Make the stakeholders aware that they need this information to take decisions on measures concerning the quality of the test object.

Create a reporting plan, defining the type of reporting that will be produced. Include the target groups for reporting, the frequency, means and content of reporting. The reporting plan can be part of the (master) test plan.

Agree on reporting templates that are used within the test process. This makes it possible to reuse parts of the reporting (like risk mitigation tables).

Establish that the reporting includes both the quality of the test object and the status of the test process.

Reuse parts of reporting content that only need limited adjustment. Create awareness that reports are part of testware (management) and should be available for reuse.

4.6.2 Reporting at an Efficient level

> Reporting is tuned to specific target groups to support the decision making process.

Reporting is tailor-made for specific target groups, such as the defect meeting participants, project, business and senior management groups. Project management will be interested in a detailed overview of the status of planned activities versus the actual situation. Business management is likely to be primarily interested in the quality of the test object, and senior management typically only wants a high level overview of the test process. Creating different views (like aggregations) or reports on the same base data for different target groups will probably mean additional work for the test manager. But the goal of reporting is to provide solid information for the decision making process and information tuned to the reader makes this more efficient. The test manager will weigh the effort of creating separate reports for specific target groups against the benefits to the decision making process.

> **In more detail - Fine tuning reports**
> Two reports that can be tuned very well for specific target groups are the progress report and the risk report. This can be done by changing the level of detail for the progress report or 'filtering' the risks in the risk report for different target groups.
> A progress report typically contains the status of the test object (results), product risk and strategy adjustment, progress of the test process (time and costs), and problem areas/points of discussion.
> A risk report typically contains a description of the event / scenario, the consequences of the event for the test project, the significance of the event to the degree to which the various product risks are covered, possible countermeasures and recommendations.

Providing stakeholders with information by reporting extensively can 'distract' the test manager from actually managing the test project, especially in very dynamic test projects or when managing multiple test projects. For a good balance other ways of communication can also be applied to suit the information needs of stakeholders. Alternative means of communicating are addressed in the Communication Key area.

Checkpoints
1. Fulfilling the reporting demands of stakeholders, needed for an efficient decision making process, is balanced against the effort for providing it.
2. The reporting contains trends and recommendations concerning test process progress and project risks.
3. The reporting contains trends and recommendations concerning test goals and product risks.

Enablers
- None.

Improvement suggestions
Make sure that the defined reports are tuned to the specific target groups.

Distinguish between information stakeholders 'need to have' and what is considered 'nice to have'. The latter could be provided on demand and not as part of the standard reporting.

4.6.3 Reporting at an Optimizing level

> Reporting provides information that can be used to optimize the software development lifecycle.

Reporting is used as a means to provide the different target groups with insight in opportunities to improve the software development lifecycle. This is best done when the information provided is factual and verifiable, for which the application of metrics is very useful.

An example is the reporting on comparing estimations with actual results, trend analysis and comparing and benchmarking of test projects. The conclusion based on the reporting could for example be that the test process has failed to produce an adequate planning and that a different way of estimating is necessary. The 'cause analysis' can be substantiated with other metrics, like test environment down times or slow test design progress.

In this form of reporting the recommendations do not merely point at test activities, but also to the activities outside the test process, meaning the software development lifecycle. For example recommendations to perform (extra) reviews on the functional specifications.

Checkpoints
1. Reporting provides data and/or measurements that can be used for current and future improvements of the test process and the software development lifecycle.
2. The data and/or measurements for software process improvement are handed over to a line organization at the test project closure.

Enablers
- Software process improvement: discuss improvement opportunities with a running initiative for software process improvement.

Improvement suggestions
Collect information during the test project that can be used as a basis for improvement of the software development lifecycle.

4.7 Test process management

> Managing the test process maximizes the execution of the test assignment within the required time, costs, and results.

The goals of testing are too complex to reach within one simple activity. Dividing the activities is worked out by distinguishing a number of phases, such as planning, preparation, specification, execution and completion. Each phase consists of defined activities with a number of actions and deliverables.
Testing should be organized as a process, either within the software development project, or as a separate project besides development. One of the first and essential deliverables from the test process is a test plan where the expectations of all stakeholders are set: what result does the principal stakeholder expect, how can the test team reach these goals and what does the test team expect from other stakeholders in order to be able to reach the goals. It is essential that all stakeholders agree on the test plan.
By executing the activities according to the agreed plan, the goals will be reached… in theory. In practice, there are always project risks that influence the execution of the test plan in a way that unplanned measures have to be taken. Test process management verifies to which extent the test plan can be followed and the progress is regularly reported to the stakeholders. If deviations between the actual progress and the plan occur, these deviations are reported. This report also contains measures that the test team takes to be able to continue according to plan again. If the test team is not able to do this by itself, the help from stakeholders will be called in and the choice can be made to adjust the test plan.

Initial level
At the initial level the test process seems to have only one phase: test execution, There is insufficient insight from the test team about the expectations from the stakeholders. It could very well be that the stakeholders don't know what to expect from testing. The scope of testing might be wrong, test activities start once the test object has been delivered and some activities are executed too late or not at all. Other activities may take too much time afterwards because they were not prepared and estimation of costs and time are not provided. This makes proper control and management rather difficult.

4.7.1 Test process management at a Controlled level

> Proactive management of the test process enables the fulfillment of the test assignment.

4 Key areas

At the Controlled level there is a shift in attitude: from reactive toward increasingly proactive. Activities are being planned, prepared, scheduled, monitored and where necessary adjusted. Before testing starts, a test plan is created where activities are described in a work break down structure. The plan is propounded to the principal stakeholder, who gives his consent and who feels committed to the plan.

The test activities address the core business of testing (creating and executing test cases) but also secondary activities like reporting and installing and maintaining environments. The deliverables are defined and thus predictable for all participants. The time line for the deliverables is clear and can be known by all involved.

The test plan is also laid before other stakeholders to agree not only upon possible prerequisites that the stakeholders need to fulfill but also upon the approach of the test.

The path that is laid out in the test plan, but the test team - with the help of all the stakeholders - needs to make sure that they stay on track. That means that the test activities need to be monitored. Deviations of the track can be established with the help of basic metrics (see section 4.9). Possible measures against the deviations should be presented to the principal stakeholder so he or she can initiate the necessary adjustments.

Checkpoints

1. At the start of the test project a test plan is created. The test plan includes at least the test assignment, the test scope, the test planning, the roles and responsibilities.
2. The test plan is agreed with the principal stakeholder.
3. Each test activity is monitored and when necessary adjustments are initiated.
4. The test plan is agreed with the relevant stakeholders.

Enablers

- Process and product quality assurance, as this provides the organization with insight into the process and testware created.
- Project management. Project management plans, monitors and controls a project. Testing is an integral part of the project and has many dependencies with other development disciplines. Good project management therefore not only makes management of the test process easier, but also has a shared responsibility in the management of the test process. Project management and test process management have many resemblances and can exchange best practices.

Improvement suggestions

Assign budget and time for testing within the development project.

Organize testing as a separate subproject and divide this project in logical phases (at least planning, preparation and execution).

Make someone, preferably not the project manager, responsible for managing the test project.

Define and agree goals for testing.

Search for appropriate test activities in available test methods in order to break them down over the separate phases.

4.7.2 Test process management at an Efficient level

> Managing the test process with clear authorizations makes instant adjustments possible to keep the test project on track.

The progress of all activities is closely followed. The test lead anticipates quickly and accurately to trends and deviations. He or she has clearly defined authorizations to act upon them within certain margins. With the decision-making authority close to the source of where complications occur it is possible for the test lead to, for instance, reallocate resources and to directly address problems to stakeholders and make arrangements. Project issues that will result in significant deviations and that endanger the test assignment are discussed with the principal stakeholder. Together with other relevant stakeholders solutions are determined. All adjustments to the test plan are documented (for example by adapting the test plan or making an exception report) for reasons of traceability and accountability.

For being able to steer and control the test process in more detail the test plan needs to be more detailed. Day to day activities need to be organized as such that data needed for substantiating measures can be derived from standard deliverables. No additional investigations or data gathering are needed.

Checkpoints
1. (Anticipated) Deviations of the test plan are discussed with the principal stakeholder and other relevant stakeholders.
2. Adjustments to the test plan are documented.
3. The test lead has a delegated mandate for the (re-)allocation of resources.

Enablers
- None.

Improvement suggestions
Reserve time for test process management in the test plan. Ensure to use this time, also when there is much pressure in the project. Realize that when the pressure is high, the time you'd save by not monitoring the test process, will probably not solve the problems. Instead, taking the time to

4 Key areas

sit down and analyze the problems is more productive in solving the problems.

Identify project risks in the test plan, together with measures to minimize or avoid the risks. During the process, review the project risks: add new risks when you see them and remove the risks that didn't show up. Inform the stakeholders of all risks, especially the ones that they need to handle.

Verify that the progress that is expected is actually made. If not, find out what caused the problem. If you can solve the problem yourself, do it. Otherwise, escalate the problem.

Whenever the actual progress is different from the planned progress, review the planning: what do we need to do to continue as planned? Is an update to the plan necessary?

Always inform the stakeholders about progress versus plan, risks, measures, as well as incidents that happen during the test process.

4.7.3 Test process management at an Optimizing level

> Lessons learned on test process management advance the effectiveness and efficiency of steering test projects to their required end result.

Lessons can be learned from the way the test process is managed. Evaluation is done regularly and may be part of the evaluation of test projects, during and/or at the end of the test. What is going well and what could be done better? To get a broad and open view the relevant stakeholders are being involved in the evaluation. The lessons learned are documented and available to all test projects.

At the start of a test project the test leads lays to heart the lessons from previous test projects to avoid stepping in the same pitfalls and to embrace best practices. The objective is to stimulate repetition of positive results and to avoid repetition of negative results. This should result in more a more effective and efficient approach in fulfilling test assignments.

Checkpoints
1. Test process management is regularly evaluated, internally (by the test organization) and with stakeholders.
2. Lessons learned from earlier test projects are used for improving test process management.

Enablers
- Project Closure Report. If the software development project performs a self-evaluation, testing can be part of this evaluation. The results can be added to the Project Closure Report of the project.

Improvement suggestions

Embrace change! Encourage people to look beyond their own project borders and witness testing in other projects, departments or even organizations

Make someone in the line organization responsible for evaluating the test projects, or at least for the evaluation results.

4.8 Estimating and planning

> The proper use of appropriate estimating and planning techniques makes the test process planning and estimating predictable and reliable.

This key area indicates how and which activities, techniques and methods are used to define the correct estimation and planning of the test project. High quality estimating and planning techniques are very important because these are the basis of allocating the right resource capacity.

This key area is closely related to Test process management, since it provides the baseline for monitoring the test process. The distinction between the two is that this key area addresses the activities to put together, discuss and agree on budget and planning topics whereas Test process management takes the outcome of Estimating and planning as a given and addresses how it is monitored and how deviations are dealt with.

One of the purposes of planning is to create the possibility for management to take action when needed. This requires planning to be 'fine grained' enough to recognize potential deviations and yet to be 'coarse' enough not to become outdated too quickly. Reliable planning and estimation will help to prevent delays because sufficient resources have been allocated at the right time. In practice, a budget is often imposed by the client, or a planning can only be developed within the boundaries of strict milestones that are unlikely to be renegotiated. This does not mean that a test manager should desist from estimating and planning within these constraints, but that he/she should be realistic in defining resource requirements.

Initial level
At the initial stage of testing maturity, a test project is usually estimated and planned in a relatively unstructured way, so that the resources required and planned activities are roughly estimated and sometimes not carefully planned.

4.8.1 Estimating and planning at a Controlled level

> The amount of resources per activity required is predicted.

A test project comprises several phases or activities than can be budgeted, scheduled and monitored separately (such as test preparation or test execution). A budget is allocated to every phase or activity of the test project. The allocations are based on simple techniques such as the use of certain ratios. Which activities are identified depend among other things on the development method used and the test level or type at hand. For a test level performed by a dedicated test team other activities can be recognized than for development testing or unit testing in an agile delivery team. The activities should not be too small or too big. As a rule of thumb, activities should not be budgeted separately on a level below 40 hours per activity. An important first step in gaining control of the planning and estimating of the test effort is that the results of these activities can be substantiated. In this way, the planning and estimating is usually of a higher quality, and is more reliable and predictable when allocating resources.

Checkpoints
1. For test effort estimation, simple techniques are used such as ratios.
2. For each test activity there is an indication of the period in which it runs, the resources required and the products to be delivered. Activities to be identified are: test planning and management, defining test cases and executing test cases.
3. The dependencies between test phases or test activities are plotted in a test planning. A certain overlap of test phases and test activities is allowed.
4. Test estimations and test planning are discussed with the principal stakeholder.

Enablers
- Project management can provide information about the time and budget allocated to the various work packages. This information can be used for estimating the test project. This could happen the other way round as well, whereby the test project estimation can help the project estimation.
- Information about the size of development.

Improvement suggestions
Gain insight into the quality and method of estimating and planning; for example by analyzing the estimating and planning of previous projects, how they were substantiated and how reliable they proved to be.
Try to validate estimates in different ways, including the following:
- Take a percentage of the total effort, based on experience of similar projects. For example:

functional design:	20%
technical design, realization and unit test:	40-45%
system test:	15-20%
acceptance test:	20%

- Employ standard ratios in testing, based on experience of similar test projects. Some of Sogeti's own experience ratios include:

Preparation:	10%
Specification:	40%
Execution including one retest:	45%
Completion:	5%

  Execution of a retest takes only 50% of the execution of a first test, because the testware is now 'tested' and reusable.

4 Key areas

Budget the overhead at an additional 10-20% of the phases mentioned above.
- Estimate the number of hours of the separate activities and then extrapolate them. For example; specifying test cases for 1 function takes 4 hours. There are 100 functions, so 400 hours are needed. Add to this an estimated 50 hours for other activities in the Specification phase (such as infrastructure!), and that makes a total of 450 hours. Further extrapolation is possible by means of the standard ratios; see the item above.

Work out a procedure to set up test estimation (for example a minimum 2 rules of thumb should be applied)
After finishing the project, reassess the estimates and the estimation procedures and if necessary, adjust for future projects.
Agree beforehand how to deal with learning time, excess work and waiting times.
In planning, take into account the required time for:
- The transfer from a previous phase and installation of the test object
- Rework and retests.

In practice, a good working method for planning is to plan the entire test project comprehensively and make a detailed plan for the next 3 to 4 weeks that is refreshed frequently.

4.8.2 Estimating and planning at an Efficient level

> Formal techniques make estimating and planning reliable.

For all test phases and/or test activities, the estimates are based on the use of formal techniques such as function point analysis and test point analysis. It is preferable that metrics from previous projects are analyzed and used to update the estimating and planning techniques or methods.
When a project has to be re-estimated because of delays, the experience of the project so far should be taken into account.

Checkpoints
1. To be as accurate as possible, at least two estimating techniques are used.
2. The test phases and/or test activities are estimated and planned, using formal techniques.
3. Metrics are used to support the estimating and planning activities.
4. The test planning includes a testability review of the test basis and the evaluation of the test project.

Enablers
- Project management can provide information about the time and budget allocated to the various work packages, which can be used for estimating the test project. This could happen the other way round as well, whereby the test project estimation can help the project estimation.
- Function Point Analysis or any other formal estimating technique for software development.

Improvement suggestions

Define a set of formal estimating and planning techniques, suitable for use within the project.

Collect figures from the overall project that can be used as a basis for the test project planning and estimating.

Define milestones in the timeline of the test project that will be used for evaluating the estimating and planning used. This allows the timely adjustment of these values if required.

4.8.3 Estimating and planning at an Optimizing level

> Estimating is based on experience data from the organization.

The organization has defined the estimation techniques to be used and will also provide key data in order to 'ground' the techniques used.

Checkpoints
1. The test planning includes the conservation of testware for future reuse.
2. A set of estimation techniques and principles are maintained at an organizational level.
3. Key figures/data for the defined estimation techniques are provided at an organizational level.

Enablers
- The measurement and analysis for defining and monitoring the collection of metrics on test project effort, throughout the organization.

Improvement suggestions

Define a set of techniques that can be used and adapted to the organization's specific needs.

Collect key figures/data for use in combination with the defined techniques.

4 Key areas

4.9 Metrics

> Metrics provide objectivity by quantifying observations.

Metrics are quantified observations of the characteristics of a product or process. Metrics are used within the test process to estimate and manage the test process, to give justification for the test process, to substantiate test advice and to compare systems or test processes.

Metrics are also important for improving the test process. The effects of certain improvement measures can be assessed by comparing metrics before and after the implementation of the measure. This is explored in section 6.2.4.

The Metrics Key area is about the process of defining and managing metrics covering the test process itself (for instance test object, progress, testware, test project or the test process). Examples of metrics that can be used are described as part of the Improvement suggestions per Maturity level.

Commitment of management and other stakeholders is a necessary condition for retrieving metrics. In practice, gathering the necessary data from the different departments or making comparisons between different branches within large organizations can be rather expensive or difficult. Relevant data may be shattered over different disciplines, departments or organizational units and they may not have been recorded in the same way.

Therefore the effort of collecting and analyzing data should always be taken into account when deciding to implement metrics. The metrics should also be kept as simple as possible and one should start with a limited set of metrics. Setting the wishes and the need for information of senior management as a starting point improves commitment.

The process of managing metrics distinguishes the following aspects:
- Define goals and find suitable metrics.
- Specify the characteristics of those metrics.
- Collect the metrics from test projects.
- Analyze and maintain the collected metrics.
- Publish the metrics.
- Act upon metrics.
- Adapt and optimize the metrics if necessary.

Initial level
A test process is at the Initial level when it is impossible or difficult for the test team to provide well-founded answers to questions about the quality of the test object or the test process. Comparison of projects or test processes is based on rather subjective observations.

4.9.1 Metrics at a Controlled level

> With the defined metrics it is possible to estimate and monitor the test process.

Within the test process metrics are defined that will help to estimate the test process. In order to collect the right metrics the required information needs to be recorded uniformly and stored systematically. Metrics are collected and analyzed as a part of the process and related activities, for example, testers routinely log their hours spent in a detailed way. In addition, the metrics collected are based on mutual agreement with the stakeholders of the test process, because they may need to contribute to the data for the metrics and because they should consider the metrics to be meaningful.

Checkpoints
1. In the test process metrics are defined and used to estimate and control the test project.
2. The necessary input for the metrics is recorded uniformly and the defined metrics are systematically stored.
3. The input (data) for metrics is provably accurate.

Enablers
- Measurement and analysis as a formalized process within the software development lifecycle. This process will provide information on the specific metrics required by the organization and will:
  - Specify the objectives of measurement and analysis so that they are aligned with identified information needs and objectives.
  - Specify the measures, analysis techniques and mechanisms for data collection and storage, reporting and feedback.
  - Implement the collection, storage, analysis and reporting of the data.
  - Provide objective results that can be used in making informed decisions, and taking appropriate corrective actions.

Improvement suggestions
Determine a person, group and/or department within the (test) organization that is responsible for defining and collecting metrics.
Next, define to which goals the metrics are related and how these metrics will indicate reaching the desired results. Than decide on which (set of) metrics supports the goal best. Example: if the goal is to have more insight in the time that is spent on testing, define metrics like:
- Hours spent on test planning and control (drawing up a test plan, negotiate with stakeholders, ...).
- Test preparation (intake of the test basis, design of test cases, ...).
- Test execution.
- Meetings (within the test team, outside the test team, project, ...).

4 Key areas

- Idle time (waiting for the test environment, waiting for the test object, ...).

Define an approach for the administration of metrics. In many situations the projects time registration will not be sufficient because it is not detailed enough.

Example metrics appropriate for the Controlled level

Elementary metrics on used resources (hours), executed activities (hours and lead time) and size and complexity of the test object (function points, 'kilo lines of code' (KLOC), number of functions etc.) can be used to control and steer the test process in order to fulfill the test assignment. The following metrics are an addition to that.

Some examples of metrics are:

Measure	Metrics	Contribution/Remark
Test coverage rate	Percentage of test situations, as defined by the coverage type, that is covered by the tests.	This metric enables you to determine to which degree you tested all possibilities described in the test basis.
Test design rate	Number of specified test cases divided by the number of planned test cases.	For monitoring the progress of the test case design to keep the test phase off the project's critical path.
Test execution rate	Number of executed test cases divided by the number of specified test cases.	For monitoring the test execution progress, to keep this test phase as short as possible on the project's critical path.
Progress of test execution	Number of executed test cases, split up in: - Passed (successfully executed) - Failed (test case led to one or more defects) - Blocked (test blocking)	These metrics give insight in the number of test cases that still need to be (re)tested.
Defect severity	Defects, split up in: - Solved / unsolved - Severity	This metric gives information on the quality of (parts of) the test object and the progress in solving the most important defects.

4.9 Metrics

Measure	Metrics	Contribution/Remark
Defects in production	Defects found in production. In other words, the number of defects not found as part of the test process.	This metric is an indication of the effectiveness of testing.
Budget utilization rate	Test budget used (hours or money) divided by the test budget available.	This metric helps to determine if the remaining test budget is sufficient to perform the planned test activities.
Test phase ratio	Number of hours spent per test phase (preparation / specification and execution).	Metrics collected from previous projects support allocating appropriate resources for each planned test phase.
Waiting time rate	Idle time / working hours in 'standstill' as percentage of the total test hours.	Metrics collected from previous projects give a means to include a realistic amount of 'slack' in the test planning.
Exit criteria	Composition of other metrics, e.g. progress of test execution and defect severity.	Indicates when the satisfactory quality level is reached to continue to the next test level or to production.

4.9.2 Metrics at an Efficient level

> The provided objectivity through metrics outweighs the effort of collecting and analyzing the measurement data.

At the Efficient level there is a balance between the effort necessary to gather, analyze and maintain the metrics and the actual result (e.g. a well founded advice). Collecting and analyzing data should never cost more effort than is gained by a metric. If the benefits do not outweigh the effort then the application of this metric needs serious consideration with all parties involved. The more difficult it is to collect data, the bigger the chance that it will not be accepted.

Checkpoints
1. The required effort to collect, analyze and value the necessary data is measured against the benefits.
2. Collecting metrics does not conflict with the progress and quality of the test process.

4 Key areas

3. In the test process metrics are defined and used to measure the efficiency of the test process.
4. Conclusions coming from analyzed metrics are discussed with stakeholders and are acted upon.

Enablers
- None.

Improvement suggestions

Keep the metric simple. Avoid the use of a variety of formulas.

Using templates may make it easier to record data.

Implement a process that will take care of collecting metrics from projects, compare them, analyze them and then publish the results.

Check with the stakeholders regularly if the metrics are still necessary and useful.

Example metrics appropriate for the Efficient level

The following metrics give the test team means to control and steer the test process in such a way that costs and benefits are optimized.

Measure	Metrics	Contribution/Remark
Test basis stability	Number of added, updated and removed test cases.	Gives an indication of the quality and stability of the test basis. The test process efficiency benefits if test case design can be done 'first time right' due to a stable test basis in sufficient quality.
Testware quality	Number of found 'defects' caused by wrong testing, compared to the total number of found defects (in %).	Enables you to get insight in the efficiency of test execution, especially when subdivided to specific parts of the test basis and/or a specific test team.
Budget ratio	Ratio between test costs and development costs (design / development).	Gives you a means to create a basic estimation for the required test effort within a project.
		The norm is *design : development : test* = 2 : 5 : 3. This ratio is organization and even application specific, so that it should be determined within your organization.
(Re)tests	Number of tests and retests.	Indicates how many (re)tests are necessary in order to test a part.
		In some instances the amount of (re)testing may be determined by the nature of the product, the precision of the test or the history of the test object.

4.9 Metrics

Measure	Metrics	Contribution/Remark
Defect resolving bottleneck	Defect per defect status (new, opened, retest).	Makes it possible to determine the bottleneck in solving defects. This can for example be resolving defect by the developers or retesting by the testers.

4.9.3 Metrics at an Optimizing level

Metrics meet the ever changing information need.

The need for information constantly changes. Provided information on questions answered through metrics may result in new questions. The use of certain metrics may become obsolete and others need to be introduced. Another question that constantly needs to be answered is if the metrics tell the truth (for instance because the wrong aspects are measured or the base data is incorrect or incomplete) and if they are interpreted in the right way[1]. So metrics themselves need to be analyzed, possibly adjusted or optimized.

Checkpoints
1. The way metrics contribute to the information need is monitored.
2. Changes in information need lead to new or optimization of metrics.

Enablers
- None.

Improvement suggestions

Be sure that the process will maintain and, if necessary, change the definition of metrics.

Example metrics appropriate for the Optimizing level

The following metrics give the test team means to make sure the right activities are kept being done in the right way in the future.

---

[1] The 19th century British Prime Minister Benjamin Disraeli once said: "There are three kinds of lies: lies, damned lies, and statistics." The statement refers to the persuasive power of numbers, the use of statistics to bolster weak arguments, and the tendency of people to disparage statistics that do not support their positions.

4 Key areas

Measure	Metrics	Contribution/Remark
Defect Detection Percentage (DDP)	The number of defects found per test level divided by the sum of defects found in that test level plus all subsequent test levels and production times hundred.	The DDP indicates the effectiveness of defect finding per test level. This metric can be used to optimize the test strategy and/or test case design. To calculate the DDP the defects found in production during a 1 to 3 months period is commonly used.
Defect Introduction Rate (DIR)	The rate at which defects are introduced, per lines of source code added or changed (i.e. the number of defects that occur after changes in the test object and/or the number of defects that were not found in previous tests because they were covered by unsolved defects).	The defect introduction rate can be used to estimate the number of new defects introduced in the source code. It is usually calculated over a sufficiently long period (e.g. 6 months). This metric is not a precise measure. It can vary due to factors other than quality of submitted code, e.g. the level of testing (based on the test strategy). On average, each 6th code change (by fixing defects and other modifications) leads to a new or previously undiscovered defect.
Test design effort	Average time spent on designing a test case.	This metric over the course of several test projects helps to optimize resource estimation. Significant deviations from the average should be analyzed to find the cause and to determine possible improvement measures.
Waiting time per cause	Idle time / working hours in 'standstill' as percentage of the total test hours.	Shows where measures should be taken to eliminate future obstruction of the test process.

4.10 Defect management

> Defect management treats defects both at an individual level and at a group level where root causes are analyzed and guidelines are available.

Within BDTPI, a defect is any kind of difference between the actual behavior of the tested system and the expected behavior. Different names exist for different kinds of differences, like 'fault', 'finding' and 'error'. BDTPI does not make such distinctions.

Although the administration of defects is a matter for the entire software development project and not specifically for testing, testers will always be the most involved group. Good administration is able to monitor the lifecycle of a defect and give various (statistical) overviews. These overviews are, for instance, used to make substantiated statements on product and process quality. Also, every party involved should be able to access the defects in accordance to their project role and authorization to avoid abuse; this is especially important when for example development has been outsourced.

In practice there is sometimes confusion about the difference between test blocking and production blocking. A relatively simple defect, like a misspelled piece of text, can be 'blocking' for production when it is part of a web page.

It is important to keep in mind that defect management is a means to an end: correcting defects as quickly and cheaply as possible on the one hand, but also to learn from mistakes that might help preventing them in the future on the other.

Defects will contain a number of items. The items that at least should be identified are: the person who observed and reported the defect, severity category, priority, problem information and status. Additional information could be the related test cases, subsystem, test basis and its version, test object and its version, suggested problem solution, version of the test object when solved and the problem solver.

Initial level

At the Initial level, defect management is quite informal. Data on defects may or may not be logged in a consistent way and defects are usually communicated verbally or in a free-format (e.g. by email). There is insufficient overview of the number of defects and their status. As a result, there is no clear insight into the product quality.

4.10.1 Defect management at a Controlled level

> Defects are tracked at an individual level and defect status is monitored.

4 Key areas

All defects found during test execution are registered using uniform defect administration. This administration provides good handling and monitoring of the defects between the various stakeholders across a predefined defect lifecycle.

The decision about if, how, when and by whom a found defect is to be handled is taken by the right people in the team, for example the project manager, senior architect and test manager together. For this, the project might organize regular defect meetings. If no agreement about a defect can be reached, or a defect has a large impact, the defect may be passed on to a higher-level decision forum, where the project leader and possibly even the customer could be present.

Another important function of defect management is that an overview of all defects found (and their status) provides an indication of the quality of the system as far as it has been tested.

Checkpoints
1. The defect lifecycle is defined (including a retest) and applied.
2. The following items are recorded for each defect: unique ID, related test case ID (if applicable), person reporting the defect, date, severity category, description (the actions to reproduce the defect, expected and observed result) and defect status.
3. For further handling of defects the responsibilities are defined.
4. All those involved in assessing and solving defects have access to the relevant defect management tool.

Enablers
- Project management; at an early phase of a project, the various stages of a defect need to be defined and aligned to the specific version of the SDLC. Specific situations, such as agile development or external supplier involvement, will require a different version of the workflow than the 'standard' one.
- Tasks and responsibilities with respect to defect management should be included.
- Problem/incident management; the working agreements and terminology used in problem and incident management can be used as examples when establishing defect management.

Improvement suggestions
Set up administration for defects based on a spreadsheet or text document. If a large number of defects is expected, or more complex reporting is required, the use of a more comprehensive defect management tool is recommended. These tools can be either be dedicated to defect tracking or can be part of broader test management tools.

Define the task 'intermediary' in the test team or the project. The aim of this task is to channel the defects and their solutions adequately. The intermediary has external contacts at an executive level to handle these issues. The intermediary focuses on defects on the one hand, and solutions on the other. The advantages are that the quality of the defects and solutions are guarded better and that communication is streamlined.

Ensure that all defects are reported as soon as they are found. Assign a unique ID to each defect to make it traceable.

Update the defects immediately if more information becomes available.

Inform stakeholders about the product risks in case a specific defect will not be solved.

Introduce a defect life cycle with the following status values:
- *New:* a defect that is observed and reported. A decision needs to be made on whether, how, when and by whom it will be solved.
- *Open:* a reported defect will be solved.
- *Rejected:* a reported defect will not be solved, e.g. it is a duplicate, the defect is the result of problems in the test environment, or a defect in the test case specification.
- *Fixed:* an open defect is solved and is ready to be retested.
- *Closed:* the defect is retested successfully.
- *Reopen:* the retested defect turned out not to be solved (entirely).

4.10.2 Defect management at an Efficient level

> Common aspects of defects are analyzed to find similar defects.

At the efficient level, it becomes increasingly possible to solve a defect as close to its source as possible. The first step to making this happen is to register and correct defects in the test basis. If this is done before the system is developed, potential defects in the system are more likely to be avoided. Also, more detailed insight into the quality of the system can be provided, especially in terms of trends. An example of a trend is an observation that most of the defects relate to (a part of) the functional specifications, or that the defects are mainly concentrated on screen handling. This information can then be used to take timely measures. In order to analyze such trends, more information about defects has to be reported in a fixed format.
Also, trend analysis can be used to identify error-prone areas of the system. The test effort spent on those areas can then be increased to find more similar defects.

Checkpoints
1. The defect management tool enforces the authorization structure for status transitions of defects.
2. All persons involved in logging and/or tracking defects use the same defect management tool or separate defect management tools with a seamless connection.

3. The defect administration lends itself for extensive reporting possibilities, which means that reports can be selected and sorted in different ways.
4. Trends are identified. For this, more information is recorded about a defect, the subsystem, priority, program and version, test basis and version, root cause, all status transitions and problem solver.

Enablers
- None.

Improvement suggestions

Highlight the importance of prioritizing the defects, which makes discussions easier, procedures run faster, and helps gaining more insight into the test results. Prioritizing should by default be based on the test strategy. A special point of interest is to arrange the quick handling of defects that can block the test progress.

Make sure that the tool used to support the defect management process is accessible, provides the correct authorities, and is used by all involved.

4.10.3 Defect management at an Optimizing level

> Defects are analyzed for common properties to avoid future defects.

At an optimizing level, defect management supports not only the monitoring of product quality by tracking defects, but also by avoiding defects. Defects from all projects are analyzed and common root causes (like problems in the test environment) are detected. In addition, guidelines are produced to enable a uniform way of logging defects, thus enabling reporting at an organizational level.

If projects are to be compared, the classification of defects must be described in a uniform way and guidelines must exist to prescribe how to handle certain properties of defects - the most important being 'priority' and 'severity'.

There must also be a 'minimum' set of values for the property status that must be included in every workflow; projects are allowed to have additional values if this is necessary for the project (for example if external suppliers are part of the workflow).

Examples of root causes are:
- The test environment.
- Lack of a quality system in the development process (unit and/or unit integration tests are not properly executed).
- Requirements from a specific business department.

Checkpoints
1. A set of guidelines for defect management is provided by the line organization or project management, and used for each test project.
2. Defect management is the responsibility of the line or project organization, where the test process provides the necessary data.
3. Defects are analyzed for common properties and recommendations are made to avoid future defects.

Enablers
- Causal analysis and resolution; defects are structurally analyzed for their causes and these are then addressed in solutions.

Improvement suggestions
Define possible targets for analyzing defects; this could be certain functionality, the development process, specific roles (analysts, developers) and others.

Start a project that produces guidelines at an organizational level for defect administration.

Classify known errors, tell what the risks are and also, if possible, what the costs are if this issue is not solved (but only handled with for example workarounds).

4.11 Testware management

> Testware management ensures coherence between test artifacts, and between test artifacts and their related design documents.

Testware management is the activity of handling (receive, store, maintain, provide) test artifacts that:
- Are produced in test activities, such as a test plan or test cases. This is the common definition of testware.
- Are used as input to the test process, like the test basis and the test object. The artifact's authorship and ownership lies outside the test team. As these artifacts are essential to the test process, they are within scope of Testware management.

More examples of testware include test scripts, regression test sets and a description of the test environment. Management of the actual test environments (the test environment configurations) is outside the scope of Testware management.

A prerequisite for testware management is the unique identification of all individual test artifacts. Just stating in a test plan that "use cases are used as test basis" is insufficient to assure consistency between a specific, individual use case and its related test cases.

Good testware management increases the efficiency of testing:
- In the test project because all artifacts can be uniquely identified; therefore it is possible to check if changes were made to the correct or out-of-date version of the test artifact. Insufficient testware management brings the risk that the version of the software going into production is not the tested version.
- In future test projects; if the testware has been conserved in earlier similar projects, it can easily be reused.

> **In more detail - Development methods**
> The development method largely influences how testware management is put into practice. A large top-down managed project, dispersed over several locations, requires a much more stringent and prescriptive testware management than a typical agile environment. The important issue is always whether everyone knows what the current and relevant artifacts are.

Initial Level

At the Initial level, testware management is ad hoc and not organized. Several versions of test artifacts can be in use and none of them is considered to have been formally approved. In the case of changing requirements, there is no clear overview of which test artifacts will have to be updated, nor in which version of the test object these changes are to be implemented. There is also no guarantee that the version of the tested system or program is the same as the version that goes into production.

4.11.1 Testware management at a Controlled level

> All used test and design documents in an approved state, are individually identified and registered.

All items relevant to the test process are under version management, and access by everyone in the test project is assured.

With good testware management in place, it should be possible to answer a question like: "Am I using the latest version of the test basis for designing my test cases?" or "What are the differences between two versions of the same artifact?".

Checkpoints
1. The test basis, the test object and all testware are identified by name and version.
2. Each test case is related to a test basis document in a transparent way.
3. The test team has access to all items under testware management.
4. The procedure by which testware, the test basis and the test object are managed is explicitly laid down and known to the test team.

Enablers
- Planning: the project's product breakdown structures acts as starting point for testware management: which test relevant artifacts are defined and which should be managed.

Improvement suggestions

Make someone responsible for testware management within the test team.

Provide a section in the testware templates for information on the version, author, etc.

Collect examples of what went wrong as a result of wrong version management, so that you gain awareness of good testware management.

Include requirements in the test basis. Often this will mean doing some research to obtain (written) requirements.

Look into the possibility of using a version management tool.

Ensure good communication with other disciplines within the project, as they create and update certain artifacts that the test team needs, like the project planning and the test object.

Keep a list of all approved artifacts that are relevant to the specific test level.

4.11.2 Testware management at an Efficient level

> The relations between all (test) artifacts are known and kept up to date.

4 Key areas

There is full transparency of the relationships and dependencies between test artifacts. The most important are shown in figure 4.1 below.

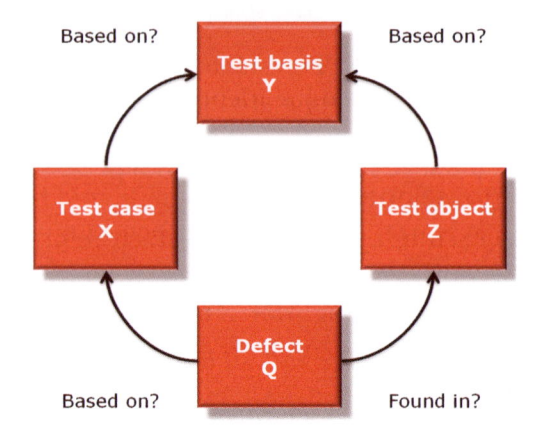

Figure 4.1: Full traceability up to the test basis.

For example, it should be possible to confirm that Test case X was based on design document Y, and determine that the Test case X and Test object Z are based on the same Test basis Y, and - as part of defect management - in which test object the Defect Q was found using what test case.

Particularly when regression tests are carried out, a clear overview is needed of which test results belong to which version of the test object. When automated testing is carried out, multiple versions of tool scripts have to be synchronized with the test cases that they implement, and the test object versions that they work with.

By having traceability between test cases and requirements and looking at the requirements coverage, it is possible to check for unacceptable omissions, in which not all risks are covered by test cases. When, under time pressure not all test cases can be executed it is possible to leave out test cases that are used to cover requirements of low risk.

Another important benefit of traceability is the possibility to quickly conduct an impact analysis on the test design, in case of a potential change to the test basis.

Checkpoints
1. The test basis, the test object and all testware are referenced by name and version.
2. Traceability is provided between test cases and the requirements.
3. Testware management is supported by a logical storage structure, roles and an authorization structure.

Enablers
- Configuration management: the delivery, registration, archiving and references to configuration items can be done uniformly throughout the project or organization.
- Requirements management: Traceability of requirements and design documents is enhanced by unique identifiers provided in the specification.

Improvement suggestions
Add a reference to each test case, showing which requirement(s) the test case covers.

Investigate the process for configuration management of the project and give recommendations for improvement and sharing its use.

4.11.3 Testware management at an Optimizing level

> Testware is made available for reuse in future test projects and actually reused.

At the Optimizing level, the testware is reused in test projects saving time and providing the reassurance that the testware is known to be of a proven quality.
In practice, this ambition puts demands on the test project: it requires effort to make the testware available for reuse. While everyone is aware of the future benefits, the current project may not directly benefit. It requires discipline for the project to expend this effort, especially if the project is already running out of budget and time.
Not all testware of a test project will be conserved. A selection should be made of the testware considered to be well worth reusing.

Checkpoints
1. It is agreed at test project start and rethought during the test project which testware will be conserved at the closure of the test project.
2. Guidelines for conserving testware for reuse are available and the reuse of testware is measured.
3. At the end of the project, the testware that will be handed over to maintenance is easily separable from the testware that is not going to be maintained.

Enablers
- Project management: conserving products should be a project responsibility and must be coordinated.

Improvement suggestions
Encourage the reuse of testware.

Make sure that the client of the project demands reusable testware as part of the delivery. In this way, testware will be on the radar of project management, and stay there even if the project ends up under pressure when all other corners have been cut.

Answer these questions to determine what testware to conserve:
- How many times is the testware going to be (re)used?
- How much time will it take to conserve it now and how much time will the reused testware save in future?

After it is decided which items will be saved for future use, make sure that they are cleaned up and updated properly.

Ensure that a line organization exists that will take ownership of the conserved testware after the project has finished.

Ensure good communication with the maintenance organization (who are expected to reuse the regression test set) or the next project.

4.12 Methodology practice

> A described method for testing directs and supports the test projects.

Testing is usually carried out in projects. Typical for projects is that the goals and preconditions are unique and for each project, the activities to reach its goals, as well as how to perform them, the tasks and responsibilities and the technical infrastructure, have to be figured out from scratch. This results in a very time-consuming and expensive way, with little control of quality.

The exact opposite of a project is a process: a series of the same steps that, with similar input, results in a predictable output with a known quality. The steps to reach its goals are usually optimized to ensure that the goals are reached as quickly and cheaply as possible.

While these are opposites in theory, in practice many aspects of a project are similar. The more the activities in a project are approached as a process, the more the project can benefit from a known quality and more efficient execution.

The way to approach testing as a process is to describe how testing is done, in a method. The method describes how the goals of testing are reached, with a known quality. At the same time, the method provides concrete support by means of guidelines, templates, examples and tools, which accelerates testing.

Describing a method is not sufficient: it needs to be used by the projects. The people working in the projects have to be familiar with the method, and they have to consider the method to be helpful. Alternatively, the use of the method can be required by the stakeholders. In that case, measures like checklists have to be built-in in the test method, to be able to verify that the method is applied sufficiently.

There should always be the possibility for deviating from parts of the method, if agreed with the stakeholders. However, if too many aspects of the method are ignored for the wrong reasons, the benefits of the method are lost.

A described method allows also for improvement of testing. By making evaluation of the test process a standard step at the end of the project, lessons learned can be fed back to the method where necessary. Also, the test method has to be adapted if new developments occur that result in that the test method is not as effective anymore, e.g. when introducing a new development method. This requires that someone in the organization is responsible for actively maintaining the method.

Test methods like TMap® [1], ISTQB [11] and the test discipline in Rational Unified Process (RUP) [21] are already defined. In practice, these methods do not really fit many organizations and need to be adapted. Also, a method can be home grown, based on best practices in the organization. A combination of both is usually the most effective.

4 Key areas

The methodology should not only describe test activities, but offer tools, such as a template for a test plan, and techniques too, such as for estimation or a set of test design techniques. A solid test method helps to achieve a balance between result, risk, time and costs in the test project.

Initial level
At the Initial level, no test method is developed by the organization, or it is not used. The method is essentially a 'paper tiger' that misses its targets entirely. The way testing is performed is entirely dependent on the individual test manager and tester and the quality of testing, nor an efficient execution, can be guaranteed.

4.12.1 Methodology practice at a Controlled level

> A described test method enables predictable execution of test activities.

When testing starts, stakeholders expect the test project to apply a described test method that provides the information and deliverables required by the stakeholders. Applying the test method correctly ensures that certain steps are taken within the test project at a predictable quality level. This requires that the method is a good fit for that particular project. Deviations from the test method are acceptable if the deviations are agreed with the stakeholders. However, too many deviations means that the test method is not being used at all, and the project team is in effect throwing away the method's benefits.

Checkpoints
1. The test process follows a documented test method: the test method describes a set of test activities, the test products delivered by the test project and additional requirements on the way of working.
2. The test method fits the development method applied by the project.
3. The test projects consider the implemented test method to be of practical use.

Enablers
- Organizational process definition: Described methods for e.g. development or maintenance can be enhanced by including a described test method.

Improvement suggestions
If no test method exists, it cannot be improved. In that case, establish a new method from scratch, i.e. from the best practices that already exist in the organization, and combine them with (parts of) existing methods.

Decide with the stakeholders what the goals of testing and the direction of the test projects should be. Align the test method with these goals.

Ensure that the method is sufficiently clear in its expectations of the test project, in terms of test products, test activities and other requirements of the project.

4.12.2 Methodology practice at an Efficient level

> The described test method provides practical support for the test projects.

While the test method puts demands on the test project, it also provides concrete support for how to fulfill these demands. Techniques are described that explain how activities are performed and how tools automate certain activities. While some aspects of the test method are mandatory, others are optional, and the method describes when to use which aspects. It is also important that the method is easily accessible to everyone in the organization. A few hardcopies on a shelf is much less accessible than a method description available in digital format and on the intranet.

Checkpoints
1. The test method describes for all test activities the goal, the responsible role, any techniques to be used and preconditions.
2. A complete and comprehensive set of templates is provided as part of the test method.
3. Mandatory, conditional and optional elements of the test method are indicated.
4. The mandatory and conditional elements are put into practice.

Enablers
- None.

Improvement suggestions
Organize training in the test method for all testers in the test organization.

Enhance the test method with best practices from other projects.

Create and provide templates based on existing test products, with sufficient help text.

Provide existing test products as examples.

Investigate where tools can support or automate certain activities.

Describe which parts of the test method are mandatory (and under which conditions), and which parts are optional.

4 Key areas

4.12.3 Methodology practice at an Optimizing level

> Deviations from the test method are evaluated and lead to enhancing the method.

The test method is regularly evaluated and updated based on experience gained in the test projects. New developments (i.e. agile, model-based testing) are evaluated for their relevance to testing and where appropriate, are used to adapt the test methodology and/or provide a guideline for tailoring.
Feedback is collected from evaluating test projects and changes implemented. If deviations occurred, and similar deviations are expected for comparable test projects, those deviations themselves are added to the test method as well.

Checkpoints
1. Test teams structurally provide feedback regarding the test method.
2. The implemented test method is continuously enhanced and improved.

Enablers
- Organizational maintenance and innovation of IT processes.

Improvement suggestions

Use a line department to perform the evaluation of test projects, based on the test method.

Create a maintenance plan for the test method (and supporting documentation) and claim resources for this maintenance.

Take care that the products of maintenance and innovation are included in the generic method and communicate the adaptations to the organization.

4.13 Tester professionalism

> Tester professionalism includes the right mix of the various skills, competences, disciplines, functions and knowledge that are necessary to perform test activities to the levels expected.

A test process requires a large set of skills: familiarity and understanding of the business and the organization, knowledge of the test object, general IT know-how and technical skills. In addition, testers need to have specific test skills, from expertise in methodologies through to the ability to communicate with stakeholders effectively (social competence).

Test skills can roughly be divided in two categories: test management skills and test engineering skills. Test management skills comprise many standard project management skills such as estimating, planning and reporting. The skills that set a test manager apart from other project managers are the ability to think consistently in terms of risks and to align test activities to the specific needs of the situation (like iterative development). Test engineering skills comprise applying test design techniques and/or knowledge of specialized test tools.

The basic attitude of a tester is substantially different from that of most other IT specialists: a tester tries to demonstrate the (lack of) quality of the system and therefore actively searches for defects or deviations. Conversely, most other specialists focus on demonstrating that the system is 'good' or 'works'.

Initial level
At the Initial maturity level people who hold the role of tester frequently have expertise in business or have specific technical skills, but do not always have sufficient testing skills. Testing is often not regarded as a profession, has a low status within the IT department and there is lack of opportunity to develop a career in testing.

4.13.1 Tester professionalism at a Controlled level

> With specific test method skills and competences the tester makes the test process more predictable and manageable.

The professional tester uses his skills and knowledge to plan, execute and control his activities and those of his colleagues. This professionalism makes the process more stable, predictable and manageable.

Test managers deliver the test activities based on identified product risks and a defined test strategy, even if the project environment is not conducive. They deliver progress reports on a regular basis, even if the client does not request them. Test engineers vary test design in test depth and test technique. During test execution, they assess whether or not to deviate

4 Key areas

from planned activities and how to communicate this deviation. Test tools are skillfully used.

Checkpoints
1. Testers have received specific test training and/or have sufficient experience in the field of structured testing.
2. Testers are familiar with the adopted test method and they apply it.
3. All required expertise - whether industry, business or technical - are available to the test team.
4. Testers are regularly evaluated on specific testing skills as well as general IT abilities in an employee performance appraisal.

Enablers
- Human Resource Management; HRM and line management consider testing a professional skill with its own merits.

Improvement suggestions
Provide test personnel with opportunities for training and education.

Facilitate test expertise development by organizing or encouraging Special Interest Groups or regular cross-department meetings, where testers can share their experiences.

Include function descriptions in the project or test plan and define who should perform which task.

Arrange the required subject matter expertise in a timely fashion (especially in the case of the acceptance test and/or improper test basis).

4.13.2 Tester professionalism at an Efficient level

> Test personnel have a dedicated role or function for testing and they fulfill their task in line with expectations.

Test personnel are very well trained, skilled and experienced in their profession. They are equipped with knowledge about methods, tools and techniques. They use these skills to provide the right information at the right time, enabling decision makers (stakeholders) to control the test process in the right direction. The test team has a strong focus on both the results of their activities and the results for the business of the test process as a whole. Their skills make it possible to achieve the required results with a minimum of effort and resources.

There are risks however; training in certain skills, or the successful application of a particular technique can result in people remaining in their 'comfort zone'. Having applied a certain risk assessment technique or test design technique in a situation with positive results makes it very appealing to apply it again, even if not appropriate. True professionalism proves itself by applying the appropriate techniques in the appropriate circumstances!

In addition to employing skilled testers, it is also important to arrange specialist support for larger more complex projects. Methodical support is needed to draw up and implement instructions, help to define the test strategy, etc. Technical support is necessary to organize and operate the infrastructure. Functional support helps to answer functional questions that come up during testing. In these situations, support is required from parties outside the test process, so it is important to co-ordinate these efforts well and on time.

Checkpoints
1. Testers are certified in testing (such as TMap NEXT [17] or ISTQB [11]).
2. Testers can explain the rationale behind chosen techniques that have been applied.
3. Test personnel enjoy their job and have a good relationship with other skill groups in the project.
4. Test tasks are defined, allocated and executed in line with expectations.

Improvement suggestions

Especially in planning and resourcing, consider the support tasks and ensure that these support roles are really used.

If there is insufficient knowledge and experience for the support role to be properly executed, consider specific training.

4.13.3 Tester professionalism at an Optimizing level

> Test personnel act from a Quality Assurance point of view thus constantly developing and improving their skills.

Test personnel are aware of the Quality Assurance role of testing as a detective measure. Using their knowledge, skills and experience, they contribute to other quality measures such as prevention (standardization, methods, training) and correction (indication of possible repairs or solutions). From the Quality Assurance point of view, it is clear to test personnel which requirements are for their own work and how these can be evaluated and measured. This enables continuous improvement of the tester and his activities.

Furthermore, testers stay in touch with new developments in the testing world and in IT generally. This to ensure that newly-developed test methods and practices, not currently widely used in the organization, can be applied when the time is appropriate.

Checkpoints
1. Testers actively participate in Special Interest Groups, attend test seminars or read test literature to keep their skills up to date.
2. Test functions are part of the organization's Human Resource Management and personal career development.
3. Testers strive towards accountability and responsibility for their own work and continuous improvement of their work process.

Enablers
- Quality Management. A well-defined and organized Quality Assurance approach views testing in relation to all the other development processes. The Optimizing level of Tester professionalism benefits from a mature and efficient development process. It is of little use if the tester is very aware of 'Quality' if the rest of the development team is not. On the other hand, testers can profit from a mature development process: they learn how Quality can be controlled with preventive and corrective measures.

Improvement suggestions

Create career paths for test personnel, i.e. define test functions at an organizational level.

Define and allocate the role of internal Quality Assurance.

Produce an internal Quality Assurance report for all stakeholders - not just the test manager, but also the project manager, the customer and/or line departments. Issues to include in the report:

- Are test personnel able to follow the method? If not, what were the reasons?
- What was the performance of the tester? What was his contribution to the team, to the process, and to the project?
- What are lessons learned for future test activities?

4.14 Test case design

> Test case design directs test execution to search for defects according to the test strategy.

A test case is used to examine whether the system displays the desired behavior under specific circumstances. Test cases provide differentiation on test coverage based on the test strategy. The test strategy determines the coverage of a test with the goal of testing precisely enough - not too much and certainly not too little. Designing test cases in an unambiguous way helps to do just that.

Furthermore, designing test cases before test execution - as is common in scripted testing - gives structure to the test execution phase. An additional advantage of designing test cases before the test execution is that it is actually the best review technique for evaluating the test basis.

> **In more detail - Test case design and Test strategy**
> In practice it is not possible to test everything. Choices have to be made. Depending on determined product risks a test strategy is created to give an overview of what will be tested and how intensively. Test design techniques provide a justified elaboration of this test strategy.
> Because test design techniques focus on achieving a specific coverage to detect specific types of defect, they require a specific test basis. The availability of the test basis is therefore a factor in the choice for using certain test design techniques and hence the thoroughness of the test.

Describing test cases in a structured way also contributes to testware management. A standard format and test design techniques make test cases reusable and transferable. It improves the execution of future tests (e.g. regression tests) and it also makes the automation of the test execution feasible.

> **In more detail - Test case design within exploratory testing**
> An alternative approach to scripted testing is exploratory testing. There are several movements within exploratory testing: from being very informal and averse to the use of any structure or techniques, through to giving support for a more structured approach. No matter the approach, currently there is a commonly-held view that documented test cases are helpful or even necessary for retests and regression tests. A feature of exploratory testing is that you start thinking about what to test at the moment the test object is delivered. Even at that stage it is possible to write down the steps that have been taken, and even to focus on certain kinds of coverage.

A test case commonly includes:
- The purpose of the test.
- Special hardware requirements, such as a modem.
- Special software requirements, such as a tool.

4 Key areas

- Specific setup or configuration requirements.
- A description of how to perform the test.
- The expected results or success criteria for the test.

> **In more detail - Test case design within agile testing**
> In iterative or agile development, there is a strong emphasis on regression testing, preferably automated, for which a good quality (and quantity) of test cases is essential. A complicating factor however is that detailed requirements are not always available from the beginning. It is - to a certain extend - the responsibility of testers to gather a detailed understanding of the customer's expectation via for example stakeholder interviews. The tester then writes test cases using the regular test design techniques. The resulting test cases will become the detailed requirement specifications for developers. This is one example of Test Driven Development (TDD).

Initial Level

Even at the initial level usually test cases are being designed without a standard. The way they are described is very person dependent, from just some keywords to a description of consecutive actions that need to be performed. It is however very hard to hand over the test cases from one person to the other, for instance in the situation that someone moves to another project, illness, etc. Above all, it is almost impossible to get any certainty about the coverage of the tests. Did the test cases cover all requirements, determined products risks or most important functionalities? What has really been tested?

4.14.1 Test case design at a Controlled level

> The test cases make the test execution repeatable and person independent.

Test cases are described according to a standard format, but there is much freedom in how to design test cases. The quality of test cases is very much dependent on the test skills and business, system or program expertise of the specifying person. The way the test cases are described makes it possible to have them executed by someone else or to reuse them. Test cases should at least be understandable for the person who will execute the test cases. There may be demands on the subject matter expertise of the tester who is executing the test cases. An important demand is to uniformly describe test cases, which makes them better understandable and which makes it easier to predict or fine-tune the time needed for execution.

Test cases need to describe in logical terms the circumstances in which the system behavior is examined (indicating which test situations are covered by the test case). Designing physical test cases directly from the test basis without making logical test cases first makes it very hard to understand and trace back for others what the test case was supposed to cover. The test case descriptions also include expected results, in order to facilitate the

4.14 Test case design

assessment of the actual result during test execution. For reasons of gaining insight they also describe their relationship to the test basis.

Checkpoints
1. The test cases are recorded on a logical level.
2. The test cases consist of a description of: a) initial situation, b) change process = test actions to be performed, c) predicted result.
3. The test cases provide insight into which part of the test basis, describing a specific system behavior, is subject to the test.

Enablers
- Design Process. Testing is the process of determining the deviation between the required and actual behavior of a system. The better the required state is described, the easier it is to make the right test cases in order to determine deviations.

Improvement suggestions

Describe a standard way of notation of test cases, possibly supported by templates. Try to include as many practical instructions as possible as guidance, particularly when the freedom for the test designer is too large. The test cases should be described in sufficient detail so that another person, other than the test case author, has enough information to execute the cases.

Use generic information sources on finding bugs. There is literature available about generic test cases and what defects to look for in certain circumstances. Agree upon a limited set of items to focus on.

4.14.2 Test case design at an Efficient level

> Designing test cases that focus on achieving a specific coverage provides a justified elaboration of the test strategy.

In order to give insight in the quality of a system testers perform tests. These tests should be performed with a minimum of effort, finding the right defects and finding the most important defects first; different systems, or parts of systems, require different levels of thoroughness of testing. Test design techniques are a powerful means for achieving this efficiency in testing: just enough test cases covering the defined risks, being realized within the available time and costs. The use of formal test design techniques has several advantages:
- They focus on achieving a specific coverage to detect specific types of defects.
- They are suitable for a specific test level (development test, acceptance test) or test type (functional test, performance test).

4 Key areas

- A more substantiated judgment is possible about the completeness of the test.
- It becomes easier to adjust and reuse test cases.
- The test process becomes less dependent on the designer and executor of the test cases.
- The test process is more manageable because an estimate can be made in advance of how many test cases are needed. This allows for a better planning and progress monitoring.
- Within Model Based Testing (software testing in which test cases are derived in whole or in part from a model) it is possible to have test cases designed automatically with the help of specific coverage tools.

The most common way of testing is dynamic testing, where the test object is manipulated and its behavior evaluated. This is where regular test cases are used. However, some properties (like some quality characteristics) of the test object can only be evaluated by observing the test object itself or its related documentation. Checklists rather than regular test cases can be used to direct this static testing.

Checkpoints
1. The test cases are understandable to and maintainable by peers within the test organization.
2. The coverage level of the test basis - as reached by the test cases - is known.
3. Formal test design techniques are used to design test cases.
4. Checklists are used for the testing of quality characteristics for which no test cases can be designed.

Enablers
- Design Process. Certain test design techniques require specific input.

Improvement suggestions

Arrange training and coaching for the testers who will be working with these techniques.

Investigate which coverage types are already being applied even if only implicitly. Even without knowledge of test design techniques, testers often apply certain coverage types without realizing it - most often in syntactic testing, equivalence classes, boundary value analysis and validation (semantic) testing.

Most test techniques are described in literature, for instance by Beizer [3], Kaner a.o. [14], Kit [15] and in TMap NEXT [17], so it is not necessary to re-invent the wheel. It is advisable to refer to these techniques. If the way the coverage type is applied deviates from a standard technique, get it described.

Start with a limited set of test design techniques to get acquainted with them. When more knowledge and experience is acquired you can expand the range of test design techniques to be used.

In a situation of frequent changes to the test basis and the test object, consider the extent to which the test script should be drawn up. It might be more efficient to keep this at a high level. The same applies to the situation in which there are restrictions on building up test data. In that case, it is possibly more efficient to keep the physical test cases and the necessary starting point for test cases at an abstract level.

4.14.3 Test case design at an Optimizing level

> Evaluation of test cases, test design techniques and defects provides a way to increase test effectiveness.

Each test should find those defects it is supposed to find. Therefore, a constant monitoring of test effectiveness is desirable. The test team (or others) should check if the test cases are correct and valid. Also defects from the next phase should be analyzed: who should have found the defect and why didn't they? The analysis may result in the adjustment of or in applying different test design techniques.

Checkpoints
1. Defects that occur in the next phase (the next test level or production) are being analyzed, leading to improvements in the accuracy and effectiveness of test cases.
2. Test cases are checked and evaluated independently on validity and maintainability.
3. The test design techniques are evaluated and adjusted for further re-use.

Enablers
- Incident management. In the case when the next phase is the live situation, incidents that are occurring in production need to be administrated uniformly and be available for analysis purposes.

Improvement suggestions
Allocate resources to verify test cases. Determine how much time should be spent on this; improving the test cases should always be cheaper than the cost of the prevented damage in the next phase.

It is even possible to organize an inspection or walkthrough of the test cases before their executions by different stakeholders from within the software development life cycle. Designers, developers and key users may

4 Key areas

give all give from their own point of view a judgment on the right interpretation of the test basis and on how realistic and valid the test cases are.

Indicate the importance of a good registration (according to the procedure) of defects and/ or incidents and their availability. This will help to produce better test cases and therefore to find defects as soon and as cheaply as possible. (See Defect management).

4.15 Test tools

> Test tools enable or accelerate specific test activities.

There are situations where a test project cannot 'escape' using a test tool. The test tool is simply necessary to be able to execute certain test activities and to reach the test goals. The use of a test tool enables the test process. This aspect is addressed at the Controlled level.

Test tools can also provide features to make the test process faster, cheaper, better (provide more insight into quality) or making the test process better manageable. The use of (a combination of) test tools accelerates the test process. This aspect is addressed at the Efficient level.

When the way and the degree test tooling accelerates the test process is continuously evaluated, its contribution to the test process becomes identifiable. Based on the evaluation, the use of test tools can be improved. This aspect is addressed at the Optimizing level.

Test tools include any and all tools that can be used during testing, both commercial and open source tools as well as tools and utilities created by test teams themselves (spreadsheet utilities etc.).

There are different types of test tools, each used in different test phases[1] of the test process and having different objectives and benefits, some examples:

- A generic tool for project planning is valuable during the planning phase of a test project.
- Test management tools contribute to progress and quality reporting during the control and completion phases.
- During test specification a test modeling tool (for model-based-testing) can be used to generate test cases.
- Tests can be executed automatically with record & playback test tools and performance test tools.
- A query tool can be used for preparation of the test environment and database validations during test execution.
- Stubs are used to simulate an interfaced system that is not available in the test environment to facilitate test execution.

The use of a test tool is never a goal in itself. A test tools must serve a purpose. While being essential to one test project, the same test tool can be superfluous to others. The simple fact that test tools are used within the test process - or not - is no indication for test process maturity. The Matu-

---

[1] Referring to the test phases according to TMap NEXT [17]: Planning, Control, Preparation, Specification, Execution, Completion and Setting up and maintaining infrastructure.

4 Key areas

rity level of the Test tools Key area is not related to the use of specific test tools.
But a specific test tool can be used in a less or more mature way. Refer to the first appendix for a description of the maturity stage of the use of some specific test tools, being test management tools, automated test execution tools and performance test tools.

Initial level
At the Initial level test tools might be used to support the test process, but not the ones necessary to fulfill the test assignment. Using and managing test tools within the test process is not done in a structured way.

4.15.1 Test tools at a Controlled level

> Test tools needed to execute specific test activities are available and used.

At the Controlled level the test tools are available to the test project that are needed to execute specific test activities and to reach the test goals. The test project can very well use other tools in addition, but at least the test tools enabling the test project are used.

The use of a test tool enables the test process when there is no other way than to use a test tool to perform an activity. Alternatively, there could be no realistic alternative for the use of the test tool given the expectations and project restrictions (time and costs).
Examples of test activities that must be executed with a test tool are the use of a driver to send messages to an interface or the use of a query tool to check the correctness of data in a database.
An example of the use of a test tool that is needed because of project restrictions is to test performance in a 50,000 user scenario. Theoretically it would be possible to execute the performance test with 50,000 testers, but organizing this would exceed project restrictions. The only alternative is the use of performance test tools.
There are test tools for:
- *Test engineering*, needed because of technical system characteristics or needed to test specific quality characteristics (like performance and security) defined in the test strategy.
- *Test management*, needed to plan and control the test process and provide the required information to stakeholders in the agreed frequency.

Checkpoints
1. The test tools needed to execute specific test activities and to reach the test goals are available to and used by the test team.
2. Knowledge about the test tools in use is available.

4.15 Test tools

3. Everyone involved, including the purchasing entity, considers the specific test tool used to be beneficial.

Enablers
- None.

Improvement suggestions
Make sure that the test team knows how to use the test tools. One common pitfall is poorly-trained users, which can easily result in inefficient use or even counter-productiveness. For example using a performance test tool and simulating a load that is too small or too large because the test run configurations are not fully understood. This can lead to wrong conclusion on the needed hardware resources.

4.15.2 Test tools at an Efficient level

> Test tools are used to accelerate specific test activities.

Test tools that accelerate the test process are used for making testing faster, cheaper, better or making the test process better manageable. However, this comes with a price: the test tool needs to be purchased, staff needs to be trained and the tool needs to be adapted and maintained. The benefits of using the test tool have to justify the investment for implementing and maintaining the tool.

The most common example is the use of a record & playback test tool for regression testing. It can be sufficient to manually execute regression tests. However, a record & playback test tool could execute a much larger set of test cases in the same time (providing a higher test coverage), or the same set of test cases in less time (being faster). But a record & playback tool takes initial and other investments that can only be earned back by recurrent use.

A business case is therefore created to obtain an overview of all these aspects and provide a decision base for introducing the test tool. This business case can be negative on the financial side, meaning that the investment will not be returned, but at the same time the use of the test tool may be worthwhile because of the benefits in quality (higher test coverage) or time-to-market (faster testing).

Checkpoints
1. Test tools currently used have been selected for testing faster, cheaper, better or making the test process better manageable.
2. The test tools are at the testers disposal at any required moment.
3. A business case has been created for each introduced test tool within the test process.
4. The use of these test tools is integrated in the test process.

Enablers
- The used tools in other processes of the software development lifecycle.

Improvement suggestions
If the organization believes a test tool offers the opportunity to accelerate specific test activities, start a process in which the criteria for the tool are defined, based on a business case with clear goals for using the test tool. Select and implement the test tool that has demonstrated the best results in the selection process, in terms of saving time and money.

4.15.3 Test tools at an Optimizing level

> Test tools, and their use, are continuously evaluated and improved.

The business case that has been created for implementing a specific set of test tools is a basis for the evaluation. Metrics on the usage of test tools are compared to the goals that have been set in the business case. When the goals have not been met, improvements that focus on reaching those goals are defined and incorporated. But even if the goals are reached, the focus lies on looking for further improvements.

A tool policy can be introduced as part of the test policy. The tool policy describes in an uniform manner what the purpose of the implementation of test tools must be. Furthermore, the tool policy describes the approach to be followed for the initiation, realization and operation of test tools. A tool policy constitutes the basis on which the organization can base the use and implementation of tools (in the future). It is not a one-off document that is archived. The tool policy must be updated and adapted to new developments and insights regularly.

As part of the tool policy test tools and their use by the test teams are regularly evaluated, leading to changing their usage, adapting their technical implementation or even replacing test tools.

There has to be a business case for implementing a tool policy in addition to the business cases for individual tools. A tool policy is based on the expected scope of test tool use both in the number of tools as well as the size and scope of the implementation (number of users and departments involved).

A general improvement is maximizing the reuse of test tool knowledge, best practices and test tool products. This requires publishing and maintaining of these items at an organizational level.

Checkpoints
1. The tool policy is created and kept synchronized with the existing test policy.

2. The expertise, best practices and test tools products are collected and published for future projects.
3. Test tools are regularly evaluated on reaching the goals that have been set in the business case for implementing the test tool and the test tool policy.

Enablers
- None.

Improvement suggestions

Create a tool policy as an addition to existing development and test policies. A tool policy is aimed at creating a commitment for procedural and organizational changes to support the introduction of multiple tools if the individual business cases are positive.

Focus on the different aspects of creating and maintaining a tool policy for your organization. These include the phase initiation, realization and operation.

Maintaining the tool policy requires a periodic evaluation of the business case for the tool policy itself as well as the business case for individual tools. In addition the way the tool policy is integrated with the test policy is to be reviewed.

As part of the tool policy the following activities are performed:

- Perform a periodic evaluation of the test tools that are being used.
- Scan the market for any new test tools that could be of benefit to the organization.

4.16 Test environment

> The test environment is explicitly designed, implemented and maintained with the goals of the test level in mind.

The test environment is one of the critical success factors of testing. No matter how well developed test cases are, how well educated the testers are, whenever the test environment stops, all testing stops.
In practice, many testers just have to make do with what they have. And they often do not have the skills or knowledge to discuss the set-up of the test environment. Increased test maturity essentially is deciding to control what the test environment can do and how this is to be achieved.

The test environment consists of a number of distinct areas [18]:
- Client environment
- Network
- Storage
- (Enterprise) Server
- Middleware
- Test data

But that's not all. To be really useful, there is more than merely installing the right hardware and software components. The test environment also needs to be kept in good working order; rules must be enforced that define how it should be used, and by whom.

> **In more detail - Client environment**
> From a Business Driven TPI point of view the client environment (client as in 'client/server', not as a stakeholder) comprises more than just a desk and a computer. Meeting rooms, telephones, video conferencing facilities, network connections, access authorizations, office software, printers, special peripherals, etc. are all examples of easily forgotten resources. Especially in geographically spread organizations and in case of outsourcing the client environment needs special care in order not to become a bottleneck.

Installing and maintaining test environments is a specialist job and not something that a tester can do 'on the side'. Even for the specialists themselves, it is a multi-disciplinary effort. Few people know all the 'ins' and 'outs' of the areas mentioned above. So the proper test environment usage and maintenance relies heavily on co-operation with internal and external suppliers.
Test data deserves special attention. In most organizations the first five areas are considered the responsibility of 'the techies', the department(s) that also maintain these areas for the production environment. This is not the case for Test data. Knowledge and ownership of Test data is usually

spread across the organization and in the standing organization no one really feels responsible for the quality of the data.

The term 'test environment' can cause some confusion, since there is also a development environment in which testing takes place, an acceptance environment in which acceptance testing takes place and sometime testing even takes place in a production environment. Many organizations have adopted the DTAP model[1], which sets the test environment apart from other environments. In this book, the term 'test environment' is used to address the environment in which testing takes place, irrespective of its place in the DTAP model.

Initial level
At the Initial level, testing takes place in the test environment that has been placed at the tester's disposal without prior design or requirements.

4.16.1 Test environment at a Controlled level

> Changes to the test environment do not happen unexpectedly.

Test environments to date are complex and intricate. Ownership is unknown or obscure at the best, not least because no-one is really able to gain a complete overview of all the test environment's components. For a test manager to be in control of his test environment, he must at least have regular contact with the other stakeholders of the test environment - whether they are suppliers of (parts of) the test environment and/or other users. This puts the test manager in a position in which upcoming changes are discussed with him, as well as with the other suppliers and users. This allows him to prepare for, and react to planned changes. It also ensures swift escalation of situations that have not been foreseen, because no time is wasted finding out who to contact.

Obviously, having the right contacts is not enough to install and maintain a well-suited environment. It is essential to define in advance what is needed and to state explicitly at least the minimal characteristics of the required environment.

Checkpoints
1. Test environment requirements are documented.
2. Working agreements are made with the parties supplying the test environment. These agreements contain tasks and responsibilities.
3. The test environment is available to the test team during the agreed time.

---

[1] Acronym for Development, Test, Acceptance and Production environment.

4 Key areas

4. The test manager is timely informed whenever a change to the test environment is planned.

Enablers
- Processes like release management, change management, build/deployment management, etc.. In other words: all processes that ensure that changes to the production environment are carried out in a controlled fashion. The owner of the test environment can use these processes as a blueprint for similar test environment processes and as a starting point for identifying stakeholders.

Improvement suggestions

Appoint a test environment specialist to streamline communication with supplying parties.

Seek contact with architects. In many cases, blue-prints, maintained by architects, are available 'somewhere' in an organization, and although they might not perfectly suit the needs of testing, they are good starting points.

Seek contact with maintenance departments of the operational environments. These departments have a huge amount of knowledge, experience and ready-to-use documentation. Re-use it.

Try and agree on (a limited) high priority defect status. Supplying parties tend to underestimate the importance of test environments. To some extent they are right, since damage due to malfunctioning test environment is, in most cases, relatively small, compared to the damage due to malfunctioning operational environments. So try to identify situations in which a test environment malfunction will noticeably cause damage and agree on a high priority status for those defects.

4.16.2 Test environment at an Efficient level

> The test environment is directly related to the demands of the test level or test type at hand.

In every aspect of delivering products, we recognize the importance of good design. Yet, designing a test environment is not something that comes naturally to test professionals. The requirements of an environment for executing a performance test differ substantially from those of, for example, a usability test. So the next step towards creating an environment that fulfils all the tester's needs is to specify those needs in detail. This includes acknowledging different types of environments, each with its own characteristics.

Checkpoints
1. Acceptance of the test environment takes place using a checklist created in advance.
2. A logical or functional design of the test environment is put together. It addresses applications, systems and their connections, and the use of stubs and drivers (mock-ups).
3. Supplying parties deliver a technical design of the test environment that is formally accepted by the test manager or the test environment specialist.
4. Agreements with supplying parties have a Service Level Agreement nature.

Enablers
- Service Libraries. Many companies rely on models such as ITIL [13], ASL [2] or BiSL [4] to shape their maintenance departments. These departments hold a huge amount of knowledge and experience with respect to installing and operating both infrastructure and applications. Best practices from these departments can be (partly) copied and used as starting point for best practice procedures in the test project or organization.

Improvement suggestions
Formalize working agreements used by other parties.

4.16.3 Test environment at an Optimizing level

> Test environments are offered as a service to testers.

All too often, testers rely on several departments for setting up and maintaining their environment and as a result not one of the suppliers feels or is responsible for the environment as a whole. So, when for instance messages are 'lost' between two platforms that are maintained by different departments, finding out why the message doesn't arrive at its destination stays the responsibility of the tester, who doesn't have the skills and knowledge to perform a proper analysis. It is therefore essential that there is one main supplier who feels responsible for an up and running environment with agreed service levels and who acts as an intermediary between the testers and other suppliers.

For the main supplier to ensure the existence of proper, flexible test environments that are attuned to every specific test need, an organization must implement certain roles and responsibilities within the line organization. One should not expect projects with a limited life span to learn and maintain all the necessary knowledge and skills required to run a complex chain of systems and platforms. However, appointing one or more persons with the responsibility for setting up and maintaining environments

4 Key areas

is not necessarily the answer under every circumstance, either. Whatever role or department is designated, it should have the competence to enforce certain rules and regulations aimed at providing stable and predictable environments.

Checkpoints
1. The ownership of test environments lies with a distinct department.
2. Usage of test environments is laid down in a standard contract.
3. Services in scope and out of scope with regard to test environments are laid down in a Service Catalogue.

Enablers
- None.

Improvement suggestions

When dealing with services that offer test data, ensure client sensitive data protection and try and differentiate between real production data and synthetic or artificial data.

Ensure development and test environments are logically and (preferably) physically segregated to avoid developer testing (or worse: development) in the test environment.

Part 3
Improving Test Process Maturity

5 BDTPI follows the steps of a generic change process

Each test process improvement is a separate change process and each change process follows a certain structured path with the following activities:
1. *(Generate) awareness:* an understanding of why the test process needs to be improved.
2. *Determine goals, scope and approach:* where does a specific test process need to be in the near or far future and how do we start from now?
3. *Assess current situation:* where are we now, what are the strong points, what needs improvement?
4. *Define improvements:* what do we have to do, or change, to reach our goal?
5. *Make plan of action:* how do we get there, with whom, within what timeframe, what resources do we need?
6. *Implement actions:* apply the improvement actions, start using the new procedures, templates, etc, and practice, practice, practice, etc.
7. *Evaluate and redirect:* have we reached our goals, is this what we wanted, how should we continue, do we need to take a new direction?

The change process is illustrated in Figure 5.1.

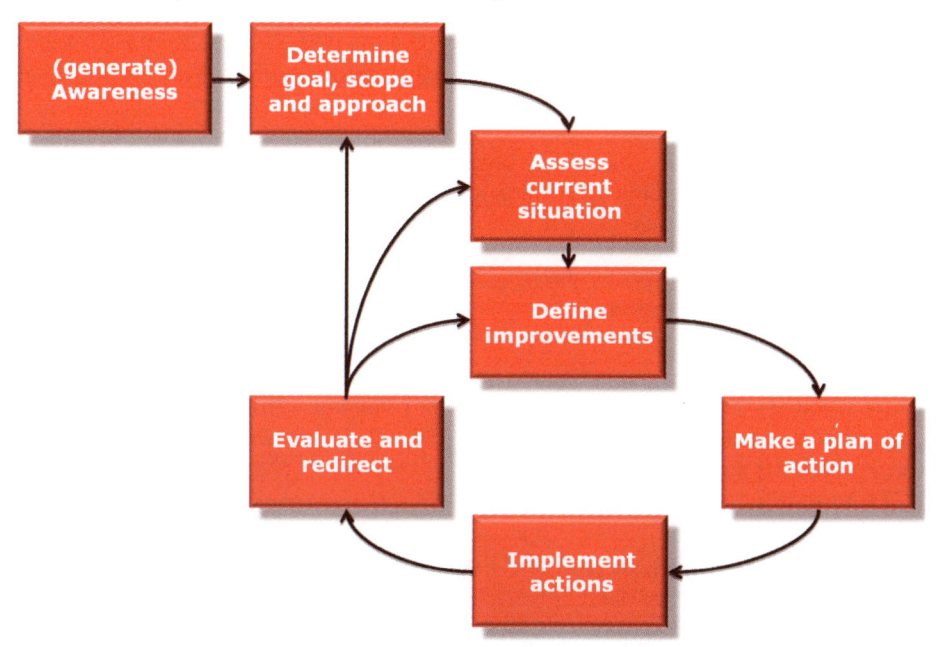

Figure 5.1: Change process follows a structured path with key activities.

5 BDTPI follows the steps of a generic change process

In a change process there are many success factors, the most important one having the commitment of the people undergoing the change. Getting their commitment and overcoming resistance (which is certainly present) may be difficult and an ongoing process. The same applies for monitoring the change process. These are all activities however that are common to change processes in general and will not be described in this chapter.

The following sections explicitly describe the test process improvement specific elements within the steps in the change process, based on the actions for a full BDTPI assessment and implementation. For each step (or sometimes per sub-step) of the change process a table is presented, which lists possible activities to be performed within that step. Depending on for example the size and approach of the test process improvement project and the size of the organization one can decide which activities need to be executed in a specific context.

5.1 (Generate) awareness

There is a wide range of business drivers or triggers for changing and improving the test process, which are described in section 6.1.1. For the change process it is beneficial not only to generate awareness, but also to receive sufficient support from stakeholders. If you, as a tester, think that the process can be improved, it is recommended to involve senior management in your ideas and plans. Likewise, if you are an IT manager with the objective that it should be possible to perform the test process in less time, it is wise to involve the testers in your plans and ideas.

> **Tip - Awareness is an essential pre-condition**
> To many it may seem that the people involved in the test process know very well the process doesn't run smooth and needs to be improved. This is certainly not always the case. Usually there is a general idea of possibilities for improvement, but parties involved mostly do not have a mutual agreement on the scope, degree and cause of the experienced problems. So, the awareness phase should in fact not be regarded as a detached step in the change process, but rather as an essential pre-condition.

The motivation for improving the test process may be the assumption that there is something 'wrong' within the test process, while this in fact may be a symptom of a different cause. Therefore all involved should become aware of, and support:

- The need for improving the test process, the purpose and the (possible) benefits.
- The acknowledgement that the use of the BDTPI model in this change process is the way to do it.
- The recognition that a test process improvement project requires or will lead to a change in the way people work.

Typical actions in this stage are to indicate to people involved the benefits of an improved test process, for example:
- A business manager may gain more certainty of the possible risks when a new or modified system is launched.
- The maintenance department may have a better insight in the ability to maintain their system.
- The help desk may be relieved by a reduction in production failures.

> **Example - Bottom-up approach**
> In a large organization, with 40-50 employees directly involved in testing, management decided that the test process could be significantly improved by using a new testing method. The employees however strongly opposed this plan, arguing that: "We have always done it in our own way and look how stable our systems are". Both management and employees agreed to follow a bottom-up approach: how could the testers be supported to improve their own test activities? Applying this approach created the awareness among the employees that improvement was possible and even necessary. The end result was successful employee training and a more structured and transparent test process.

Possible actions and deliverables in this step

Action	Deliverables	Remark
Preliminary discussion	Presentation Problem description	Presentations (e.g. about the value of testing) and other means of communication to define: what is the problem and who is involved

5.2 Determine goal, scope and approach

An improvement project can be approached in many ways, but 'failing to prepare is preparing to fail'. In order to perform a BDTPI project, you have to know: what goals you want to reach, what can and must be expected from improvements, which specific test process(es) should be focused on, who has the relevant information and how much time is needed.

5.2.1 Setting the goals

Goals can be set in terms of time, money and/or quality, either for a short-term timeframe (months) or long-term (years). A typical quality-related goal for test process improvement would be to receive more and better information from the test process. In using the BDTPI model, it is important to know that specific goals lead to a specific focus on certain

5 BDTPI follows the steps of a generic change process

BDTPI Key areas (chapter 4 describes the Key areas; section 6.1 describes the focus on certain Key areas through certain business drivers).

> **Tip - Assess the feasibility of the goals**
> Prioritize the goals based upon either the ones that are "low hanging fruit", gain the most with the least effort, or the ones that resolve critical issues. The goals have to be realistic. In other words can BDTPI achieve these goals? And are we solving the right problems with BDTPI? Is the problem a cause or a symptom? It may very well be that what is regarded as a problem is actually caused by something else. So, at this stage of the change process, it is wise to assess the feasibility of the goals.

A BDTPI assessment will help to find out if you are solving the right problem. The findings can be used as substantiation for an improvement business case. Another example of a goal would be: to develop and implement a well-controlled and repeatable process. The essence of this goal is that testing activities have been determined and described. The timeline for a test project can be planned and the necessary resources (knowledge, competences and budget) can be estimated accurately. This can be obtained by using a standardized testing method (like TMap® NEXT) and the application of lessons learned and best practices. In a controlled test process, the test efforts are aimed at the most critical parts of a system in such a way that the most relevant defects are found at the lowest cost.

> **Example - Translation of business goals**
> A test process improvement project in a large financial organization started by translating the business goal (higher efficiency) to specific goals for testing:
> - *Strategic:* testing should be more efficient
> - *Tactical:* the most important defects should be found as early in the project as possible
> - *Operational:* by January 1st next year, the number of severe defects found in production should be eliminated by 75%.

Note that when you start describing goals, you also have to consider the issue of being able to demonstrate their achievement. How will you or your stakeholders know that your improvement efforts have reached the expectations and goals? This can be achieved by defining indicators. Examples include: the number of defects in production in the first month after launch, user satisfaction that can be measured by a checklist and the ratio between the number of test cases. See also section 6.2.4. 'Working with Indicators'.

5.2.2 Determining the scope

The area of consideration of the change process can be various:
- One specific test in a project (for example the performance test).
- System or acceptance tests (in a project or in general).

- All test levels in a project (including development tests).
- All tests of one certain test level in the entire organization (for example all system tests).
- All test levels in the entire organization.
- The tests performed by an (external) supplier.

Considerations could include a certain project or a certain test level that would benefit the most from any improvements (e.g. the system test in a system upgrade), or a specific test level that has the highest chance of successful results for the lowest expenditure of effort.

Another consideration is that in some situations the test process is the final phase of the project and therefore under constant pressure. In this situation, will the improvement project have enough time and stakeholder commitment to prove its worth and achieve the required results?

It should be noted that the choice of scope may affect the priority of Key areas that you focus on. The unique situation of a test process and its particular issues may lead to specific Key areas to be considered.

> **Example - Narrowing the scope**
> An energy supplier had expanded significantly in recent years, together with its IT department. Because of the increased size of the organization, it was no longer possible to depend on short communication lines and domain expertise. Due to the increasing importance of the quality of the output of the IT organization, the energy supplier wanted to improve its current test process.
> As the existing test process was small-scale and largely ad hoc, the principal stakeholder explicitly requested to leave out test tools, tester professionalism and metrics from the assessment, since it was clear to him from the start that there had been no activity in those Key areas.

> **Tip - Cover all Key areas**
> It is possible to leave out Key areas from a BDTPI project as mentioned in the example above. But be reluctant with leaving out Key areas just like that. Focusing on particular Key areas only or discarding certain key areas should be justified by specific situations (e.g. agile environment) rather than on an assumed maturity of the test process under consideration.
> The additional effort needed to cover all Key areas is rather small, especially when the test process is rudimentary. In order to have complete insight and options to realize quick wins it is recommended to perform an analysis across all Key areas.

Possible actions and deliverables in this step

Action	Deliverables	Remark
Initiation of the improvement project	Assignment formulation	Define the goals and scope of test process improvement and the assignment, including definition of activities

5.2.3 Define the approach

Once you have set your goals and scope, the next step is to determine how to continue from here. Needless to say, the next steps depend very much on the outcomes of the previous stages - awareness of test improvement, and choices made such as the people to be involved, the defined goals and scope.

If you realize that you have a testing problem, but at the same time you do not have the time or resources to do something about it right now, in that case, wait and perhaps begin to raise awareness about the issue.

If the scope is broad, for example aimed at all test activities in the organization, then assessing all projects would be too great an effort. In that situation it may be an option to find a reference project or process. If for example the scope is acceptance tests, you could take a recent project and its acceptance tests to be assessed. The most important criterion for such a reference is that it must provide enough useful information to produce generic statements, and that the information should be easily accessible and suitable for being analyzed.

> **In more detail - Multiple test processes**
> Special consideration is needed when assessing an organization with multiple test processes. Many questions need answering:
> - Can any of the test processes function as a reference?
> - Should the test processes be compared and, if yes, how?
> - How should the results be presented?
>
> For more information see section 7.3.

Part of defining the approach is to establish how many interviews are necessary, who they should be conducted with, which documents need to be studied and if a kick-off meeting is needed. Additional aspects to consider are: additional people to be involved, what elements (such as progress, preliminary finding, and issues) of the test improvement process should be reported on, and how the report should be delivered (to whom, when, etc).

> **In more detail - Kick-off meeting**
> In a kick-off meeting the goals, process and procedures are explained to the people involved. A possibility is to ask some preliminary questions to get them acquainted with the kind of questions they may expect.

Another important question for the organization is: who will perform the actual assessment? Should one of your test employees be appointed to carry out the task, or should it be an independent, experienced, probably external BDTPI consultant? An outsider is often more objective and the test team may be more comfortable opening up to an outsider instead of to a colleague. Or maybe a test employee should take the lead and the BDTPI consultant take an advisory role.

In the assessment plan considerable time should be reserved to:
- Gain a mutual understanding of the goals and the approach (for people in the organization who are part of the project).
- Organize, schedule and carryout interviews (including question preparation).
- Manage and provide information (documentation).
- Review reports.
- Attend presentations and other meetings.

Possible actions and deliverables in this step

Action	Deliverables	Remark
Make Assessment plan	Assessment plan	Describe activities and the time that will be required of the people involved
Make appointments with those involved	Schedule	This is always time consuming. Tip: have someone from the staff division take care of appointments

5.3 Assess current situation

"If you don't know where you are, a map won't help!" - Watts H. Humphrey[1]. If you do not know your starting position, you may take inadequate steps on the way to your goal. It is important to know the strengths and weaknesses of the current test process to know where to put most effort, which Key areas need additional attention, and/or which aspects are beneficial and should be retained and leveraged.

The current situation is defined by executing the following steps:
1. Gather information from people and documentation.
2. Analyze the information by using the BDTPI model as a reference.
3. Describe the strengths, weaknesses, opportunities and threats, and draw conclusions

Section 3.6 provides a visualization of the current situation of a test process.

---

[1] A fellow of the Carnegie Mellon University Software Engineering Institute (SEI).

5 BDTPI follows the steps of a generic change process

5.3.1 Gathering information

Interviews

The most valuable sources of information are those people who are actually involved in the test process, either in a dependent role (such as management who want to take decisions based on the test results) or in a execution role (like testers, programmers repairing the defects, and possibly a support center). The information can be obtained via interviews, where the Key areas and their Checkpoints can be the basis for the questionnaire (see chapter 4). In interviewing, decide in advance on the level of information that you require: what will be useful and when will the (amount of) information collection be sufficient?

Not all opinions or information that you gather will relate directly to the test process, but will throw light on other aspects of the project or organization such as the quality of the designs and the general atmosphere or culture in the organization. All this may be relevant information for the BDTPI project. For instance, if you hear in the interviews that testers are demotivated by a recent reorganization, this information can be useful for developing the improvement plan.

These aspects strongly relate to the Enablers from the BDTPI model: information from other processes in the software development life cycle (SDLC) can be used to strengthen the test process and vice versa.

> **Tip - Check and recheck**
> Keep in mind that people usually tend to see their own work more positive than it actually is. Most people see problems within testing caused by other people/organizational units. This requires an experienced interviewer who critically checks the answers. For experienced BDTPI consultants it is not unusual to ask the same question three times to the same person - and to receive three different answers.

Interesting sources of information include:
- Principal stakeholder
- Project manager
- Test manager (test coordinator)
- Testers (test engineers, test analysts)
- Line management
- Key users
- People responsible for the test environment(s)
- Head of System development/developers
- Defect manager
- (Internal) auditors
- Maintenance.

> **Tip - Objectify the information**
> In a situation in which you perform an assessment on your own test process, be sure that your information is as objective as possible. When in doubt, contact a peer for a review or deliberation on your findings.

A special way to get information about the ongoing test process is to have one or more group sessions with people involved. This might be the most practical mechanism for managing larger assessments such as organization-wide BDTPI projects or projects with different parties, such as suppliers and clients. However, there is a great downside to group sessions where people are interviewed jointly. There may be large discussion, information may be colored, or people may not open up, especially in the situation of staff members who are not independent of each other. Further, even among equals, the input of talkative persons may impede shy individuals to render their input. Of course, a mix of individual interviews, group interviews or sessions is possible.

> **Example - Group session**
> In order to carry out a quick view of the test processes in an organization with 6 autonomous divisions, an assessment session was organized. Each division had at least 2 representatives in this group. They were expected to provide the most relevant information for the BDTPI Key areas, both from a high level overview (helicopter view) as from their test engineering point of view. The session was prepared and managed by two BDTPI consultants, one to lead the process and the other to observe and take notes. In one day, all Key areas and relevant Checkpoints were addressed. This resulted not only in a clear BDTPI matrix for the whole organization, but also, much more importantly, in a common understanding of the general test process and a vivid exchange of ideas and opportunities.

Documentation

During the interviews you may need to verify the information. One way is to cross check the findings with other interviewees or relevant stakeholders. Another way is to examine key relevant documents such as (master) test plans, test cases, defects and progress reports. For an overall view, it is also important to review project plans and functional specifications.

> **Example - Verify information from the interviews**
> BDTPI Consultant: "Before the actual interview started, the Test Manager sent me a Master Test Plan. The document looked excellent: all items were there and adequately worked out. However, for verification, I checked with the test manager's principal stakeholder. It appeared that he had never seen the Master Test Plan, let alone he had reviewed the possible product risks and test strategy. The test manager had developed the plan but had overlooked the importance of sharing and checking it with his principal stakeholder."

> **Tip - Documentation analysis before interviews**
> The best practice is to read documentation first and use this information for preparation of interviews.

5 BDTPI follows the steps of a generic change process

If there is nothing else that can be used for verification, ask for emails. While this might sound strange, in some cases emails are used by the tester to report defects, general findings or the evaluation of the test at the end of the project.

Alternatively, you may be inundated with documentation. In this situation, it is wise to set a time-box. In general, do not spend more than one day to examine documentation, so if there is a lot, prioritize the documents and only review the most relevant parts. For example, if you receive a complete administration of defects, select some (still) open severe defects and some closed less severe defects to have a good representative mix.

Auditing by walking around

The informal contacts during or between working hours are a very useful source of information. You could consider sitting next to a tester while he is working or even perform some tests yourself to check the user-friendliness of the test cases. Also a friendly chat at lunch or during a coffee break often provides helpful information.

Possible actions and deliverables in this step

Action	Deliverables	Remark
Kick-off	Hand-out, providing (general) information about the approach of the BDTPI project	For larger assessments, a kick-off will help to gain mutual understanding of goals and approach
Interview testers and other involved parties	Interview reports (for internal use)	Allow about 2.5 hours per interview: preparation, actual Interview time of 1-2 hours per interviewee, and processing

5.3.2 Analyzing the information

Gathered information is checked against the BDTPI model, checking all relevant Key areas and Checkpoints, as soon as possible (already parallel with the interviews). The complete picture of the test process under consideration is elaborated step by step. Gaps regarding the information obtained so far can easily be identified and closed during remaining interviews. What may help is to document all your notes, remarks and findings in a BDTPI spreadsheet, cross-referencing them to the relevant Key areas. This 'Justification table' helps to verify which Checkpoints match your findings and which have not been checked, and is the basis for the description of the current situation.

Example - Justification table

Key area	Findings, remarks	Improvement suggestion
Test strategy	The Test Strategy guides the test process towards an optimal allocation of effort and resources. The Test strategy defines the distribution of the test effort and the coverage over the parts to be tested or aspects of the test object. The Test strategy aims at detecting the most important defects as early and cheaply as possible. The qualification 'most important' is driven by the test goals such as business processes, critical success factors or perceived product risks. - The goal and scope of a test level with regard to other test levels is unclear in practice. There is a test policy and test process model in which this scope is determined and in which is established that deliberation is required at the start of a test project about the distribution of test effort over the different test levels. However, the test policy and test process model are not being followed and this is not managed. - There is factually no differentiation in coverage of the tests. The test approach offers limited coverage. What needs to be tested and with what coverage is not discussed explicitly, causing differences in expectations with the project manager and the principal stakeholder.	Arrange a test strategy meeting at the project start. Tune work load between the different test levels. Determine which risk are run if a defect won't be found during test. Involve explicitly the user and maintenance departments.

Possible actions and deliverables in this step

Action	Deliverables	Remark
Analyze the interviews	Interview log/protocol	After finishing all the interviews, analyze the results. What are the similarities and the deviations? Do I really have all the answers? Do I need additional input or to verify certain issues?
Study documents		Sometimes there is an overload of documentation. Limit the time spent to a realistic amount.
Justify the Checkpoints	Justification table	Remarks and findings per Key area or per Checkpoint.
Progress report (and discussions)	Progress reports	Only for large assessments and if agreed with the principal stakeholder or project owner.

5.3.3 Describe the strengths, weaknesses, opportunities and threats

For many people interested in the results of a BDTPI assessment the table of Checkpoints and findings may be too detailed. Although very powerful the Checkpoints remain a means. A BDTPI assessment should give insight into what is going well already and where are possibilities for improvement. For most people involved, especially senior management, it is more interesting and thus necessary to summarize the results, for instance in a report containing a description of the strengths and weaknesses of the current test process.

In an accurate analysis of the current situation, the reader should recognize all the SWOT aspects (Strengths, Weaknesses, Opportunities and Threats):

- *The Strengths:* what works well now and should be maintained; what are the positive trends?
- *The Weaknesses:* what are the problems and bottlenecks?
- *The Opportunities:* where do we see changes; which circumstances (Enablers) may have a positive effect on the test process?
- *The Threats:* which circumstances may have a negative effect on the test process?

During the assessment, aspects often arise which are not directly related to the test process. For example: a high staff churn rate, an uncontrolled development process or a new development approach (such as Agile) that does not meet the defined expectations. In many cases, these aspects can be linked to the described Enablers. Another solution is to describe them separately, and then discuss with the stakeholders what action can be taken.

Example - SWOT analysis

Strengths
It is evident that much has been done to achieve a formal Test Process. Developers and testers can execute their tests in separate environments. User acceptance tests are carried out in a separate test room where they were not distracted by their daily work.

Weaknesses
Nobody really knows how much testing costs or what the benefits are. In fact, the overall IT costs are not known either.

Opportunities
The importance of testing is clearly recognized. The well-structured and maintained defect management tool could be the basis for increased and more accurate metrics, which will in turn provide more insight into the costs and benefits of testing.

Threats
Government regulations and IT infrastructure are becoming more and more complex. Therefore it is unclear how much longer the current software quality can be maintained using the current process.

The description of the current test situation should conclude with a short management summary of the findings. Be careful not to link problems to single persons (lack of motivation, lack of education, lack of cooperation, ...). Keep in mind that test process improvement is about assessing processes - not the persons.

If, in defining the approach, a reference project or process was chosen and a sub-set of a test process has been assessed, it is still necessary to produce a judgment on the process as a whole. One approach would be to simply project all the conclusions of the reference project onto the other processes, but this is quite risky. During the interviews, the assessor often gains some insight into other projects, test levels or processes. In this situation, the assessor can make some assumptions and estimated guesses about the higher or overall level. However these assumptions should be clearly stated in the report and not passed off as fact.

Possible actions and deliverables in this step

Action	Deliverables	Remark
Describe current situation	Current situation (part of the Assessment report)	Results of the (SWOT) analysis

5.4 Define improvements

This is the point in the change process to reflect on how to realize the target situation (described as goals for the short-, mid- and/or long-term), working from the present situation using either the base Clusters or business-driven Clusters you create.

How do I get from the SWOT to improvement measures?
1. Let the principal stakeholder, sponsor and/or other stakeholders determine the target situation. The target situation is usually extracted from the business driver(s) that were the reason for the assessment. If there was no clear business driver stated at the beginning of the assessment an (long term) improvement goal can be set, like reaching the Controlled level for the test process. The target situation should be a realistic reflection of the determined current situation. If for instance in the current situation the test process is generally still at the initial level then targeting for a highly efficient test process is just a few steps too far.
Setting the target situation limits the scope of the next steps.
2. Determine which improvement path to use. This can either be
   a. The base Clusters (see section 3.7).

5 BDTPI follows the steps of a generic change process

      b. Modification of the base Clusters by means of some elaborated business drivers. BDTPI is used to:
- 'Make sure that IT services are reliable and secure' (6.3.1).
- 'Support Effective automated solutions' (6.3.2).
- 'Shorten the time to market' (6.3.3).
- 'Improve cost efficiency of IT' (6.3.4).
- 'Improve Transparency and understanding of IT' (6.3.5).

      c. Created Clusters based on any business driver (see section 6.1 and appendix B).

3. Step through each Cluster (as determined in Step 2), starting with Cluster A up to the last Cluster needed to reach the target situation (set in Step 1). Look for Checkpoints that are not scored.
4. Establish appropriate measures for each non-scored Checkpoint within the Cluster(s) which are to be implemented first.
    a. Is it possible to simply put the Checkpoint into practice?
    b. Is the improvement suggestion feasible?
5. Identify if there is enough commitment for the measures to be accepted (by consulting interviewees or senior management).
6. Estimate how much effort it would take to implement the measures.
7. Perform a final prioritization of the measures by looking at:
    a. The Clusters once again (they already suggest a prioritization).
    b. Which Improvement measure produces 'Quick wins' or the most spin-offs.
    c. Which measures can actually be implemented and used right now.
    d. Which measures can be realized on the short- or long-term.
    e. The amount of measures that can be implemented in one time.

Tip - Determining improvement measures and their benefits

When determining the improvement measures, look beyond the obvious measures. The number of improvement measures is unlimited and each organization will choose to implement the measures that best fit their situation.

For prioritization and determination of the effects the BDTPI assessor needs input from BDTPI participants, principal stakeholder, sponsor and/or other stakeholders, because they know their organization the best and know what may work and what not. The BDTPI assessor - especially when being an external consultant - merely has an advisory role. Do not forget to relate the improvement measures back to IT or even business goals (see section 6.1.1). Or consider the following items:
- Flexibility of test resources.
- Quality of the test process.
- Test organization prepared for the future.
- Test lead time.
- Working more effective or efficient.
- Knowledge sharing and anchoring.

A session with BDTPI participants is a very helpful tool for generating improvement suggestions. It gives the various people involved the opportunity to give their views and make a positive contribution.

Possible actions and deliverables in this step

Action	Deliverables	Remark
Describe improvement horizon	Assessment report	The goals for test process improvement, short-, (mid-) and long-term
Discuss with all relevant stakeholders		Peer and stakeholder reviews (especially interviewees)
Describe improvement proposals and actions		This can be done after the acknowledgement of the defined current situation and goals
Initiate implementation		A draft and initial implementation plan
Write management summary		If agreed with your principal stakeholder
Discuss draft version with the principal stakeholder and other involved parties		Agree with the principal stakeholder whether or not the draft report should go to the wider organization
Finalize report		
Prepare presentation	Presentation	Presentation of the report for stakeholder committee. Determine, during the assignment formulation with the client, what kind of presentation it should be.

5.5 Make a plan of action

After the decision has been made to start the implementation phase, an implementation plan should be developed. However, it is possible that the implementation plan may be considered as the next 'go/no go' step in the change process. In that case, it may be necessary to spend additional time on the justification of the business case for the improvements.
In the plan of action an evaluation should be planned: at the end of the project, or no later than six to nine months after the project has started. It is advised to run an improvement project no longer than half a year. The world around the test process changes constantly and the value of an improvement action may have become obsolete. It is better to see what the BDTPI project accomplished after six month and then to reset the goals and the improvement actions.

5 BDTPI follows the steps of a generic change process

Commitment from management is absolutely vital for the implementation and improvement process. Not only for allocating resources such as time, money and personnel, but especially in times of crisis (such as when the company or specific projects are under pressure) when it is even more necessary to convince management of the benefits of test process improvement.

> **In more detail - Worldwide TPI survey**
> One of the results of Sogeti's worldwide survey on the use of the original TPI model, carried out in 2004, is that management commitment is the most important success factor for a test process improvement project.
> For the improvement of the test process training on the job is a very successful way of getting new procedures and methods put into action. Another approach is to introduce the new methods and techniques in a pilot project that is small-scale, with Quick wins or in a project where mistakes are allowed and lessons can be learned from them.

Possible actions and deliverables in this step

Action	Deliverables	Remark
Define stakeholders and participants	Statement of work	After finishing all the interviews, analyze the results. What are the similarities and the deviations? Do I really have all the answers? Do I need additional input or to verify certain issues?
Elaborate on the improvement actions		Do not limit yourself to the ones given in the book! There are countless other possibilities.
Develop a plan		Think about time lines, hours, deliverables, owners of particular actions, etc.
Describe the project organization		Define tasks, roles and responsibilities. Who will lead the project? Is advice needed?
Develop a communication plan		Meetings, reports, publications (on the Intranet). Think of involving other projects/ departments to get them inspired.

5.6 Implement actions

In this phase, the plan is executed and the consequences of the change process will have the most impact. Progress should be measured in terms of the extent to which the various actions have been executed. Intermediate surveys and quick scans on participating projects on the basis of the BDTPI Checkpoints for example are ways of doing this.
Overall, communication plays an important role: information requests, suggestions, problems and ideas must be surfaced and given due attention by the BDTPI lead (and his team as well as the project owner). In addition, as mentioned in the previous section, strong stakeholder commitment is needed. Actions can be initiated to show this commitment, ideally by having the management visible on the work floor, endorsing the importance of the project and responding to and acting on any possible resistance.

> **Tip - Involve the work floor**
> Involve the ones who will execute the new or changed activities or will work according the new procedures. Ideally they elaborate the actions themselves for optimal commitment.

Possible actions and deliverables in this step

Action	Deliverables	Remark
Execute, monitor and adjust plan	Progress reports	Communication about results creates curiosity. However, be aware that in a change process there may be some resistance as well. This phenomenon should not be underestimated, but it can certainly be managed.

5.7 Evaluate and redirect

The process of getting used to the improved method will be similar to any other change process. The results of the improvement actions are compared with the initial plans, goals and requirements. From here, the process may take different directions like a new assessment, redefinition of goals of improvement actions, or may even stop or hold the process. Also a re-assessment of the achieved situation should be executed with the BDTPI model, indicating how the maturity of the test process has grown.

5 BDTPI follows the steps of a generic change process

Note: if the implementation process takes longer than 6 months, it is also wise to perform an assessment using the BDTPI model of the current situation to evaluate the intermediate milestones.

Possible actions and deliverables in this step

Action	Deliverables	Remark
Evaluate implementation		Look at the indicators (see section 6.2.4). What are the measurable (quantitative) results of the improvement actions? But also take qualitative indicators like interview findings or surveys into account.
Decide on new directions	New or adjusted assignment or discharge	

Part 4
Business Driven Improvement

6 Business Driven Test Process Improvement

Chapter 5 describes how to apply the TPI model in a general way. In this Chapter, we describe how the aspects of 'business driven' manifest themselves. We first put into context the concept of business goals as the drivers for test process improvement and then illustrate this in more detail through five example drivers:
- Time to market
- Cost reduction
- Effectiveness increase
- Transparency improvement
- Business continuity.

Time to market, Cost reduction and Effectiveness increase have been chosen as they are very common business drivers, Transparency improvement because it is an important driver for outsourcing, and Business continuity to demonstrate the usefulness in a not so common environment.

6.1 BDTPI aims at a specific result

Test process improvement always serves a purpose. It can be used for improving the test process as a whole, targeting a broad spectrum of test aspects. This is the case when an organization has initiated a specific program, such as an SPI program, that needs to attain a certain CMMI maturity level or SPICE capability level. It can also be used for optimizing the test process for a specific business purpose such as test cost reduction or shorter time to market.

In the non-biased way the test process is gradually improved in all its aspects. All Key areas are considered to be equally important and are all treated the same. Applying the model business driven implies a biased approach in which certain Key areas are expected to contribute more to the business driver at hand than others. Consequently, it is better to achieve the requirements (Checkpoints) of these Key areas more quickly than those of the less important Key areas. This is the core assumption behind the 'business driven' approach of test process improvement. It translates into rearranging the Checkpoints over the Clusters, moving the important ones to the early Clusters and the less important ones 'backwards'.

The next sections describe a 4 step approach for rearranging the Clusters in a business driven fashion, starting with identifying the business driver and its related IT goals, prioritizing the BDTPI key areas and finally presenting guidelines on how to move the checkpoints around. After this section some practice based examples are presented.

6.2 The BDTPI model used in a business driven manner

With business goals, IT goals and Key areas in mind, business driven TPI follows this four step approach:
1. Identify the business driver
2. Translate business goals into IT goals
3. Identify the more and less important Key areas for the IT goals
4. Rearrange the Checkpoints in the Clusters.

Step 1: Identify the business driver
Research by the IT Governance Institute (ITGI™)[12] identifies business goals and how they can be linked to IT goals. This research can be helpful in determining where the the pain is really felt, but this list is by no means exhaustive. The advantage of recognizing a 'known' business goal lies in the fact that the next steps have most probably already been undertaken and documented. Some of the most common are described in this book. Some of the business goals distinguished by the ITGI™ are:
- Improve customer orientation and service
- Ensure compliance with external laws and regulations
- Establish service continuity and availability
- Manage (IT-related) business risks
- Offer competitive products and services
- Improve and maintain business process functionality
- Provide a good return on (IT-enabled) business investments
- Acquire, develop and maintain skilled and motivated people
- Create agility in responding to changing business requirements.

An important part of this step, Identify the business driver, is to describe how to measure progress against the driver. This step is typically executed during the phase when the assignment is being set up. If the business driver is formulated well, it can serve as the basis for reporting. It can also prevent future disappointments, since discussions on how to measure often reveal implicit expectations on the client's side.

Step 2: Translate business drivers into IT goals
ITGI maps the business goals to IT goals as demonstrated in Table 6.1. This is especially helpful since test process improvement is not always initiated in a business department. Often the IT department recognizes the need for improvement and acts accordingly.

6.2 The BDTPI model used in a business driven manner

IT Goals	Business Goals								
	Improve customer orientation and service	Ensure compliance with external laws and regulations	Establish service continuity and availability	Manage (IT-related) business risks	Offer competitive products and services	Improve and maintain business process functionality	Provide a good return on (IT-enabled) business investments	Acquire, develop and maintain skilled and motivated people	Create agility in responding to changing business requirements
Make sure that IT services are reliable and secure	P	P	P	P	S	S	S		S
Ensure IT compliance with laws and regulations	S	P		S	S		S		
Translate business, functional and control requirements into effective and efficient automated solutions	S		S	S	S	P	S		S
Deliver projects on time and on budget, meeting quality standards	S			S	S	S	S		S
Drive commitment and support of executive management	S			S	S	S		S	S
Improve IT's cost-efficiency					S		P		
Acquire, develop and maintain IT skills that respond to the IT strategy	S			S				P	S
Provide IT agility (in response to changing business needs)	S			S	S	S			P
Offer transparency and understanding of IT costs, benefits and risks				S			S		
Ensure that IT demonstrates continuous improvement and readiness for future change				S	S			S	P

Table 6.1: The cross reference of business goals to IT goals (P=primary, S=supportive) [12].

Step 3: Identify the more and less important Key areas for the IT goals

The next step is to translate the (primary) IT goal to BDTPI key areas. BDTPI comprises 16 key areas. For the identified IT goal, these Key areas are categorized in terms of importance: High, Neutral and Low. High indicates that the Key area is of 'above average influence' on the IT driver and Low indicates the opposite. The Key areas are equally distributed across the categories (e.g. 5 Key areas 'above average', 6 'average' and 5 'below average'), but this is not mandatory.

161

6 Business Driven Test Process Improvement

Table 6.2 illustrates how these Key area categories can be aligned to some example IT goals. Please note that this is not a universal truth! The rationale behind the categories is described in the following sections and is based on years of experience in test process improvement projects. But it may not be applicable to the specific situation in your organization. As an example: if the cost of a test environment (hardware, maintenance, licencies) is taken into account in the case of the Cost reduction goal, the Key area should score High. These costs may be a substantial part of the test process!

Key areas	Make sure that IT services are reliable and secure	Translate business functional and control requirements into effective and efficient automated solutions	Deliver projects on time and on budget, meeting quality standards	Improve IT's cost-efficiency	Offer transparency and understanding of IT costs, benefits and risks
Stakeholder commitment	H	L	N	L	L
Degree of involvement	L	H	H	H	L
Test strategy	N	H	H	H	H
Test organization	L	N	N	H	L
Communication	H	N	N	N	N
Reporting	H	L	L	L	H
Test process management	N	N	N	N	H
Estimating and planning	N	N	H	N	H
Metrics	L	L	L	L	H
Defect management	N	H	N	H	H
Testware management	H	N	L	N	N
Methodology practice	L	L	L	N	N
Tester professionalism	L	H	N	N	L
Test case design	N	H	H	N	N
Test tools	N	L	H	H	N
Test environment	H	N	H	L	L

Table 6.2: The cross reference of IT goals against Key areas, indicating degree of importance (H=High, N=Neutral, L=Low).

162

Dependencies

When rearranging the Key areas also the interdependencies between Key areas need to be considered. Dependencies may take one Key area to the same category as its related Key area. However: in our case the contribution of the Key area to the business driver is the main issue! This may lead to a situation that one Key area has category High and its dependant Key area has category Low.

Step 4: Rearrange the Checkpoints in the Clusters

The 'standard' division of Checkpoints over the Clusters does not take any particular business-driven bias into account. All Key areas are equally important.

In the business driven, biased situation, Checkpoints of Key areas in the category 'High' importance now are re-allocated to Clusters further to the 'left' from their original position in the maturity matrix. Checkpoints with Cluster name 'A' remain the same, Checkpoints with Cluster name 'B' become 'A', Checkpoints with Cluster name 'C' become 'B', etc. The Checkpoints in these Clusters need to be achieved first. Checkpoints in the category 'Neutral' stay where they are and Checkpoints in the 'Low' importance category move to the 'right' (Checkpoints with Cluster name 'A' become 'B;', etc.).

Note: The Appendix "Creating New Clusters" offers the clustering technique with an example of the business driver 'cost reduction'.

6.3 Business drivers affect the use of the model

The previous sections show how business drivers can be translated into one or more IT goals. These IT goals can be rephrased into goals for test process improvement, for example like this:

Business driver	IT goal	BDTPI goal
Establish service continuity and availability	Make sure that IT services are reliable and secure	Improve Business continuity tests
Improve and maintain business process functionality	Translate business, functional and control requirements into effective and efficient automated solutions	Improve the effectiveness of testing
Create agility in responding to changing business requirements	Deliver products on time/shorten Time to market	Reduce (the critical path of) test execution
Provide a good return on (IT enabled) business investments	Improve IT's cost efficiency	Reduce the cost of testing
Manage (IT related) business risks	Offer transparency and understanding of IT costs, benefits and risks	Increase the transparency of testing

6 Business Driven Test Process Improvement

We will now look in more detail at these five examples of business drivers and IT goals and evaluate how BDTPI can be used.

6.3.1 BDTPI used to make sure that IT services are reliable and secure

The concrete goals for improvement
In coping with a disaster, it is extremely important for an organization to have the business up and running again, according to predefined priorities. To actually test that the production environment can be reinstated after a disaster is a difficult and expensive exploit that in most cases is undertaken no more than once a year at the most. The goal of such a disaster recovery test is to verify that all primary systems can be up and running again in the shortest possible time - usually in a matter of hours! In-depth testing of specific applications or functionality is not required, but wide coverage is.

Key areas categorized in terms of helping to achieve the specific business continuity goal
Based on table 6.2, the Key areas are categorized as follows:

High	Neutral	Low
Stakeholder commitment	Test strategy	Degree of involvement
Communication	Test process management	Test organization
Reporting	Estimating & planning	Metrics
Testware management	Defect management	Methodology practice
Test environment	Test case design	Tester professionalism
	Test tools	

The following 5 Key areas support business continuity and therefore have increased priority:

- *Stakeholder commitment*
  Disaster recovery testing is pre-eminently a joint effort. Testers cannot perform such a test on their own.
- *Communication*
  Again, disaster recovery testing is a joint effort. Moreover, it is one that needs to be performed in a very limited timeframe. Interdepartmental co-operation is of the utmost importance. Anything but optimal communication will frustrate the process.
- *Reporting*
  Disaster recovery testing is very costly and performed under the close attention of board members or even an external supervisor. Reporting must comply to the highest of standards.

- *Testware management*
  The tests conducted are those used after a catastrophe, to decide whether or not systems can be released again for use. These test cases need to be accessible and well-understood.
- *Test environment*
  In a sense, during disaster recovery testing, the environment is the test object. So this Key area is of crucial importance.

The 6 Neutral Key areas are:
- Test strategy
- Test process management
- Estimating and planning
- Test case design
- Test tools
- Defect management.

These Key areas are neutral in terms of Business continuity and are listed here for the sake of completeness, but they are described in more detail in Chapter 4.

The 5 Key areas in the Low category are:
- *Degree of involvement*
  For disaster recovery testing there is no real SDLC in which testers can be involved.
- *Metrics*
  Trend analysis or the need to substantiate proposals or decisions with figures that have been collected over a long period of time plays no significant role in disaster recovery testing.
- *Tester professionalism*
  Subject matter expertise is more important than knowledge of, for instance, test design techniques. In fact, most of the time, the disaster recovery testing is performed by maintenance or support staff, and not by dedicated test professionals.
- *Methodology practice*
  There is little need to align the methods or techniques used with other test projects, since disaster recovery testing is usually separate from regular tests.
- *Test organization*
  Disaster recovery testing is mostly executed as part of an overall project in which testing is an integral part.

There are pitfalls that prevent improvement
There is a possible pitfall in Business continuity:
- *Awareness*
  Business continuity requires a lot of initial investment, but in practice the need for those investments will fade away in time. Having a test pro-

6.3.2 BDTPI used to support Effective automated solutions

The concrete goals for improvement
Testing is all about finding defects. Actually, it is about providing insight into the quality of whatever is being tested, but the means by which this insight is gained is through identifying defects. Or, when no or few defects have been found, testing provides the insight to explain why this should be the case. In finding defects, two aspects are equally important; finding the most severe defects and finding them as soon as possible.

- *Finding the most severe defects*
  Resolving defects costs money. The higher the cost, the more severe the defect. This is undeniably true, but it does not mean that cost is the only aspect to be taken into account when determining the severity of a defect. Another important aspect is the way a defect interferes with the progress of testing. If an unsolved defect means that a large part of the system can not be tested, it also counts as a severe defect.
- *Finding defects as soon as possible*
  To be more precise, defects should be found as close to their origins as possible. Do not aim to find technical issues in a functional test or vice versa. The first goal is to find defects through evaluation, even before the software has been written. Every error that slips through from this point on should be found in the test level or test type associated with the relevant test basis.

Key areas categorized
Based on table 6.2, the Key areas are categorized as follows:

High	Neutral	Low
Degree of involvement	Test organization	Stakeholder commitment
Test strategy	Communication	Reporting
Defect management	Test process management	Metrics
Tester professionalism	Estimating & planning	Methodology practice
Test case design	Testware management	Test tools
	Test environment	

The following 5 Key areas are the most important in helping to achieve a more effective test process:

- *Degree of involvement*
  Early involvement of testers has proved be a good measure to find flaws in requirements and design documents. No matter how early in the process a defect is detected, preventing it from being built is always better!
- *Test strategy*
  In aiming to find the most critical defects as soon as possible, you must decide in advance what the characteristics of these errors are and tune the test efforts accordingly. That is exactly what the test strategy is all about! Evaluation of design documents should be part of the identified activities.
- *Defect management*
  Finding defects without having the appropriate means to resolve them is not very effective. Another positive contribution of proper defect management is the ability to recognize trends or identify specific parts of the software that are very error prone.
- *Tester professionalism*
  Deciding, by means of a test strategy, what to aim for means nothing if the chosen strategy cannot be executed. The test design techniques that are the most appropriate for finding certain specific defects require training and experience.
- *Test case design*
  Applying test design techniques makes it possible to focus on the kind of errors that have been identified as the most severe in the Test strategy.

The 6 Key areas are Neutral are:
- Estimating and planning
- Test environment
- Test organization
- Testware management
- Communication
- Test process management.

As before, these Key areas are neutral in terms of Test effectiveness and are listed here for the sake of completeness, but they are described in more detail in Chapter 4.

The 5 Key areas in the Low category are:
- *Metrics*
  Metrics need to be gathered to measure progress, but this activity does not in itself constitute an improvement to the effectiveness of testing.
- *Test tools*
  This is a tricky one. In many situations, tools can speed up the process but they play a minimal part in enhancing the effectiveness of testing - hence, its position in the low Key areas. But in other situations a test tool can be a prerequisite for performing a test! A fitting example is perfor-

mance testing. So, with the right situation and motivation, this Key Area can be promoted to a higher category.
- *Reporting*
Reporting does not have added value for testing activities in this specific context.
- *Stakeholder commitment*
The positive influence of the stakeholders manifests itself in the Test strategy which has already been taken into account.
- *Methodology practice*
A common understanding and application of test techniques, language and methods does not in itself increase the chance of finding defects.

There are pitfalls that prevent improvement
There are some possible pitfalls in improving the test effectiveness:
- *Functional regression test tools*
The use of functional regression test tools requires long-term investment such as money, training of staff, etc. In addition, the quality of the use of such a tool depends heavily on the quality of the test cases used.
- *Estimation and Planning*
Without adequate and well-motivated estimation, planning and monitoring of the test process, it will soon become the critical time factor and concessions to the level of quality that can be achieved are very likely.

The causes of poor quality of deliverables are often due to the test process itself, but they may however be arbitrary. Sometimes the root causes are outside the test process and so we would recommend investigating the most effective measures in the overall software development lifecycle.

Some pitfalls that relate to subjects beyond testing:
- *Project management*
Poor project management, notably in terms of planning, will result in focusing on delivering on time rather than on delivering quality.
- *Change management and requirements lifecycle management*
To deliver quality, it is essential that testers are sure that they are using the actual versions of requirements and test basis that are related to the test object that is the subject of testing, including actual changes.

6.3.3 BDTPI used to Shorten the Time to market

The concrete goals for improvement
The goal of Time to market is especially important in industries where products become quickly outdated or where new regulations are regularly introduced. In addition to being a business objective, there may be other reasons for concentrating on the time aspect of the test process. A frequently heard remark about the test process is that it remains too long on

the critical path of the project; the deadline has almost been met and yet testing is still being carried out; or testing always seems to be delayed, thus causing other problems that require 'desperate measures' or postponement of the deadline.

When focusing on time to market for testing, it is important to establish a common understanding between all parties involved as to what constitutes 'testing lead time'. Several non-testing aspects significantly influence the lead time of testing:

- It's about test *execution* lead time
  In most cases, the reason behind shortening testing lead times is fed by the wish to 'make the date'. More or less all testing activities can be kept off a project's critical path except for test execution, which is *always* at the end of the line. So measures must aim primarily at keeping this stage of testing as short as possible and secondly at developing a well-founded and realistic plan, not only of test execution, but of all activities. This to prevent other test activities interfering with test execution.
- Waiting for developers is *not* testing
  The general practice is that testers usually have to re-use a large number of test cases, sometimes over and over again to re-test fixed errors or bugs. It is not unusual for a tester to wait for several days before a defect can be retested. Especially at the end of the test time, it is the development team, rather than the test team, that becomes the bottleneck for the 'OK to go live'! Therefore, it is important that measures address non-testing (i.e. development) activities as well.
- Waiting for the test environment is *not* testing
  Over the past decade, information systems have become heavily integrated with one another; indeed 'monolithic' systems are virtually non-existent nowadays. Testing these integrated systems, especially from an end-to-end perspective, relies heavily on an integrated test environment. Installing such environments and keeping them 'up-and-running' is continually cumbersome. End-to-end test teams regularly report environment outages of 50% and higher over the entire planned testing period. Measures to shorten test lead time must address improving the availability of the test environment.

In general there are two ways to approach time to market. The first is to improve the individual steps within the test process. The second is to skip some steps and/or to actively apply tools and techniques that will shorten some steps.

Key areas categorized in effectiveness for shorter time to market

Based on table 6.2, the Key areas are categorized as follows:

High	Neutral	Low
Degree of involvement	Stakeholder commitment	Reporting
Test strategy	Test organization	Metrics
Estimating & planning	Communication	Testware management
Test case design	Test process management	Methodology practice
Test tools	Defect management	
Test environment	Tester professionalism	

By improving certain test activities, avoiding others altogether or supporting them with tools and techniques, the Key areas focus on efficient test execution, lowering the 'idle time' ratio or preventing other test activities from interfering with the execution.

- *Degree of involvement*
  The sooner the test process is involved in the development process or project, the better the test activities can be prepared and planned. A good preparation helps to keep as much activities off the critical path.
- *Test strategy*
  Establishing a test strategy, based upon a product risk analysis, lets the principal stakeholder decide which test items have the highest priority. It is the means of making substantiated choices when time is strictly limited, including reducing or skipping some test activities.
- *Estimating and planning*
  A well-thought through and agreed plan enables not only the optimal allocation of resources at the right time, but also makes last minute changes possible, ensuring that only the test execution is on the project's critical path. Applying estimation techniques (*ultimo* the use of metrics) makes estimations, and consequently planning, more reliable.
- *Test tools*
  If properly managed and applied in the right way, test tools can speed up the test process. Test automation makes it possible for instance to carry out labor-intensive regression testing during out-of-office hours.
- *Test environment*
  A test environment is needed for executing test cases. Composing and organizing the test environment in time and having control over it, reduces *the chance of disruptions leading to idle time.*
- *Test case design*
  One of the most time consuming activities is the design of test cases. As stated with Degree of involvement this activity should be performed as soon as possible but at any case not of the critical of the process. Another aspect of Test case design is the use of design techniques: they help to limit the amount of test cases to a minimum, thus shortening the time for test execution.

6.3 Business drivers affect the use of the model

The 6 Key areas that are Neutral are:
- Stakeholder commitment
- Tester professionalism
- Communication
- Defect management
- Test process management
- Test organization.

These Key areas are neutral in terms of reducing Time to market and are listed here for the sake of completeness, but they are described in more detail in Chapter 4.

The 5 Key areas in the Low category are:
- *Metrics*
  Metrics are most important for substantiating proposals, plans or decisions and do not play an important role in test execution.
- *Methodology practice*
  This Key area is important for facilitating co-operation between parties. It does not bear much importance for lead-time reduction.
- *Reporting*
  While reporting is important for providing information about product quality and risk and for monitoring the plan, basic reporting practices will suffice. Improving reporting in itself does not contribute to reducing lead time for testing.
- *Testware management*
  Well-maintained testware contributes to faster and more controlled test preparation and test case specification. It does not support test execution.

There are pitfalls that prevent improvement
Often the causes of a time-consuming test process are sought within the test process itself. However, these causes may actually be symptoms of a completely different problem that lies outside the test process. Therefore it is important to look for the most effective measures in the overall software development lifecycle.
Some external pitfalls:
- *'Garbage in garbage out'*
  Testing does not improve the quality of the test object; it merely states the degree of quality. Having to test and retest over and over again indicates that there's probably more to gain within the requirements, design and/or engineering process or within for instance project management.
- *Limited insight*
  Often there is little understanding of how much time testing takes within a project. This is especially the case for organizations that have always tested on an ad hoc basis and are now facing challenges such as an expansion of IT, growing systems complexity or tighter regulations.

6 Business Driven Test Process Improvement

The necessity, value and complexity of testing are not always understood. Testing is regarded as expensive and time-consuming. Many managers are unaware of how many incidents occur in production, that may cause a lot of damage and need to be fixed. So, although not testing is a much worse option, a manager may see only the time testing takes rather than the benefits. Ironically, providing more rather than less time to testing could prevent many of these incidents.

- *Change management*
  Testing requires solid planning and preparation. Changes in specifications (RFCs) may cause changes to the plan and rework of some of the preparation stages. Particularly when the test object is already under test and test cases have been executed, changes may lead to redeliveries and retesting, but also to adjusting the test cases, which will take additional time. Reducing last minute changes, or at least doing a proper impact analysis on them, might reduce the test time even further.
- *Project management*
  To make sure that test execution starts at the moment when the test object is ready for testing, (only test execution should be on the project's critical path), testers should be able to start their preparation in advance. Project management therefore needs to allocate test resources at an early stage of the project. Project management also needs to ensure that certain preconditions are met on time. For testing, preconditions include timely availability of the test environment, planned availability of developers to fix defects found by testing, and timely delivery of input and steering information.
- *Configuration management*
  When testing you want to be confident that you are testing the right (version of the) object. If not, it is not only a waste of time, but it will also take additional time to test the 'correct' object.

6.3.4 BDTPI used to Improve cost efficiency of IT

The concrete goals for improvement
Reducing the costs of testing will be a constant driver for most organizations. Controlling costs can be fundamental to improving a business's competitive advantage in the marketplace, or a means of survival in times of economic downturn. As a consequence, costs have to be reduced, and that includes development and testing costs as well.

Besides being a business objective, there may be other reasons for concentrating on the cost aspect of the test process. When testing is considered to be a cost center rather than providing value, the pressure to reduce testing costs can be particularly huge, and in some cases, this position is certainly valid.

6.3 Business drivers affect the use of the model

The costs of testing can be divided into three categories:
- *Cost of the test activities*
  This category includes not only the amount of man hours, but also maintenance of the test method and building up and maintaining test expertise: methods, procedures, templates, checklists, etc.. Improving the test process can help reduce such costs.
- *Test tools*
  The cost of test tool licenses, as well as maintenance of customizations, tool scripts, training and supplier support costs can be very high. Reducing such costs can be done primarily with focused efforts, such as developing a framework for automated testing. While the cost-saving effects of these tools depends largely on the maturity of the test process, test process improvement per se does not really help in producing more cost-effective use of test tools.
- *Test environment and test data*
  The increasing complexity of IT infrastructure in production is reflected by the complexity of test environments as well as test data. As a result, the cost of maintaining test environments has become huge. As with test tools, focused effort can be spent on optimizing the management of test environments and test data, but this effort is usually carried out separately from test process improvement, since it addresses the test process less than infrastructure related activities.

Key areas categorized in terms of effectiveness of reducing test costs

Based on table 6.2, the Key areas are categorized as follows:

High	Neutral	Low
Degree of involvement	Communication	Stakeholder commitment
Test strategy	Test process management	Reporting
Test organization	Estimating & planning	Metrics
Defect management	Testware management	Test environment
Test tools	Methodology practice	
	Tester professionalism	
	Test case design	

The following 5 Key areas help to reduce the costs of the test process and therefore have an increased priority:
- *Test strategy*
  Establishing a test strategy, based on a product risk analysis, lets the principal stakeholder decide which test items have the highest priority, and also what the required test coverage is. Rather than testing every-

thing equally thoroughly, the test depth can be reduced for system parts and quality characteristics that have a relatively low product risk.
- *Test tools*
  The use of test tools can significantly reduce the costs of testing. Automated test execution is in itself much cheaper than manual test execution, but also other test tools allow for efficient test management, defect management and testware management (configuration management). Without specific tools, this is hard to accomplish, especially in larger development and test teams.
- *Defect management*
  Proper defect management contributes to solving defects as efficiently as possible, especially if developers also have sufficient access to the same tools as testers. More advanced defect management assists in measures to avoid defects, for example in root cause analysis.
- *Test organization*
  Many organizations rationalize their business activities by concentrating on projects that will generate profits immediately, while keeping the line organization (viewed as a cost center) at a minimum. However, projects are limited if they cannot take advantage of economies of scale. Significant cost saving can be realized by acquiring and maintaining scarce resources, like skilled test specialists, test environments and test tools, within a line organization and then providing them as a service to projects as required.
- *Degree of involvement*
  Many problems in the development process manifest themselves in the test process - typically the project costs at the testing phase appear to run out of control. By involving testing early in the development process and allowing testing to influence the development project, many of these problems can be avoided. Sufficient involvement early in the project also results in defects being found earlier, resulting in lower fixing costs and less uncertainty about rework in the project. Moreover: it prevents surprises at the end: 'This is not what I wanted' or 'I did not get what I wanted'.

The 7 Key areas that are Neutral are:
- Test process management
- Communication
- Tester professionalism
- Test case design
- Testware management
- Estimating and planning
- Methodology practice

These Key areas are neutral in terms of Cost reduction and are listed here for the sake of completeness, but they are described in more detail in Chapter 4.

The following 4 Key areas in the Low category contribute in a limited way to reducing costs and therefore have a lower priority:
- *Reporting*
  While reporting is important for monitoring costs and managing the test process in a cost-effective way, basic reporting will suffice. Improving reporting in itself does not contribute to saving testing costs.
- *Metrics*
  As with reporting, basic metrics are necessary to provide support for saving costs, but while more intense use of metrics does provide more detailed control to test process management, it does not contribute to cost reduction by itself.
- *Stakeholder commitment*
  Testing certainly benefits from strong stakeholder commitment in many ways, but saving costs for testing is not really one of them.
- *Test environment*
  The management of test environments and test data can cost a lot of money and often there is a strong desire to reduce these costs. In this case, effort should be spent on improving test environment management.

There are pitfalls that prevent improvement

When improving the test process with the aim of reducing the costs of testing, some potential pitfalls can be identified:
- *Test tools*
  Automated test execution is often considered to be the most important solution to saving costs, but this is too simple a response. Automating test execution requires that the test design has been very well thought-through: if chaos is automated, you end up with automated chaos!
  While the automated execution of test cases is in itself certainly cheaper than manual execution, there are also associated costs. Besides the costs of tool licenses, support and the training of users, costs are incurred in the creation and maintenance of tool scripts, which are significantly more expensive than 'just' executing a test case manually. Maintenance of tool scripts is required when using existing tool scripts with new versions of the test object. The latter is typically the case in regression testing - exactly the scenario in which frequent automated test execution can recoup the associated costs. Minimizing the costs of maintenance places additional requirements on the test process itself.
- *Cause of problems in testing outside the test process*
  The fact that test process costs are often higher than expected may be the result of causes outside testing. 'Testing costs too much' is often not the real problem, it is a symptom of an 'external' cause such as poor configuration management, change management, project management, etc.

- *Limited insight*
  Frequently we find that there is little understanding of exactly how much testing really costs. This is especially the case for organizations that have always tested on an *ad hoc* basis and are now facing challenges such as an expansion of IT, growing systems complexity or tighter regulations.
  Taking a broad overview of costs, it can be the case that in fact *more* testing is cheaper than *less* testing. This point of view is rarely taken because there is limited insight into those testing costs that are beyond a manager's influence. Also when defining a project, decision makers often do not calculate how much effort is really needed and how much it costs to solve incidents and keep applications running.
- *Release management*
  Often additional 'last minute' changes are made to a release without proper testing, because the project is running out of time and there is a fixed release date. Reducing these changes will prevent a lot of unwanted rework.

6.3.5 BDTPI used to Improve transparency and understanding of IT

The concrete goals for improvement
In some cases, testing is carried out satisfactorily enough: not many severe defects show up in production. But despite this, there is insufficient insight into how testing is actually done. More insight into the test process may be needed in order to fulfill external regulatory requirements such as the Sarbanes-Oxley laws (SOX), and safety requirements such as the different levels of SIL[1], or GxP[2] as enforced by the American Food and Drug Association (FDA).
Alternatively, more insight into testing may be required by the business itself, to get a better understanding of the value of testing. Last, but not least, the stakeholders in the development or test project may suffer from miscommunication and need to get a better grip on what happens in the test process.
Increased transparency in the test process means greater focus on communicating what is done in the process. Depending on how transparent the process has to be, the fact that all activities are being, or have been, performed can be proved in documented results. Also, all major decisions,

---

1 SIL: Safety Integrity Level, defined as a relative level of risk-reduction provided by a safety function, or to specify a target level of risk reduction.
2 GxP is a general term for Good Practice quality guidelines and regulations, where the x denotes the specific practice, e.g. GMP stands for Good Management Practice.

made by the test team or stakeholders, are documented, supported by specific requirements for how these results are reported.

Proving what has been done in testing does not automatically improve the effectiveness or efficiency of the process. One can expect even some more overhead, which reduces the efficiency of the process. Neither is there any relationship between transparency and overall maturity: a test process might be very unstructured but transparent, while another process might be very efficient, but there is no evidence that the activities have actually been performed.

More transparency results in better controllability of the test process. It is clear which activities are performed and how, which helps to make better decisions. Also, better insight into the test process usually indicates potential for improvement: the test team or stakeholders may choose to follow up on quick wins or set other improvement goals.

Key areas categorized in terms of effectiveness in increasing the transparency of testing

Based on table 6.2, the Key areas are categorized as follows:

High	Neutral	Low
Test strategy	Communication	Stakeholder commitment
Reporting	Testware management	Degree of involvement
Test process management	Methodology practice	Test organization
Estimating & planning	Test case design	Tester professionalism
Metrics	Test tools	Test environment
Defect management		

The following 6 Key areas help to increase the transparency of the test process and therefore have increased priority:

- *Test strategy*
  The Test strategy is based on (product) risks. One of the major elements of product risks is the damage that may be caused by a defect. Damage may, in almost any situation, be defined in terms of damage to the business. So the test strategy is a valuable instrument to provide information on (the mitigation of) these risks. Because the analysis is performed with several stakeholders it contributes highly to transparency of the process.
- *Reporting*
  Insight provided by test process management and defect management has to be reported to the stakeholders in a way that has been agreed up front. It is also likely that reports will be saved for later reference, for audits for example or as input for future improvement activities.
- *Test process management*
  The test activities should be executed according to the test plan. The

plan offers clear insight in all agreements made between stakeholders and testers, the approach, the strategy, planning, etc.
- *Estimating and planning*
  A plan for testing, with a reliable estimation of the different activities, provides a baseline for expectations between the test team and stakeholders, as well as in the test team itself. Stakeholders can influence and approve the test plan.
- *Metrics*
  Metrics are applied to measure observations objectively. Common examples are budget, time and number of defects. These metrics can be combined to make more complex observations measurable and more objective, such as progress, test coverage, the quality of the test object and efficiency of the test process.
- *Defect management*
  Defect management keeps track of all the defects found during testing. All the important properties of each defect are registered and can be used for reporting. By aggregating all this information, defect management can provide accurate insight into the quality of the test object.

The 5 Neutral Key areas are:
- Test case design
- Test tools
- Methodology practice
- Communication
- Testware management.

These Key areas are neutral in terms of Test effectiveness and are listed here for the sake of completeness, but they are described in more detail in Chapter 4.

The 5 Key areas in the Low category are:
- *Degree of involvement*
  Improving the involvement of testing in the development process is usually the result of increased awareness of how testing can contribute to a better product quality. Typically, these measures are taken once increased transparency has been achieved. Degree of involvement in itself does not help making the test process more transparent.
- *Stakeholder commitment*
  While a certain degree of stakeholder commitment is needed (often initiated by external regulations) to agree to the overhead costs incurred in gaining greater transparency, stakeholder commitment usually is increased once the increased transparency has been reached.
- *Test environment*
  Tools in test environments can provide information about the environments themselves, and be used in reporting. Improving the test envi-

ronments beyond the use of these tools does not help transparency of the test process.
- *Tester professionalism*
Testers and test managers do not need to be highly skilled to generate a report on what they are doing. However, they may need additional training in working in a more structured way.
- *Test organization*
A test support organization can help to align reporting and metrics across projects, for example by establishing guidelines and templates, and so increase transparency in an efficient way. But the test organization itself does not contribute to greater transparency.

There are pitfalls that prevent improvement
When improving the test process with the aim of increasing the transparency of testing, some pitfalls are possible:
- *Metrics*
In asking for metrics, it is important to understand which metrics are meaningful and whether they can be measured in a pure way. Collecting too many metrics, or metrics that cannot easily be understood by the stakeholders, is an unnecessary burden on the test process. If it is not clear to the stakeholders which metrics to ask for, start with a standard set based on general best practice and experience, and then fine tune it based on the customer's requirements. Everyone involved in collecting, providing and using metrics has to be aware of this uncertainty and needs to be co-operative.

A common problem with metrics is that management likes to have them, but there is resistance to providing them! Collecting metrics appears to be an extra burden and a distraction. In addition, it gives rise to an element of mistrust as testers may believe that the metrics could be used by management to judge their performance. So be careful not to ask for metrics that can be used to measure an individual's performance and to explain carefully the reason and aim of reporting metrics.
- *Test tools*
Many test tools provide metrics. Test management tools provide reports about the number of test cases with a certain status (design, executed, passed or failed). Similarly, defect management tools provide metrics on the number of test cases with a specific status, possibly linked to test cases and requirements. These reporting facilities can be a great help so long as the information required is generated by the tool, and is not from an external source.

If information from different tools needs to be combined, collecting and then combining is much more complex. If time per activity is reported in a time reporting system and not per test case in a test management tool, it can be hard to merge this information if needed. To combine data, it should be exported from the tools into a spreadsheet with custom reporting. Alternatively, the same information should be registered in multiple tools.

6.4 Cost and Benefit of Test Process Improvement

6.4.1 Introduction

How much does it cost and how do we benefit? Two aspects of test process improvement that are obvious questions to ask, but at the same time are difficult to answer - at least in specific and financial terms. One reason for this is that it is hard to evaluate the cost of testing and to establish the precise benefits. Costs are often visualized in terms of the cost of human resources: a number of people participating in a project for a number of hours at a certain rate. But what about the cost of not testing at all? Or the cost of repair and retesting after detecting defects? And how much do we know about the benefits of testing? Can we tell to what extent the product risks have been mitigated, and how much testing has added to the quality of the product?

These questions are hard to answer, so it is equally difficult to resolve the questions about the costs and benefits of test process improvement. The following section discusses issues that influence a cost/benefit analysis and provides some suggestions for gathering the appropriate information and data.

6.4.2 Value for money

Reality or fiction

Triggers for test process improvement are usually "testing is too expensive" or "testing takes too long". However, certain issues can 'muddy' this assessment:

- It is rarely a black or white situation; there is usually more than one valid reason for a specific situation.
- The root cause may be different from that which appears to be the trigger.
- External influences may have been the trigger (for instance: testers are doing 'nothing' because the test object was not delivered on time).

For each trigger, it is worthwhile paying some attention to aspects that lie partly outside the test process. Some examples are given in the table 6.3.

6.4 Cost and Benefit of Test Process Improvement

Trigger	Possible causes
Testing takes too long	If there were many defects, a lot of time was spent on rework on design, repair and retests.
	The test object was delivered late, causing idle time for the testers.
	The test environment was not ready on time.
	Many requests for change (RFC) during the test process caused continuous change of functionality and therefore test cases and scripts needed to be changed. Sometimes a whole strategy needs to be adapted.
Testing is too expensive	The test manager reported the actual costs of the testing efforts, which had not been done before.
	Higher product risks required better skills and more resources.
	More resources were needed because the test object had been delivered late, while the deadline for production launch remained fixed.
The quality of testing is not good enough	Production errors in the first weeks after launch were caused by inadequate requirements or infrastructure.
	Management decided to launch the product despite the fact that testing had not been finished.
	False expectations between developers and testers caused gaps in test coverage.

Table 6.3: List of triggers for test process improvement and their possible causes.

6.4.3 Cost

Like any other improvement project, a BDTPI process will cost time and money. Characteristic features of test process improvement costs are:
- Assessment aspects: e.g. interviews, analyses, meetings.
- Development time for (new) methods, procedures and templates. A number of predefined templates and checklists can be found at www.tmap.net. It is wise to customize these documents to the specific situation.
- Introduction of test tools. This is often regarded as the quickest way to cost reduction. However, selecting and implementing the right tool takes time including the roll out, and incurs costs through the multiple licenses and other incidentals such as tool manuals that can use up much of the available budget. The cost and time for proper maintenance of the tool should not be underestimated.
- Training, pilot projects and try-outs.
- Monitoring and reporting on the improvements. During the process, indicators have to be developed and maintained to demonstrate the significance of the improvements.

What if we do nothing?
Doing nothing is always an option! One of the cost items might be measured by calculating the cost of doing nothing, leaving the current situation 'as is' for the (near) future. For instance, this could be the cost of having an estimated number of defects in production. Typical characteristics of these costs are:
- Detection and processing; help desk, customer support, etc.
- Repair; redesign, rebuild and retest
- Develop workarounds
- Loss of image or reputation
- Dissatisfied users and/or customers.

6.4.4 Benefits

It is not easy to evaluate definitively the cost aspects of test process improvement. It is even harder to establish the actual benefits. Assessing these benefits was one of the reasons for three world wide surveys on the use of the TPI model.

The surveys showed interesting aspects about BDTPI benefits:
- Better software quality
  61% of respondents stated improved software quality, as defined by, for example, fewer failures in production.
- More control on the test process
  Implementation of TPI leads to better or much better testing control, according to 83% of the respondents. In many situations, this leads to shorter test projects.
- Return on Investment is very good
  77% of respondents indicated that the necessary investment for implementing test process improvement really paid off.

Working on countless TPI projects around the world, we have witnessed a number of other benefits that have been achieved in practice. The following advantages have been taken from interviews with a variety of test managers:

- *Personnel*
  - The improvement of skills and knowledge of testers increased their productivity and performance.
  - Focused resource planning reduced idle time and overheads.
  - There was an increase and a more efficient collaboration in complex projects between testers and other staff.
- *Efficiency*
  - There was a bigger focus on measuring and reporting on product quality and risks.

- Defects were found (and repaired!) earlier in the lifecycle thus leading to lower costs. Improvements in the system test process led to a 50% reduction of technical defects during acceptance testing.
- By re-using well-documented and adapted test cases, there was a 50% reduction in the preparation time for test cases.

- *Reliability*
  - Prediction of the quality of the information systems was more accurate.
  - An adequate analysis of (product) impact and risks was carried out at an early stage in the process, thus supporting the project lead to steer his project.
  - Intake and review of the test basis provided adequate feedback on specifications.
  - Application of tools and techniques for budgeting and planning provided reliable figures.

> **In more detail - Reorganizing people into more efficient groups**
> During a TPI assessment, measures were already taken to train testers who each worked for one specific program in a maintenance environment. The testers were reorganized into a single pool of testers, and they learned to test other systems and different techniques of designing test cases. Idle time of the testers was cut dramatically and maintenance test projects took half the time compared to before.

The challenge of metrics and statistics

As we have indicated, common goals of test process improvement often are:

- testing costs should be cut.
- testing needs to be done quicker.

We also noted that improvement measures cost money and take time to deliver value for money and a return on investment. Moreover, how can we prove that the measures actually work and that testing time really has been shortened? We have to search for indicators and substantiated figures that will demonstrate and prove how the process has grown in maturity.

The fact that figures relating to testing activities are often missing cannot be an excuse for not proving the quality and results of the improvement actions. It is necessary to collect, analyze and report figures on test results, test cases, defects, resources and productivity. Relevant indicators, such as the ratio between development time and testing time, can help to demonstrate the value of an improvement project and create commitment for further steps.

Working with indicators

To be able to indicate the effects of more test maturity through BDTPI, it is necessary to retrieve metrics from both the current and future situations. Familiar and easy to use indicators are listed per business driver below.

- *Cost driven*
  - Development-test ratio: the time or money spent on both development and testing.
  - The cost of test as a percentage of the total project cost.
  - Defect-based cost: the ratio between test hours/cost and the total number of detected defects.
- *Time driven*
  - Waiting or idle time of testers as a percentage of the total test time.
  - The number of test hours per test level.
  - The number of test hours per phase in a test level.
  - The actual amount of time in relation to the planned and estimated time.
- *Quality driven*
  - Test level quality: the number of detected defects in one test level as a percentage of all detected defects.
  - Defect detection ratio (Test effectiveness): Defects found per single test level divided by the sum of defects found in all subsequent test levels plus defects found in production.
  - Non specific findings: defects or findings that should have been detected in an earlier stage or preceding phase. The indicator is linked to one specific test level or production.

Other indicators that will demonstrate the results of a test process improvement project can be obtained by asking people's opinion, both at the start of the improvement process and at regular intervals, say every six months. Participants are asked to give their opinion on a scale from 1 (Yes) to 5 (No). Opinions should be obtained from representatives of different stakeholder groups, including testers and project managers.

Questions for Testers					
	Yes				No
All testing activities are under control	1	2	3	4	5
The results of the test actions are predictable	1	2	3	4	5
The test tasks are easy to understand and transferrable	1	2	3	4	5
Testing contributes to the quality of the product	1	2	3	4	5
Testing is fun	1	2	3	4	5

6.4 Cost and Benefit of Test Process Improvement

Questions for Project managers					
	Yes				No
The progress of the test process is clear	1	2	3	4	5
The quality of the test object is clear	1	2	3	4	5
There is good co-operation and understanding between testing and development	1	2	3	4	5
The project and the business benefit from the testing efforts	1	2	3	4	5
Testing is fun	1	2	3	4	5

Table 6.4: Questionnaire for subjective indicators.

Produce facts and figures

The following steps can be taken to collect and analyze figures and numbers for the indicators. The steps are explained by using the example of the indicator "non-specific findings".

1. *Define the indicator*
   Findings (defects, bugs, flaws) that should have been detected in a preceding stage of the test process. Example: a defect that was found in the acceptance test but should have been found in the system test.
2. *Connect the indicator to one or more goals*
   Target: As per (dd-mm-yyyy) the number of non-specific findings of the acceptance test should be XX% less than its current figure.
3. *Define data*
   The data for this indicator are the defects listed in the category non-specific.
4. *Define sources of data*
   The data can be found in the defect administration called Defect Administration Project X that can be found on the server.
5. *Describe analysis procedure*
   - In the defect administration tool (excel sheet), an additional category should be added: non-specific.
   - The category should be filled in by the tester.
   - The tester collects the data and documents in the System Test Analysis Form.
   - The tester reports his analyses to his superior.
   - The superior collects all the Analysis Forms and summarizes them in the monthly Management Report.
6. *Reporting*
   The indicator will be reported in the System Test Analysis Form, the monthly Management Report and the Project Report.
7. *Define initial situation*
   The analyzed data of today shows the following figures:
   - Total number of defects in the System test: XXX.

- Number of non specific issues: XXX.
- The current percentage of non-specific findings of the System Test is: XX%.

> **In more detail - Tips for indicators**
> - Be aware that measuring takes time, effort and incurs costs. The implementation of metrics and indicators is often regarded as a process of its own.
> - Looking at individual indicators can lead to the wrong conclusions. Use at least three indicators.
> - Measurements in general should be taken over a longer period. In order to be able to make a comparison, data is required of the 'before' as well as the 'after' situation. Data from the 'before' situation is usually not available, so start measuring and collecting data as soon as possible.

7 The BDTPI Model can be used in any situation

Although TPI was primarily developed from the viewpoint of high level tests like system and acceptance tests, its application is by no means restricted to these test levels. This chapter describes how Business Driven TPI can be used in a number of IT environments and situations, for example agile and in conjunction with other software process improvement models[1].

The following topics are covered in relation to test process improvement:
1. Iterative development method
2. Agile development methods
3. Organizations with multiple test processes
4. Organizations starting from scratch
5. Software maintenance
6. Software Process Improvement
7. Outsourcing
8. Managed test services
9. Development testing
10. Evaluation
11. Integration.

7.1 BDTPI can be used in iterative development methods

If an iterative software development approach is chosen, the product is delivered in several iterations, where the result of each iteration is an increasing part of the product. Only in the last iteration, the final product is delivered.

This approach has specific advantages over waterfall development. First, the process delivers parts of the final system much earlier, allowing the client to fine tune the requirements. Also, the process can start earlier, even if the requirements have not been fully clarified at the beginning of the project, because the time needed for each iteration is shorter and the scope more limited, than with waterfall development.

---

1   Descriptions of further BDTPI applications will be published on the TPI site www.tpinext.com when they become available.

7 The BDTPI Model can be used in any situation

The entire project is planned at a higher level, where the decision is made about how many iterations will be used to deliver the final product, and what the goal of each iteration will be. The choice of which part(s) of the system will be developed first is often based on a mix of product, technical and project risks.

7.1.1 Iterative development and testing

It is generally well recognized that testing is and should not be an afterthought, but should be well integrated into the development cycle. Unit testing, unit integration testing and system testing is carried out at each iteration. Acceptance testing is also carried out at each iteration where the software will be deployed. In the case of 'big bang' deployment (one single full-scale integration of the final delivered product), acceptance testing is executed at the last iteration. With gradual deployment, in which the delivery of each iteration is deployed one after the other, acceptance testing is part of every iteration.

An iteration plan is developed as a lower-level project plan for each iteration. Testing is set up in a similar way, in which a high-level test plan is derived from the overall project plan, and iteration test plans are created based on the high-level test plan and iteration plans. Since the size of each test level within an iteration is limited, usually all test levels in an iteration are covered by its iteration test plan.

Reporting on the quality of the test object is usually done per iteration. Based on the quality found during testing, the scope of future iterations in the project can be adjusted.

Another feature of iterative development is that there is limited focus on documentation, especially test documentation before test execution. Test cases are not usually created in advance (scripted testing), but exploratory testing is common, in which skilled testers design test cases *during* a test execution session. Test design techniques can be used, but it is hard to prove the test coverage over different system parts.

Since each iteration builds on the product of earlier iterations, regression testing is essential in each following iteration. It is not just the functionality that has been added that should be tested, but also the existing functionality that needs to remain in place, without quality degradation (regression). Formal, reusable test cases can be valuable for accelerating regression testing; however, the focus is more on the automation of the execution of test cases.

Automated test execution certainly can be beneficial, but this is only true if the quality of the test cases to be automated is good enough. If this is not the case, the effort of automated test execution will be wasted. As a consequence, the lack of good test cases for regression testing, as well as no automated test execution, results in very limited regression tests.

7.1.2 Iterative development and test process improvement

While testing in iterative development is more focused on 'getting the job done', rather than 'proving that the job has been done' and hence documentation is limited, it may be difficult to find evidence that certain aspects of the test process fulfill the Checkpoints in the model.

At the same time, it may seem that a fully-structured test process involves too much documentation and goes against the principles of iterative development. As always a balance has to be struck. If the balance inclines too much towards too little documentation, it is even more important to focus on the benefits for the business that structured testing has within the development project.

> **In more detail - Testing in Rational Unified Process**
> Rational Unified Process (RUP) [21] is probably the most well-known iterative development method. Within RUP, a number of software processes (called disciplines) are performed in parallel from beginning to end. Testing is one of these disciplines. The development process is separated into phases; The Inception phase (1 iteration) focuses on fully understanding which business needs have to be fulfilled; the Elaboration phase (2 iterations) concentrates on defining the technical solution to fulfill these needs; the Construction phase (n iterations) on developing the solution; and the Deployment phase (2 iterations) on deploying and handing over the solution that has been built.
> RUP defines the Unit Test (UT) level as part of the Development discipline, the Integration Test (IT) level as part of the Integration discipline, System Test (ST) as part of the Test discipline and Acceptance Test (AT) as part of the Deployment discipline. Since the Test discipline focuses only on system testing, the lifecycle for testing is also limited to the system test. The same lifecycle is applied in each iteration, and also in the Inception, Elaboration and Deployment phases.
> A master plan is defined for all system tests across all iterations and an iteration test plan is created for the system test in each iteration. No explicit test case design is developed before test execution and there is a relatively heavy focus on the automation of test cases.

Stakeholder commitment

Testing is all about risk management. So the most risky or uncertain parts of the system should be delivered and tested as soon as possible in order to create ample opportunities to react on defects found. In practice the delivery sequence of system parts is usually determined by development without much influence from testers and no special attention for deploying high risk software first. It is a tester's job to try and influence project management and other decision makers to adjust delivery sequence in such a way that high risk parts are deployed as soon as possible.

Test strategy

In iterative development the test strategy focuses more on what to test per iteration than per test level. The test and development cycles are in general too short to execute all test levels separately, so some are combined or integrated. When developing in cycles counted in weeks, it is not possible to conduct a complete end-to-end test for every cycle. The test strategy in this case describes after which cycle an end-to end test will be conducted. For instance, when a project is divided in six four-week iteration, the test strategy may state that after iterations two, four and six an end-to-end test is executed, next to a developer test and system test per iteration.

The test strategy must also explicitly describe how regression testing per iteration will take place. If not, chances are that newly developed software takes up all test effort per iteration and the quality of the software as a whole slowly decreases with every iteration.

Communication
Cooperation in iterative development is informal by nature. Short lines between all parties involved are a prerequisite for success. This bears the danger of not documenting anything, making it impossible to track when decision were made, let alone why. Make sure that taking decisions and gathering or spreading information does not become chaotic, without hampering the test process.

Testware management
Every iteration builds on the deliverables of the preceeding iterations. The chances of regression are eminent and every iteration must make sure existing software still works as before (regression testing). The time available for regression testing in a iteration is very limited, whereas the amount of software to be tested grows with every iteration. This can only be achieved by creating and maintaining a relatively small regression test set that is in every iteration expanded with iteration specific test cases.

Test case design
Creating test cases can take up a considerable amount of time, and time is scarce in iterative development. Exploratory testing as a test technique arose as an answer to the challenges posed by this lack of time, providing a way for effective testing with a minimal of preparation. Well executed exploratory testing, meaning a charter has been put together before test execution and a good log of what has been tested and how, satisfies Checkpoint 2 of the controlled level.

An often seen practice in iterative development is automated regression testing. If this is the case, test cases need to be designed conscientious.

7.2 BDTPI can be used in agile development methods

The Agile Manifesto

Agile methodologies have emphasized many excellent practices from a testing perspective such as test-driven development and exploratory testing. Nevertheless, practice also shows that the overall approach and process of testing is often less than satisfactory in agile projects.

While agile has many different 'flavors', the foundations of any agile methodology in use today can be traced back to the Agile Manifesto[1] that states:

We are uncovering better ways of developing software by doing it and helping others do it. Through this work we have come to value:		
Individuals and interactions	**over**	processes and tools
Working software	**over**	comprehensive documentation
Customer collaboration	**over**	contract negotiation
Responding to change	**over**	following a plan
While there is value in the items on the right, we value the items on the left more!		

For the purpose of this book, we have chosen not to discuss a specific method like RUP [21], SCRUM [22] or DSDM [9], because, with the Business Driven TPI model, it does not matter which method is used. Whether in a traditional or agile environment, the Key areas of the BDTPI model will always be applicable and prove their usefulness. For example, the Key areas indicate which activities have to be carried out, but do not prescribe how this has to be done. You can write a test plan of a hundred pages if that works for your organization, or make a list on a whiteboard if that works better. How people work is organization-specific and may even be project-specific.

The Manifesto, together with the 12 principles that lie behind it, is the starting point for this section, covering the general concepts of agile methodologies. (See also the Section 'Agile principles linked to Key areas'.)

7.2.1 Agile development and testing

It is important to understand that agile methodologies originated from the perspective of software developers. It was formulated in February

---

1 A statement of the principles that underpin agile software development, drafted by representatives of various new methodologies in February 2001. For more information: www.agilemanifesto.org.

7 The BDTPI Model can be used in any situation

2001, with the publication of the 'Manifesto for Agile Software Development'. However neutral the Manifesto was towards the test discipline, the methods that embraced the agile philosophy never focused on how to integrate the testing discipline thoroughly in agile environments, nor did they consider what the consequences for test professionals would be. It is therefore not surprising that setting up a test process in an agile environment has not always been very successful.

The underlying thought of the agile philosophy is to deliver business value as early as possible and in the smallest workable piece of functionality. The feature or product needs to be tested in order to prove that the developed software works as required and to prove its business value. Therefore testing is certainly a vital element of agile projects.

In more traditional environments, the scope of the project is usually fixed, while time and quality may vary. But in an agile development, time and quality are fixed and the scope can vary. More traditional development methodologies bring in testing at a later stage in the lifecycle, whereas agile includes testing right from the beginning and then throughout the whole process. This means that agile project teams have to work more closely together and have to be staffed with people from different disciplines. In addition, agile projects need to be able to respond to changes more easily, which raises the need for test automation, efficient and effective documentation, and increased face-to-face communication. These distinctions require a different approach and different skills from testers.

The Agile mindset

Agile advocates often talk about the 'special mindset' that is deemed to be necessary when working in an agile environment. This mindset is based and focused on self-organizing teams, underpinned by mutual trust, team responsibility, professionalism and diversity. To be able to put this mindset into practice is probably the hardest part of becoming agile and also the most essential part of being agile.

> **In more detail - Agile in name only?**
> When using Business Driven TPI in an agile environment, the first question should be whether or not the environment really is agile - in other words does it meet the criteria of the Agile Manifesto. If not, consider using BDTPI in the same way as you would apply it to a generic test process, with perhaps increased attention being paid to the Key area Methodology practice.

When agile is implemented effectively, working in an agile way actually means: facilitating a multi-disciplinary team so that all team members are able to achieve not just their individual aims but also those of the team as a whole.

7.2 BDTPI can be used in agile development methods

The following Agile principle covers the responsibility of the individual team members as well as that of the team as a whole:

> Build projects around motivated individuals. Give them the environment and support they need, and trust them to get the job done.

The principle covers the trust that managers should have in the team to organize itself in the most efficient way. The 'whole-team approach' and the 'agile testing mindset' as described by Crispin and Gregory [7] arise from this team responsibility.
In agile environments, a lot of the traditional monitoring and control is carried out by the team itself. There is hardly any management involvement and sometimes none at all. There is a shift from 'command and control' to 'facilitate and encourage'. This is the mindset that gives direction and focus for the improvement of the test activities within an agile environment.

7.2.2 Agile development and test process improvement

In this section, we describe how, based on the mindset outlined above, to start optimizing the test process in agile environments using the Business Driven TPI model. To help you get started, we have selected a set of six priority Key areas, which are discussed below. We are not aiming to cover in depth here the subject of using Business Driven TPI in agile environments, but to show that BDTPI can be of use in such a context and to include some practical tips on where and how to start improving the test process.

Priority Key areas
When improving the test process in an agile environment, the Key areas that are most important follow from the agile mindset. 'Facilitate and encourage' sets the tone for the Key area selection. In a truly agile environment, each of these Key areas should already be at a level of considerable maturity.

Note: the list below is not exhaustive. It simply guides you on the right track. Every organization and project will have different needs and circumstances that need to be examined carefully first

The selected six priority Key areas are:
1. Stakeholder commitment
2. Degree of involvement
3. Test strategy
4. Testware management
5. Tester professionalism
6. Test environment

Stakeholder commitment
In agile environments, the stakeholders are continually and closely involved and the commitment of stakeholders is necessary to building and maintaining an efficient and motivated agile team.

Commitment is also essential for good client relationships, working in both directions - from the stakeholders to the team, and from the team to the stakeholders. One way of creating commitment is to involve the client in the process: the client receives feedback and is kept well informed, which adds to his commitment. Another way benefits the team in a more direct way: involved clients will be more available for providing additional detailed information (for example the product risk issue of damage), to discuss issues, decide on changes, etc. Short communication lines contribute greatly to this efficiency.

Improvement suggestions

Always keep stakeholders well-informed. However, first determine what information they are interested in and how often they wish to be informed. That way they will not be overloaded by superfluous information.

Whenever stakeholders give feedback, show them that you appreciate their involvement and later let them know what actions have been taken using the information provided and why.

Show stakeholders how early testing can prevent defects, and so therefore costs and delay. Make them aware of the added value of testing.

Gather metrics to show the costs and benefits of improvement to demonstrate that testing efforts have distinct benefits and a positive return on investment.

Degree of involvement
A high degree of involvement at an early stage is essential for testing in agile environments. All disciplines, including testing, must be involved as soon as possible in the process. This is an essential part of agility, as indicated by the Manifesto's value of 'Responding to change' . In agile environments, changing the requirements can be done more easily than in a non-agile environment. If the change is discussed and agreed upon within the team, including the client, then no one can really be opposed to the change. Testing in particular is of importance in the early stage of changing requirements because of the value it can add to impact analysis and risk analysis. The sooner testing can respond to changes and take actions, the better.

Improvement suggestions

At the start of an agile project, allocate specific responsibilities linked to testing to one or more specific people.

Create awareness among all team members and stakeholders of the added value of the test roles.

Collect metrics or other experience-based data, for instance on the carry-over effect of an early defect, to substantiate remarks and suggestions made.

Let testers be involved in unit testing. Helping the programmers and receiving help in return will ensure a more efficient approach (and better quality) for the entire project.

Test strategy

The test strategy is the foundation for every test action, activity, process or project. It summarizes the justification of what will be tested and how it will be done. Proper product risk analysis drives this justification: 'No risk, no test'. The test strategy describes the test goals, how they will be approached and how (product) risks are covered. Risks have a significant influence on establishing priorities, so areas that carry the greatest risks need to be prioritized the highest. Furthermore, risks will trigger the inherent flexibility of agile environments in deciding what and what not to do in terms of time, costs and quality. The test strategy thus provides guidance and direction for the whole agile team.

Improvement suggestions

Create awareness by indicating the possible risks related to the more vulnerable parts of the system and the time that could be gained by not testing those parts that represent little or no risk at all.

Involve the various stakeholders in the test strategy and persuade them to perform a Product Risk Analysis with the key people who have knowledge of the possible impact of a defect, (such as business or sales management), and of the chance of failure (such as engineers and architects).

Discuss the defects found with the agile team and stakeholders, and then set up a method to categorize the defects according to the perceived risks. Based on these categories, consider a full retest, a 'thin' retest (per defect/function/subsystem) or even no retest.

Set up and maintain a regression test that is used to test new releases of the system for regression. Such a test is often composed of existing test cases and should be suitable for automation.

Make sure the test strategy reflects the way of working according to the method used, for instance, how to approach iteration planning. This also means integrating the agile mindset into the test strategy. Ask the team what strategic steps will facilitate the project.

Testware management

In agile environments, responding to change is considered to be more valuable than following a plan. However, this means more than just responding to changing requirements. What if team members or roles change? In such situations, the transferability of for example test scripts becomes an issue. Furthermore, responding to change can be quite difficult if little or no attention has been given to maintainability, transferability and reusability. This is where testware management comes in.

An agile team has to work efficiently in order to be able to deliver working software at every iteration. Testware management improves maintainability, transferability and reusability and therefore it is an important facilitating area for an agile team.

Improvement suggestions

Implement a version control tool and make sure all team members use it.

Ensure maintainability, transferability and reusability of the testware are part of the test strategy.

Include testware management activities in the (iteration) planning.

Tester professionalism

In agile environments the team is responsible for the work to be done and for solving the problems that arise. The members of this team have to trust each other and in turn they have to be trusted by their management. Therefore, it is absolutely necessary to have skilled people on the team. However, skilled should not be confused with 'brilliant'! Testers certainly do not need to have an above average intelligence to be able to work in an agile team; anyone with an open mind can learn to work in this context. But they do need to have knowledge of the agile method used, and they need the skills and competencies that will enable them to carry their responsibilities so that they can fulfill their roles effectively. To be successful, the skills and knowledge available within the team must not be an issue. They have to be developed, preferably before the project starts or training should be scheduled at an early stage in the project. These skills should be focused on: working together, communicating both within the team and with the 'outside' world, team building, and decision-making.

One of the major differences between working together in teams that embrace an agile methodology versus teams using another methodology is that in agile teams there is a collective team responsibility. This means much is required of agile team members, because they must be able to assist other team members. So, agile testers should have an open mind towards taking on other tasks outside the scope of traditional test methods.

Motivation of the team is at the heart of agile methodologies. Teams are self-regulating and team members need to be committed to their work, particularly to finishing work within a time-boxed period.

Test roles in agile environments, although regarded as useful and essential, tend to get little attention: it is often unclear what the specific test roles are and what testers do or do not do. Well-defined tasks and responsibilities, together with on-the-job or prior training can help to make this clear to everyone involved.

Improvement suggestions

Make sure that all team members are trained in the agile method used.

Discuss the role of testing within the team. Define the specific skills needed for certain tasks, for example developing a test strategy and designing test cases, and other techniques and methods.

If professional testers who are familiar with testing methods join an agile team, they have to be able to follow the method. If they cannot, find out what the reasons are and take measures (training, practice, team building) to bring them up to the required level.

Effective collaboration between team members can often be obstructed by all kinds of cultural differences. Make sure it is clear which cultural values are embraced in the organization or project (such as how to communicate, how to behave).

Test environment

In order to deliver working software, a robust, stable and reliable test environment is essential because iterations or increments must prove their value in a short period of time. Problems that arise in the environment may block the progress of all other activities and the impact on the iteration can therefore be huge. If, for example, solving an environmental issue takes a day, the impact on a two-week iteration would be much greater than on a two-month project that has no intermediate deliverables.

The Key area Test environment also plays a major role in end to end tests, which for practical reasons is often carried out at the end of the project. However, preparing the test environment for this test can be done much earlier and will reduce the chance of failure in the integration test.

A stable test environment is one of the most important facilitating areas for an agile team, enabling it to deliver reliable working software at the end of each iteration.

Improvement suggestions

Make contact with the maintenance departments of the operational environments. These departments usually have a substantial amount of

7 The BDTPI Model can be used in any situation

knowledge, experience and ready-to-use documentation. Re-use it! Also, make sure there is commitment from them for helping out if issues arise.

Agree on (a limited) high priority defect status. Supplying parties tend to under-estimate the importance of test environments. To some extent they are right, since damage due to malfunctioning test environment is, in most cases, relatively small, compared to the damage due to malfunctioning operational environments. So try to identify situations in which a test environment malfunction will cause clearly identifiable and traceable damage (for instance delays in the iteration) and agree on a high priority status for those defects.

Try to be as self-supporting as possible. If the team has administrator rights for the test environment and the knowledge and skills to use them well, many environmental problems can be solved quickly and efficiently.

Agile principles linked to Key areas

Supporting the Agile Manifesto is a set of principles. The table below shows the mapping of the most relevant Key areas of BDTPI to the Agile principles and, as the remarks indicate, how BDTPI is supportive and helpful in an agile environment .

Agile principle	Key area	Remark
Our highest priority is to satisfy the customer through early and continuous delivery of valuable software.	Stakeholder commitment Degree of involvement Communication Test strategy	This is also the principal driver for Business Driven TPI. The client and other stakeholders play an indispensable role and their 'stakes' are reflected in several Key areas and Checkpoints. Furthermore, the Business Driven TPI model urges for early and continuous involvement of both testing (in the delivery process) and client (in the test process).
Welcome changing requirements, even late in development. Agile processes harness change for the customer's competitive advantage.	Test strategy Testware management Degree of involvement	A well defined test strategy and testware management will ensure that changing requirements are manageable and have as low an impact on testing as possible.

7.2 BDTPI can be used in agile development methods

Agile principle	Key area	Remark
Deliver working software frequently, from a couple of weeks to a couple of months, with a preference for the shorter timescale.	Test process management Test strategy Test environment Test tools	Frequent delivery means frequent testing. The impact on the test process and test object is assessed and managed. A stable test environment and appropriate tools can enable testers to work more efficiently.
Business people and developers must work together daily throughout the project.	Tester professionalism Degree of involvement	An effective team combines business knowledge, professional skills and competences, which are involved as early as possible in the project.
Build projects around motivated individuals. Give them the environment and support they need, and trust them to get the job done.	Tester professionalism Stakeholder commitment Organization	Motivation is one of the key issues for the professional tester. Stakeholder commitment emphasizes the need for support and sponsorship from (line) management.
The most efficient and effective method of conveying information to, and within, a development team is face-to-face conversation.	Communication Tester professionalism	The Checkpoints in these Key areas focus on clear communication, to ensure common understanding and alignment of expectations between all parties involved. A professional attitude is a prerequisite for this.
Working software is the primary measure of progress.	Defect management Metrics	Best way to demonstrate the quality of software is to show the (lack of) defects. A good defect administration enables reporting on progress.
Agile processes promote sustainable development. The sponsors, developers, and users should be able to maintain a constant pace indefinitely.	Tester professionalism Estimating and planning Test process management	This aspect requires both professional and social skills and competences. Estimating and planning and test process management can support a steady pace.
Continuous attention to technical excellence and good design enhances agility.	Tester professionalism Degree of involvement Test case design	These Key areas address both technical and design issues, e.g. by an early start of review activities.

7 The BDTPI Model can be used in any situation

Agile principle	Key area	Remark
Simplicity - the art of maximizing the amount of work not done - is essential.	Test strategy	This Key area aims at performing tests with the highest possible effect at the lowest cost and effort. The primary principle is: No risk, no test!
The best architectures, requirements and designs emerge from self-organizing teams.	Tester professionalism Organization	Basic elements for self-organizing teams are clarity about tasks and responsibilities, and a professional attitude. These elements are addressed in these Key areas.
At regular intervals, the team reflects on how to become more effective, then tunes and adjusts its behavior accordingly.	Tester professionalism Test process management Communication Metrics	The Business Driven TPI model encourages continuous improvement and provides all kinds of improvement suggestions, not only for the method but also for personal or team effectiveness. Metrics can assist in finding the areas that need most improvement.

Table 7.1: Mapping the Agile principles to the BDTPI Key areas.

Checkpoints

When using the Business Driven TPI model in agile environments, most Checkpoints can be used as described in the previous chapters. However, some of them need to be set in an agile context first. For example, test levels must be looked at differently; test levels, as such, are not usually found in agile testing, although this does not mean that tests traditionally belonging to a certain level cannot be performed. Agile test processes are much more diffuse and activities are performed in parallel rather than sequentially.

To give another example, documentation does not necessarily mean a pile of paper. Agile practices strive for efficient and effective documentation. If that means the test strategy is described in a picture take from a whiteboard that is fine. Checkpoints describe which activities have to be performed, not how they are performed.

In this book, we have chosen not to describe a complete 'agile' Business Driven TPI variant, so we have not included a thorough description of all Checkpoints in an agile context. The Agile Manifesto and the agile principles, together with knowledge of the agile mindset, should give a general idea of how the Business Driven TPI model can be used in this context.

7.3 BDTPI can help with multiple test processes

Several different IT processes usually co-exist in most organizations, especially those that are multinational, large, with several, relatively independent divisions or departments and have been in existence for many years. If such divisions have been formed through acquisition and/or are geographically spread, it is often to be expected that they have their own culture and traditions. The need to 'align' the different divisions may be limited if they also are focused on their own business processes and markets.

Also different technical platforms and development methods may exist within one organization, and these may have resulted in the existence of various test processes. For example, a mainframe environment where software development is based on the waterfall approach probably displays a different test process than a SOA-based approach where an iterative or agile development method is used. Also when an organization implements ERP systems or purchases standard or custom-built systems, there are different requirements to the IT processes.

7.3.1 Multiple test processes and testing

So when an organization is divided in several distinct units, each with their own technical background and perhaps even geographically apart one can expect multiple test processes to exist. It would not make sense to expect a single test process for all units, but there may be a need for some alignment.

The more interaction exists between testers and non testers, the more this alignment becomes a success factor. Cooperation with non-testing parties need to be on the same level throughout the organization, information exchange need to contain the same subjects and preferably the same look and feel to facilitate consolidating the information from various parts of the organization.

The alignment between individual test processes is described in an overall test policy. This establishes the strategic aspects of testing, while 'local' test processes extend the test policy at the operational level, which is much more dependent on the immediate cultural and technical situation. If such a test policy does not exist, there may be a need for the organization to establish one.

7.3.2 Multiple test processes and test process improvement

When performing an assessment of 'the test process' at such a dispersed organization, one must decide which Key areas should be considered on a joint, overall level and which ones can be judged solely on their own mer-

7 The BDTPI Model can be used in any situation

its, irrespective of the other test processes in scope. As a rule of thumb, Key areas in the 'Stakeholder Relations' group are good candidates for joint assessment, Key areas in the 'Test Profession' group can mostly be judged on their own and Key areas in the 'Test Management' group are assesses partly on overall aspects and partly as if the test process takes place in isolation.

Stakeholder commitment
Stakeholders are responsible for delivering a risk analysis, to be used as the basis for the test strategy. Especially in geographically spread organizations there may exist little consensus on possible risk and mitigating measures. Outspoken disagreement about possible risks can threaten a test projects success, disagreements that dwell under the surface without explicitly being addressed are a sure way towards disappointing test project results.

Test strategy
At some point all test processes converge into one final end to end test level. Development testing and system testing can be organized and conducted independent from the other test processes. The first stages of integration testing can also be carried out relatively independent, but at some point everything comes together. An overall test strategy must explicitly address the tangent planes, gaps and overlaps between the various test levels of all the test processes.

Reporting
Ensure the same kind of reporting across all different test processes, depending on the needs of the client.

Test process management
Even when it is not possible to produce one consolidated planning for all activities of the various test processes, a high level milestone planning indicating dependencies and revealing the projects critical path is a prerequisite for a controlled test process.

Metrics
Determine a uniform set of metrics to be collected and reported, to aggregate results from different test processes.

Methodology practice
Maintain the test policy at a central level and ensure that all 'local' test processes are aligned with the policy.

7.4 BDTPI can be used to set up the test process from scratch

In some, often smaller, organizations, software development is the playground of individuals with a large knowledge of the business that they support. In this situation, the methods and procedures that are used come from years of experience rather than from training, books or existing methods. Activities and actions are rarely documented and new employees learn the 'ins and outs' in a master-apprentice relationship. Here and there, initiatives are implemented to structure the processes and methods (or methods 'in name'). The same situation applies to testing: there is no well structured test method and the test approach is based on knowledge of the business.

7.4.1 Testing from scratch

Test activities in this context are commonly carried out by employees who perform test tasks supplementary to their real job: application managers, functional designers, developers etc. Testing is focused on answering the question '(how) does it work?' rather than 'does it work according to the requirements and specifications?' The largest proportion of test activities tend to be on the critical path of the project: test cases are developed once the test object is delivered, in parallel with test execution. Since testing is not a full time job, activities are often interrupted by the on-going (business) process. Although the test process is often under pressure, these circumstances lead to even more pressure, a 'quick and dirty' test process, and unwanted and unnecessary errors in production.
One of the most important issues to address is the aspect of responsibilities, both on the demand and supply side: who initiates test projects, who is accountable for test results, who decides what needs to be tested, when testing is finished, what the quality is of the test object, and when to launch for production.

> **Tip - The base Clusters provide detailed guidance**
> Considering to build up a test method from scratch likely means that the test process is currently at the Initial level. The base Clusters indicate how to establish a test process, starting at this Initial level, up to fully Optimizing. Consider therefore the Checkpoints of Cluster A first, than continue with those of Cluster B etc. The base Clusters not only support stepwise improvement, but this way the stepwise introduction of an established test method.

If you are a tester, examine the way you work: how could you do your own job better or faster? You may realize that, because of the way you work, a number of Checkpoints are already fulfilled, while some others will feel natural to adopt. Focus on quick wins: changes that do not cost much but give immediate results. Make sure that your own way of working is at a consistent Maturity level across different projects.

If other test specialists work at your organization, compare your approach to work with theirs, using the Business Driven TPI model again as a reference. You will most likely discover some best practices at each other, especially if you share examples of test products and derive templates from these examples. Adopt the templates and use them to 'drive' your work. By continuously evaluating each other's personal test processes, you can collectively make each stronger and more 'standard'. At this juncture, (methodical) training will help; look together for aspects in your work that you want to improve and ask for specific training or a workshop on that subject.

7.4.2 Test process improvement from scratch

Test strategy
Testing is a means to an end. The test strategy plays a major role in establishing a common understanding of what the end of testing is. Agreement on the test goals to be achieved, what to test thoroughly and what to a lesser extent, with parties involved, especially the principal stakeholder is perhaps the single most important step towards good testing!

Reporting
Report regularly and report about the subject that matter. This is not something a tester can decide on his own, the receiving party decides to a great extent what's useful or not. Keep in mind that ideally reporting addresses both test object and test process. Are test goals met, which risks still exist are examples of test object focused reporting. Is the deadline still feasible, how many man hours have been spent on testing, if possible in relation to the estimate, are examples of test process focused reports. Merely reporting the number of raised and solved defects does not provide insight in the status of the test object, nor in the progress of the test process.

Test process management
Next to agreeing with the principal stakeholder what to test en to what extent, it is important to decide on how to make sure that the agreed goals will be met (monitoring and controlling the test process). This is more than setting up a planning for one's own work, the planning must also reflect the efforts of other parties involved. Scope and prerequisites need to be described as well as roles and responsibilities of parties involved. Finally, all this must be agreed on by the principal stakeholder.

Defect management

Probably most communication during a test project is concerned with defects. It is therefore extremely important that everyone involved is aware of the proper procedures to handle defects and uses the same definitions (like for severity).

Test case design

Creating test cases can take a lot of time. Ideally, this investment in time pays itself back several times, every time the test case is executed. Both by the original test case designer as well as by other testers, perhaps as part of a regression test set. But a poorly designed test case will most probably be executed once or twice and only by the designer himself. So an important first improvement step is to create test cases that are accessible for other people and that are more or less self explanatory: what is the initial situation, what steps are needed to execute the test and what is the expected result. This can be achieved by applying test case design techniques, but this is not a prerequisite right from the start.

7.5 BDTPI can be used in software maintenance

The IT world recognizes broadly three types of maintenance - technical, application and functional:
- Technical maintenance focuses on IT infrastructure as the basis on which applications run. ITIL [13] can be used as a framework for this kind of maintenance.
- Application maintenance adjusts applications due to found errors, changing techniques or functional requirements. Application maintenance addresses existing applications but not completely new development. ASL [2] can be used as a framework for this kind of maintenance.
- Functional maintenance produces the requirements for applications as well as verifying that the applications adhere to them. BiSL [4] can be used as a framework for this kind of maintenance.

In this context, 'maintenance' means functional maintenance; Business Driven TPI does not address infrastructure testing, so technical maintenance lies outside the scope of this book. Testing aspects of application maintenance are described in section 7.9.

7.5.1 Functional maintenance and testing

In functional maintenance, the emphasis lies with solving production issues and implementing relatively small changes that are not really related to one another, possibly concentrated in regular releases. For functional maintenance staff, testing is more or less their second priority, the first being to ensure that the systems that they are responsible for support the business and meet predefined quality levels that are often laid down in KPIs. Furthermore, they are subject matter experts, knowing more about the system than is documented and having acquired a wealth of ready knowledge that can help them to focus their test efforts. The test process itself comprises a lot of regression testing and testing specific situations that are rarely documented.

Testing in a maintenance environment is a somewhat on-going process. It consists of repetitively performing few test cases in combination with a set of standard test cases that cover the full extent of the application, even in places one would not expect any impact from the implemented change!

7.5.2 Functional maintenance and test process improvement

In the context some Key areas can be interpreted in a slightly different way or their focus can be modified to compare to the 'standard' way of applying Business Driven TPI. These particular Key areas are discussed below; other areas not directly addressed here can be applied normally.

Test strategy
Once the test strategy for an application has been agreed, it can and must be re-used for all releases, as long as it is kept up-to-date on a regular basis. The validity needs to be reaffirmed every time it is used; applying the strategy without a second thought is just as bad as not applying it at all, but there is no need for a comprehensive strategy session for every individual change implemented.

Estimating and planning
The ratios used in estimating and planning maintenance test effort may differ from the ones used in test projects due to the greater emphasis on regression testing. Test execution takes relatively more time, whereas preparation and test case specification takes less time when re-using test cases from previous releases. In many cases, the test budget for maintenance is allocated on a yearly basis.

Defect management
Defect management administration must be implemented in such a way that defects from a maintenance or release project can be grouped together. Ideally, for proper trend analysis 'defect data' from the test process is combined with 'incident data' from the production environment. This requires a seamless interoperability between the tools supporting the test process and the functional maintenance process.

Testware management
Test cases will be reused frequently and therefore should be carefully changed and saved for the next release. If test cases are not properly maintained and testing is performed by functional maintenance staff with vast experience, the immediate repercussions for poor testware management are hardly present. But the organization is very vulnerable. If that experienced tester wins the 10 million lottery jackpot and quits, no one and nothing is available for assessing the equality of the application.

Tester professionalism
Testing is performed by functional maintenance staff and is not their highest priority. However, their test skills must be reviewed and, if necessary, improved through the provision of specific training.

Test environment
The maintenance department should have an environment of their own. One of the important tasks of the maintenance department is to analyze production defects. This can only be done in a production like environment and test environments are meant to be non-production like! Maintenance testing relies much more heavily on production like test data than any other kind of testing, requiring extra emphasis for data management.

7.6 BDTPI can be used within software process improvement

This section provides information on Business Driven TPI in relation to two key models for software process improvement (SPI) - CMMI and SPICE:
- CMMI® [6], the acronym for Capability Maturity Model Integration, is a family of process models, each of which addresses a specific domain. In this book we refer to the CMMI for Development (CMMI-DEV), which supports improvements in organizations that develop in-house software, systems and hardware. CMMI is owned by the Software Engineering Institute at the Carnegie Mellon University.
- SPICE [24], the acronym for Software Process Improvement and Capability Determination. This is the international standard ISO/IEC 15504.

There are other SPI models in use such as Trillium and BOOTSTRAP, but their application is less widespread and since they share with CMMI and SPICE the CMM (without an I) as their 'common root', there is limited added value in including these additional models here.

Business Driven TPI is used for optimizing the test process, whereas CMMI and SPICE are well-known models for improving the software development process as a whole.

CMMI and SPICE include testing as part of the overall development process, but Business Driven TPI provides a much more detailed and in-depth method for test improvement. BDTPI offers a specific and extensive set of best practices for testing, and its usage is typically justified by the significant costs for testing and the potential to reduce them.

It is important to note that if you are considering using Business Driven TPI in parallel with CMMI or followed by CMMI, please read section 7.6.3 where the business driver 'Maximizing the Return on Investment when combining Business Driven TPI and CMMI' is explained.

The software process and the test process

The relationship between the two processes - for test and software - is illustrated in Figure 7.1, which shows clearly that not only is the test process part of the overall software process, they are also actually intertwined.

The test process takes the test basis and test object as the main inputs and considers the possible risks. Reports on progress and product quality in the light of identified risks are rendered as outputs. This is carried out within the software process, which takes the client's expectations as inputs (to engineer the requirements) and delivers the software product. Each process is drawn as a cloud because each model defines its own process borders. SPICE for example uses the ISO/IEC standard 12207, which defines the standard software lifecycle processes.

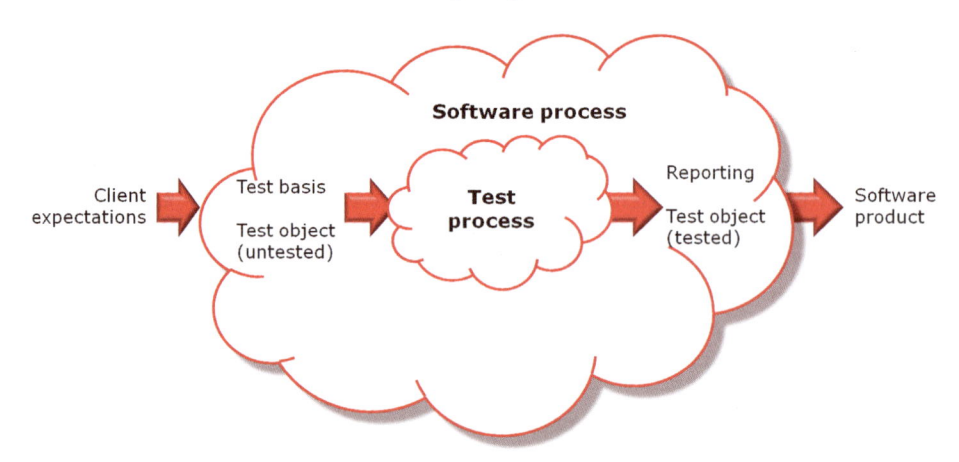

Figure 7.1: The test process is part of the software process.

7.6.1 SPI and testing

CMMI

CMMI offers two representations: the continuous and the later added staged one. In the continuous representation each process can be taken individually and improved independently. This offers flexibility as organi-

7.6 BDTPI can be used within software process improvement

zations can select those areas most relevant to their business goals. But it has the drawback that it does not guarantee an integrated approach to SPI as some processes can and probably will be omitted.

The staged representation, offering an integrated SPI approach, is applied more widely and provides a roadmap with simple levels acting as milestones and comparative benchmarks. For these reasons, we have used this representation for comparison here with Business Driven TPI.

Business Driven TPI includes characteristics of both the continuous and staged models. Please refer to Table 7.2 in this chapter for more comparative information on the three models.

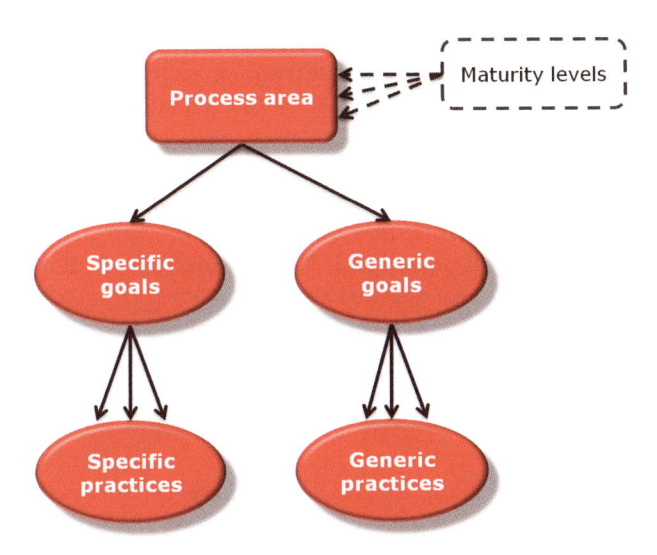

Figure 7.2: The basic structure of the CMMI model in the staged representation.

Figure 7.2 provides a basic illustration of the structure of the CMMI model, distinguishing the different process areas. A defined group of process areas produces a maturity level in the staged representation. To fulfill a process area, all the specific goals (those are exclusive to a single process area) and the generic goals (those that are shared between process areas) must be fulfilled. A goal has one or more practices that can provide help on how to fulfill the goal.

The CMMI staged representation has five maturity levels. No requirements are provided for maturity level 1 as the process is *ad hoc* and chaotic, depending almost entirely on the competence and professional attitude of individuals in the organization.

The rationale for CMMI is that many of the process areas implicitly address testing, such as Project planning and Project monitoring & control, which cover test planning, Requirements management which includes validation of requirements, Measurement and analysis which can cover metrics within the test process, and Configuration management

7 The BDTPI Model can be used in any situation

which can cover parts of Testware management. The level of detail and the lack of explicit test guidance at the practice level is addressed within Business Driven TPI. Project management creates a project plan and test management creates a test plan; both documents have much in common (like estimations and risk identification). In addition, the test plan should contain the test strategy as an important steering instrument for testing based on the identified product risks. Business Driven TPI specifically addresses the creation of the test strategy.

Testing is directly addressed by the CMMI model in two process areas, in the 'Engineering' category, which are Verification and Validation:
1. *Verification:* The purpose is to ensure that selected work products meet their specified requirements ('Is this what I ordered?').
2. *Validation:* The purpose is to demonstrate that a product or product component fulfills its intended use when placed in its intended environment ('Can I use this?').

In the popular staged representation of CMMI, both process areas are situated on maturity level 3 and only come into focus after maturity level 2 has been accomplished. Reaching CMMI maturity level 2 can easily take up to 1 or 2 years for larger organizations.

How is attention given to test process improvement during this period? By using Business Driven TPI to prepare the test process for maturity level 3 and paying special attention to the Enablers described for each Key area. Detailed information on the CMMI is available at: www.sei.cmu.edu/cmmi/

SPICE (ISO/IEC 15504)

SPICE splits the software process up into processes. Separately, SPICE defines five capability levels that are achievable for each individual process by fulfilling its process attributes, and the process attributes of the preceding capability levels. The generic practices provide help to achieve the process attributes. Outcomes address the unique results of the process and base practices are important indicators for achieving the outcomes. Figure 7.3 provides an overview of the structure of SPICE.

SPICE covers testing in 4 primary lifecycle processes, which are:
1. *Software Testing:* Confirms that the integrated software product meets its defined requirements.
2. *Software Integration:* Combines the software units, producing integrated software items, consistent with the software design, and which demonstrates that the functional and non-functional software requirements are satisfied on an equivalent or complete operational platform.
3. *System Testing:* Ensures that the implementation of each system requirement is tested for compliance and that the system is ready for delivery.

4. *System Integration:* Integrates the system elements (including software items, hardware items, manual operations and other systems, as necessary) to produce a complete system that will satisfy the system design and the customers' expectations as expressed in the system requirements.

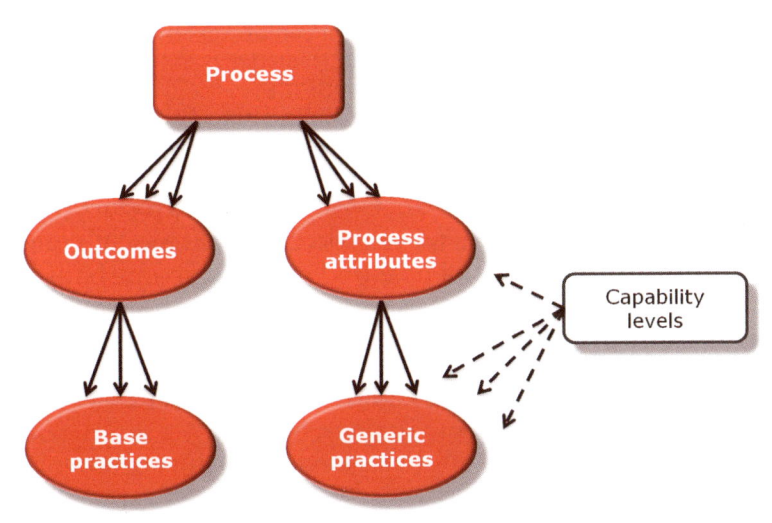

Figure 7.3: The basic structure of the SPICE model.

Additionally, there are 3 supporting lifecycle processes:
1. *Verification:* Confirms that each software work product and/or service of a process or project properly reflects the specified requirements.
2. *Validation*: Confirms that the requirements for a specific intended use of the software work product are fulfilled.
3. *Quality assurance:* Provides assurance that work products and processes comply with predefined provisions and plans.

A full description of the international standard ISO/IEC 15504 is available through the website of the International Organization for Standardization: http://www.iso.org

7.6.2 SPI and test process improvement

Business Driven TPI links each Key area to the relevant aspects of the software process through the concept of Enablers.

> **Example - The Enabler Project management**
> Project management is stated as an Enabler in the description of Key areas:
> - Estimating and planning
> - Test process management

7 The BDTPI Model can be used in any situation

> Project management in general is responsible for:
> - Project planning
> - Project monitoring and control.
>
> The Key area Estimating and planning can be linked through the Enabler Project management to the process area Project planning in CMMI and directly to the process Project management in SPICE.
> The other Key area Test process management can be linked through the Enabler Project management to the process area Project monitoring and control in CMMI and directly to the process Project management in SPICE.
> Having identified these relationships, the test team can make good use of and share the best practices (checklists, estimation techniques, etc) of the CMMI process areas and the SPICE processes.

Not all the processes have a direct relationship from model to model, so not every Key areas Enabler will be found on a one-to-one basis.

Comparing the models

Table 7.2 gives an overview of the key characteristics of each of the three models.

	CMMI	SPICE (ISO/IEC 15504)	Business Driven TPI
Model	A maturity model for software process improvement. Testing is also part of the software process.	A capability model for software process improvement. Testing is also part of the software process.	A maturity model for test process improvement. This includes: - Specific test aspects, like test case design and defect management - Test elements of generic activities that are part of the test process as well as the software process. Examples include organizational training, project planning and configuration management. To a limited extent, there is some influence on non-testing processes. See Key area Degree of involvement or Defect management which is a project matter.
Scope	Software development within a project, department or organization. The scope is defined by the client.	Software development within a project, department or organization. The scope is defined by the client.	Testing within a project, department or organization. The scope is defined by the client.

7.6 BDTPI can be used within software process improvement

	CMMI	SPICE (ISO/IEC 15504)	Business Driven TPI
Representation	Either staged or continuous	Continuous	Mixed, but more likely to be continuous. Continuous as the improvement path is not 'rigid', but chosen individually with the help of Clusters available for different business drivers. A selection of Key areas to improve can be made, while others can be omitted from the scope as defined in continuous models. Each Key area can be improved to Controlled, Efficient and Optimizing Maturity levels separately. Staged, as Business Driven TPI provides a roadmap with the Maturity levels Initial up to Optimizing acting as milestones and comparative benchmarks.

Table 7.2: A comparison of CMMI, SPICE and Business Driven TPI models.

Table 7.3 compares some specific model elements, describing the elements they have in common but not defining those elements as equivalents.

CMMI	SPICE (ISO/IEC 15504)	Business Driven TPI	Explanation
Process area	Process	Key area	Entities used to structure the respective model. Key area vs. Process (area): A Key area is an aspect of the test process, but not necessarily a process. This does not make the models incompatible with each other. At a more detailed level (like goals, process attributes and Checkpoints) comparisons can be made.
Maturity level	Capability level	Maturity level (Controlled/Efficient/Optimizing)	Describes the recognized and fixed steps within the respective models. Business Driven TPI offers the Maturity levels as steps, including smaller improvement steps through the Clusters. Maturity level vs. Maturity/Capability level: Business Driven TPI Maturity levels can be translated into a maturity or capability level, by comparing the content of the models (like goals, process attributes and Checkpoints).

7 The BDTPI Model can be used in any situation

CMMI	SPICE (ISO/IEC 15504)	Business Driven TPI	Explanation
Goals (specific or generic)	Process attributes	Checkpoints	The common factor is that they are all criteria that must be fulfilled in order to reach a certain level of the respective model. In general Checkpoints are more specific than goals or process attributes.
Practices (specific or generic)	Practices (base and generic), work products	Improvement suggestions	The commonality is that they are informative elements that help meet the level criteria within the respective models.

Table 7.3: An evaluation of the common elements of each of the three models.

7.6.3 Maximizing ROI when combining Business Driven TPI and CMMI

Improvement of the test process should align with the improvement of the software development process as a whole. If CMMI is used for assessing and improving the software development process the Clusters in table 7.5 can be used to maximize your return on investment when using both Business Driven TPI to support and partly replace efforts of the CMMI assessment team.

Each CMMI maturity level has its own Cluster in the Test maturity matrix. These Clusters are an interpreted view on the test process improvement priorities for each CMMI maturity level.

The Initial level corresponds to the CMMI Initial maturity level. In both cases no requirements are set by the models. The corresponding Cluster for each individual CMMI maturity level is listed in Table 7.4.

CMMI maturity level	Business Driven TPI Cluster
Level 1 - Initial	Initial level
Level 2 - Managed	Cluster A
Level 3 - Defined	Cluster B
Level 4 - Quantitatively managed	Cluster C
Level 5 - Optimizing	Cluster D

Table 7.4: BDTPI Cluster per CMMI maturity level.

7.6 BDTPI can be used within software process improvement

If your organization's target is to reach a certain CMMI maturity level you can take the following approach:
1. Start with assessing the current situation of the test process by using the Business Driven TPI Checkpoints. The result is a filled out Test maturity matrix.
2. Make a list of the missed Checkpoints of the Cluster that corresponds to your target CMMI maturity level.
   Example: If the CMMI maturity level 2 is your organization's target, check which Checkpoints of Cluster A you did not reach.
3. Define improvement actions to achieve those missing Checkpoints by negotiating with the CMMI initiative (responsible for implementing the target CMMI maturity level):
   - Which improvement actions the CMMI project will take care of (organization wide). This prevents a double investment, first by the test organization and later by the CMMI project.
     Example: By establishing the process area Configuration Management as part of CMMI maturity level 2 failing parts of the Testware management Key area can be covered directly.
   - Which improvement actions can be done through cooperation between the test organization and the CMMI project. This generates benefits for both sides.
     Example: The maturity of the Metrics Key area is improved through participating in establishing the process area Measurement and Analysis as part of CMMI maturity level 2.
   - Which improvement actions of the BDTPI team make that the CMMI goals are met.
     Example: The CMMI process area Verification as part of CMMI maturity level 3 is about testing so when the BDTPI team improves the test process there's little left to do for the CMMI team.
4. Finally, the test organization will take care of all other necessary improvement actions to improve the test process. We advice that the Clusters presented in Table 7.5 will be used as just one aspect to consider for test process improvement. Also take other aspects like your business drivers and your specific situation into account for sensible improvement of the test process.
   Example: The test organization decides to bring the Test strategy Key area to a Controlled level, improving the allocation of effort and test resources. According to the Cluster A this improvement action would not be necessary yet.

If you use Business Driven TPI for improving the test process according to the Clusters in Table 7.4 you will cover the practices of CMMI that are relevant to testing and thus BDTPI and CMMI can be combined efficiently.

7 The BDTPI Model can be used in any situation

	Initial			Controlled			Efficient			Optimizing		
1 Stakeholder commitment	A	A	A	B	B	B	B	B	B	D	D	D
2 Degree of involvement	A	A	A	A	A	A	A	B		D		D
3 Test strategy	A	A	B	B	B	B	B	B	B	B		D
4 Test organization	A	A	B	B	B	B	B	B	B	B	C	C
5 Communication	A	A	A	A	A	A	A	A	A	B		D
6 Reporting	A		A		A	A	A	A	A	B		D
7 Test process management	A	A	A	A	A	A	A	B		D		D
8 Estimating and planning	A	A	A	A	A	A	A	A		B	B	C
9 Metrics	A		A		A	A	B	B	B	C		D
10 Defect management	A	A	A	B	B	B	C	C	C	C	C	D
11 Testware management	A	A	A	A	A		B		B	C	C	-
12 Methodology practice	A		A		B	B	B	C	C	C		D
13 Tester professionalism	A	A	A	B	B	B	B	B	B	B	B	D
14 Test case design	A		B	B	B	B	B	B	B	B	B	D
15 Test tools												
16 Test environment												

Table 7.5: Clusters for the business driver Maximizing ROI when combining Business Driven TPI and CMMI.

Justification

Of course various practices of CMMI are not relevant to the test process (for example the specific practice "assemble product components" which refers to the actual construction of the test object and thus is out of scope for testing and test process improvement) so they can be marked as not applicable.

Looking at the Clusters in the Test maturity matrix various things leap to the eye. The order in which improvements are made differs. For some Key areas the Efficient level must be reached to get to CMMI maturity level 2. For the Test case design Key area meeting only one Checkpoint is enough to reach CMMI maturity level 2 for the test process. About half of the Key areas have no CMMI maturity level 4 equivalent, this can be explained by the fact that the BDTPI model has 4 Maturity levels where CMMI has 5 and we see the CMMI maturity level 4 as a step "in between". Three Key areas don't match with any CMMI maturity level 5 practice, therefore if reaching CMMI maturity level 5 is the ultimate goal additional action may be needed after the BDTPI Optimizing level is fully reached. Checkpoint 3 at the Optimizing level for Testware management cannot be matched with any CMMI practice since this Checkpoint is very specific to the test process. So this Checkpoint is not applicable for reaching a CMMI maturity level.

Finally we must explain that the Key areas Test tools and Test environment are greyed-out because CMMI does not define practices for tooling and other supporting facilities. Only the CMMI process area Verification has one practice for this purpose which would imply that both Key areas totally match with CMMI maturity level 3 but we are of the opinion that in practice this would not work well while improving the test process. We advise you to define your own improvement goals for these Key areas, additional to reaching CMMI maturity levels, or refer to the base Clusters in Chapter 3.

7.7 BDTPI can be used with outsourcing and offshoring

Outsourcing can be defined as subcontracting a process, such as product design or manufacturing, to a third-party company. Organizations decide to outsource certain activities to gain several advantages, which may include:

- *Save costs:* The lowering of the overall cost of the test services to the business. This can include limiting the test services made use of defining quality levels, repricing, renegotiation, cost restructuring.
- *Focus on core business:* By outsourcing for example IT support to specialized IT services companies, companies can free up IT resources to develop the core business.
- *Improve quality:* Achieving a change in quality through contracting out the service with new service level agreements.
- *Knowledge:* Access to intellectual property and wider experience and knowledge.
- *Contract:* Services are provided via legally binding contracts with financial penalties and legal redress. This is not the case with internal services.
- *Operational expertise:* Access to operational best practices that would be too difficult or time-consuming to develop in-house.
- *Access to talent:* Access to a larger talent pool and a sustainable source of skills, in particular in science and engineering.
- *Capacity management:* An improved method of capacity management of services and technology, where the risk of excess capacity is borne by the supplier.

> **In more detail - Offshoring**
> Outsourcing has been widely adopted as a cost-saving measure, especially in combination with offshoring. Offshoring is a special form of outsourcing where the third-party company is located in a different country, in practice often to lower-wage countries like India, Mexico and East European countries. Offshoring has its own specific advantages and challenges related to cultural differences, language issues and time zone differences.

The test process, either partially or in its entirety, can also be outsourced. Typical examples of test outsourcing are the design and manual execution of test cases, automating test cases, and planning, preparing and executing performance tests. In addition, the hosting and management of test environments are often outsourced, especially when the production environment has also been outsourced.

7.7.1 Outsourcing and testing

From an outsourcing point of view, two specific challenges exist where the Business Driven TPI model can be helpful. First, the quality of testing performed by the supplier needs to be assured; how can the client trust the test results provided by the supplier? The client can impose on the supplier demands relating to transparency of the test process and the maturity of the test process. These requirements can be part of a service level agreement between the supplier and client.

The second challenge for the client is that outsourcing testing also puts obligations on the client. Clear communication between client and supplier is needed as early as possible. In addition to the client's acceptance criteria which need to be defined and agreed in advance, business knowledge and system knowledge, which is often *implicitly* available on the client side, needs to be made available to the supplier. Clear agreements need to be made in advance, to ensure that the supplier has ready access to this knowledge.

While the client may expect that the supplier will define a test strategy, the client needs to provide the necessary input; for example when the client performs the acceptance tests, this must be included in the overall test strategy.

In creating a test plan, the client needs to provide input to the supplier and show his commitment once the test plan has been agreed. The test plan can be based on a master test plan or test policy provided by the client, and should be considered as a contract between client and supplier that respects mutual expectations. If during the execution of the test plan deviations occur, the supplier needs to signalize the necessity to renegotiate the test plan.

The management of defects has to be agreed with the supplier. One can choose a separate defect administration or a shared administration. Agreements must be reached about tools and access, as well as what information will be exchanged.

Last but not least, there will be challenges around integration testing: the client will use the product in a test environment and with (possibly production like) test data that is not necessarily available to the supplier. Agreements have to be made to deal with the consequences of these limitations.

7.7.2 Outsourcing and test process improvement

Essentially, the Business Driven TPI model can help the client measure the quality of the supplier's test process and improve the transparency of the test process. At the beginning of an outsourcing engagement, the client can perform a Business Driven TPI assessment on the suppliers test process, and agree on improvement goals and suggestions for both the

7.7 BDTPI can be used with outsourcing and offshoring

supplier and the client. This assessment can be repeated for example every six months.
Below are some suggestions for several Key areas in an outsourcing situation:

Test strategy
Assure that the client contributes to the analysis of the product risks and that the supplier bases the test strategy on these products risks. Have the supplier discuss with the client if the created test strategy can sufficiently cover the product risks as perceived and analyzed by the client.

Communication
Define an overall communication plan in the master test plan that includes the communication between client and suppliers. Pay additional attention to communication using internet, conference calls and the possible time difference.

Reporting
Have the supplier focus on reporting on the quality of the test object / covered product risks. Reporting on progress or project risks is less relevant, as suppliers normally control their own performance and are responsible for their results.

Metrics
The most important metrics to consider are those that can be used to measure the effectiveness of testing by the supplier. One example is to measure the number and severity of defects found in the next test level or production.
For metrics provided by the supplier on the test process efficiency/supplier's performance (like: test cases designed / hour) the base data should be accurate and verifiable.

Tester professionalism
To assure sufficient test methodical knowledge and support is available at the supplier, the client can require that (a certain percentage) of the testers is trained and certified. To assure that industry, business and technical knowledge is actually available at and used by the supplier, the client can have (some) testware like test cases regularly reviewed as a quality assurance measure.

Test environment
In general two situations may occur: the client provides the test environment in which the supplier performs the outsourced test execution, and secondly the supplier sets up a test environment on his own and the test assignment can be conducted completely independent from the client. In

7 The BDTPI Model can be used in any situation

the first case strict agreements must be made on the service level of the test environment. This way the influence of the quality and availability of the test environment on agreed deliverables can be assessed as objectively as possible. One of the advantages of testing in the clients environment is less configuration issues when deploying software to the clients acceptance environment. This can be very cumbersome when the supplier has performed all his testing in a separate, dedicated environment of his own. It is good practice to agree up front that the supplier can only be discharged when software has been deployed in the clients target environment and a basic set of test cases has been run successfully.

7.8 BDTPI can be used with managed test services

Section 7.7 addresses the way Business Driven TPI can be applied at the client side in case of test outsourcing. Business Driven TPI can also be applied at the receiving end of an outsourcing engagement, where testing is conducted in a process like manner and is offered as a managed service.

7.8.1 Managed test service

Organizations often decide to set up a permanent test organization (see Key area Test organization) that offers a range of test services. In contrary to project-based testing, a permanent test organization does not execute a specific element of the test process on a per project basis, but across all projects.
Usually a permanent test organization offers one or more managed test services. A managed test service can be defined as a permanent set of technical components and related procedures (test environment), which has been dedicated to:
- A specific (client) organization and/or specific systems (applications) which are part of the scope of the test process.
- A group of clients who are in the scope of the test process and who collectively use the managed test service for efficiency reasons; usually each client has a limited use of the managed test service at any given moment.

When a permanent test organization offers multiple managed test services for several (internal or external) customers, there is a pressing need to measure the performance and quality of the services in an objective way.

7.8.2 Managed test services and test process improvement

Periodical TPI assessments are used in a permanent test organization. The information gathered is used to monitor and then improve the quality of the offered services, and also to prove that the services are offered according to the contractually agreed key performance indicators and procedures.

When supported by a low threshold tool and containing multiple choice questions, these TPI assessments can be conducted by the testers themselves. The information and analysis reports are kept at a high level. The power of such a TPI scan tool lies in the low threshold and ease of use of the questionnaire. The results from the previous assessment form the default for the new assessment so the test manager responsible for the quality of the test service can directly focus on those areas in which improvements have to be made. The results for each specific test service and an overview of all offered test services are provided on a quarterly basis, and deviations from the desired standard can be acted upon quickly. This approach has the advantage of giving a quick evaluation across the different test services. From this top-level data, it is possible to identify significant deviations, which determine the focus for an experienced TPI assessor to perform a more profound assessment.

However, there is a risk of working towards a particular result: test service managers may 'polish up' the findings of the assessment in order to meet the required result. Random samples prevent this and, on a yearly basis, an experienced TPI assessor will also perform a reference check to assess whether the standards are being interpreted identically for all test services.

Specific Enablers

In addition to Key areas, some Enablers are of specific interest for the assessment of a managed test service:

- *Supplier agreement management:* this process is, amongst others, used to establish and maintain agreements with the test service supplier. Obviously it is very important that agreements are clearly defined and understood by all parties involved.
- *Customer collaboration:* As well as the existence of formal agreements, collaboration with the client of the managed test service is of great importance. Are unexpected issues solved without endless discussions? Is there good will on both sides when questions arise that are not clearly defined in the agreement, etc?
- *Requirements management:* The quality of the test basis, especially its usability - the ease with which testers can understand the test basis - is important to ensure a solid test process.

7 The BDTPI Model can be used in any situation

- *Release management:* New versions of the software to be tested must be deployed according to a well-defined process, in order to avoid unexpected surprises within the permanent test organization.

Some of the Key areas of the Business Driven TPI model are more important or have significantly different impact than others when assessing a managed test service. They are:

Test strategy

Usually one of the very important Key areas that require attention every time a project or release is initiated. In case a client closes a contract with a test service supplier for several releases over a period of time, a test strategy can be agreed for the whole period or a periodical re-evaluation of the test strategy is planned. This overall test strategy is part of the agreement between client and supplier. Such a document that focuses on testing in substance is commonly known as the Generic Test Agreement or the Generic Master Test Plan. So it is not uncommon for a specific test assignment between the test service supplier and the client to be without a test strategy. The result of the test service to be delivered is unambiguously described in terms of scope, number of test cases and test cycles to be executed, etc. and follows the guidelines of the overall test strategy.

Reporting

Reporting is always an important part of the test process. In the context of managed test services extra emphasis lies with timely delivery of complete and consistent reports. When client and supplier are both acting within the same organization, informal communication can compensate poor reporting. This is not the case when the relationship is strictly businesslike and should adhere to rules and agreements laid down in binding contracts.

Test process management

In most situations, it is good practice to discuss the test plan with the principal stakeholder and mutually agree upon the contents of it. When a client buys a service, he is usually not interested in how the service is rendered, he is interested in the end result. Indeed, the wish not to be bothered with the specific details of a service is often one of the drivers for buying services.

Metrics

There are two kinds of metrics: process metrics, substantiating how well or poor the test process is conducted and product metrics, substantiating how well or poor the subject under test fulfills its requirements. When rendering test services, process metrics are of major importance to the internal organization but hardly of interest to the client. Product metrics however, are the means by which the client can measure his value for money.

Testware management
Often, managed test services are bought for an extended period of time, for instance all acceptance testing in a certain business domain for a number of years. All test deliverables created in rendering such a test service stand a good chance to be reused or referenced in the future, when testing a next release. To keep the quality of the service high and the cost low, reusability of the test deliverables is an important prerequisite. Secondly, many clients have contractually stipulated that the ownership of the testware ultimately lies with them, not with the supplier. This to make sure that when the service period ends they can safely switch to another service supplier without losing all investments so far.

Test environment
The features a test environment must deliver play a decisive role in the nature of a test service offered. If the test service supplier can control the test environment completely, without interference from other parties, a solid service level agreement is feasible. When the test service supplier depends on the client for (parts of) the test environment, for instance in case of large legacy systems being indispensible for test execution, the result of the service rendered depends on the result of yet another service rendered: from the client to the supplier!

7.9 BDTPI can be used in development testing

Development is not testing, and developers are not testers! No one would dispute these statements, yet testing constitutes a significant part of the workload of a developer. Well-known low-level testing are the unit test and the integration test. Similarly to evaluation, these tests can find defects at an earlier stage of the system development path than high-level tests do. Low-level tests are efficient, because they require little communication and because often the finder is also both the error producer as well as the one who solves the defect.

No matter who performs the testing, it always involves thinking what and how to test, creating test cases, executing them, often using tools and a dedicated environment, investigating and reporting mismatches with expected results, reporting status and progress of testing, etc. In many cases special skills are required, so training and education becomes necessary. But this by no means implies that Business Driven TPI can be used in the same manner for development testing as for other test levels such as system testing or acceptance testing.

7 The BDTPI Model can be used in any situation

We will now look at the key success factor of any test - the people who perform it, and in this case, the developer.

The tester's mindset

An important prerequisite for good testing is the mindset of the tester. Table 7.6 outlines a number of strengths of both testers and developers.

Good testers ...	Good developers ...
Get up to speed quickly	Thorough understanding
Domain knowledge	Knowledge of product internals
Ignorance is important	Expertise is important
Model user behavior	Model system design
Focus on what can go wrong	Focus on how it can work
Focus on severity of problem	Focus on interest in problem
Empirical	Theoretical
What is observed	How it is designed
Skeptics	Believers
Tolerate tedium	Automate tedium
Comfortable with conflict	Avoid conflict
Report problems	Understand problems

Table 7.6: Summary of strengths of Testers and Developers [19].

As this Table demonstrates, developers look at and handle software in a very different way compared to testers. However, testers and developers have one important quality in common: they take pride in what they do! This should be reflected in the way Business Driven TPI is put into practice.

7.9.1 Development testing

Development testing is testing using knowledge of the technical implementation of the system. This starts with testing the first/smallest parts of the system: routines, units, programs, modules, components, objects, etc. Within this book, the term unit and therefore unit test is used exclusively in this context.

7.9 BDTPI can be used in development testing

> **In more detail - Test levels in development testing**
> **Unit Test (UT)**
> The unit test is a test carried out in the development environment by the developer, with the aim of demonstrating that a unit meets the requirements defined in the technical specifications.
> **Unit Integration Test (UIT)**
> The unit integration test is a test carried out by the developer in the development environment, with the aim of demonstrating that a logical group of units meets the requirements defined in the technical specifications.

When it has been established that the most elementary parts of the system are of sufficient quality, larger parts of the system are tested integrally during the unit integration tests. The emphasis here lies on the data throughput and the interfacing between the units up to subsystem level.

A pitfall in organizing development tests is the temptation to set up the test process from the viewpoint of a system test. When development tests are compared with the system test and acceptance test, a number of significant differences come to the fore.

In contrast to the system test and acceptance test, development tests cannot be organized as an independent process with a more or less independent team. These tests form an integral part of software development, and the phasing of the test activities is integrated with the activities of the developers.

Because development testing uses knowledge of the technical implementation of the system, different types of defects are found in addition to those found by system and acceptance tests. It may be expected of development tests, for example, each statement in the code has been executed at least once. A similar degree of coverage is, in practice, very difficult for system and acceptance tests to achieve, since these test levels focus on different aspects. It is therefore not easy to replace development tests with system and acceptance tests.

With unit tests in particular, the discoverer of the defects (the tester) is often the same individual who solves them (the developer), which means that communication regarding defects may be minimal.

The approach of development testing is that all defects found are solved before the software is transferred. The reporting of development testing may therefore be more limited than that of system and acceptance testing.

Development testing is the first test activity, which means that all the defects are still in the product, enabling cheap and fast defect adjustment. To achieve this, it is important to set up a flexible test environment with few procedural barriers.

As has been noted, development tests are often carried out by developers themselves. The developer's basic intention is to demonstrate that the product works, while a system or acceptance tester is looking to demonstrate the difference between the required quality and the actual quality of the product (and actively goes in search of defects). This difference in mindset means that sizeable and/or in-depth development tests run counter to the developer's general approach and so these tests can meet with resistance and/or be carelessly executed.

Well executed development tests pay themselves back double. Firstly, because the defects found are solved relatively cheap. Were they found in system or acceptance testing, cost of rework would be considerably higher (as was demonstrated by Boehm in 1981 [5]). Secondly, test execution of later test levels is shortened and planning of these test levels becomes more reliable.

7.9.2 Development testing and test process improvement

Test strategy
An often heard complaint of testers is that they find bugs that certainly would have been found if that part of the software had already been executed at least once. The test strategy states where the developers commit to the type and degree of coverage (for example 100% statement coverage) that should be realized before handing the software over to the next development of test phase.

Estimating and planning
Testing is an integral part of system development. Introducing unit testing as a separate phase does not work, but planning should take into account that a certain amount of rework and refactoring is required after the initial coding has taken place. Unit integration testing on the other hand is a good candidate for being viewed as a separate activity in the test plan.

Metrics
Separate metrics for test products, such as defects found and solved or testing activities, add very little value and can even have a counterproductive effect. Be specific about what and how you measure. The '90% done' syndrome (reporting three weeks in a row that you are 90% done) is prevalent especially when unit testing and refactoring are poorly addressed.

Defect management
Defects often are solved by the testers who detect them. It is therefore often acceptable that defects are not formally registered.

Tester professionalism
This is where the different developer and tester mindsets are relevant. Not all 'testing best practices' should be translated to development practices entirely and unchanged. But some test design techniques like Elementary Comparison Test (ECT) and Decision Table Test (DTT) can very well be applied in development testing (see [17]).

Test environment
Developers usually test in their development environment, which can be a 'sandbox environment' with little or no interface with other platforms. Therefore the freedom that developers have in configuring and adjusting their environment can be considerably greater than that of testers in a 'standard' test environment. When taking development testing in scope of an assessment be specific about the way this key area is assessed: does it address the development environment as well ? The characteristics of and roles and responsibilities with respect to the development environment can differ substantially from those of a separate test environment.

7.10 BDTPI can be used for evaluation

This section on evaluation also explains static testing as these two activities are easily mixed up.

7.10.1 Evaluation and static testing

Evaluation is *not* the same as static testing, although both engage in the examination of documents and both apply the same techniques. Evaluation is the assessment of *intermediary* products in the system development lifecycle. Testing, including static testing, is applied to end products in the system development lifecycle. Static testing and evaluation are both done without any program being executed.

There is a clear difference in definition between the two but this is not always intuitively understood. The reason lies in the perception of what an *intermediary* or an *end* product is. An end product can be regarded as an intermediary product by one tester, and *vice versa*. Therefore for the purpose of clarity, the products relevant to the test process are categorized below.

Evaluation of intermediary products:
- *Test basis:* requirements, design documents
- *Testware:* (master) test plan, test cases, defects etc.

- Static testing of end products:
- *Test object:* the source code
- *User documentation:* manuals, procedures etc.

Certain quality characteristics are very difficult if not impossible to test by executing a program and are therefore tested statically.

Examples of such quality characteristics are:
- *Maintainability:* Highly dependent on the source code structure, like the code complexity and the presence of comments in the source.
- *Security:* Particular security vulnerabilities can only be found in practice by investigating the source code.

Other quality characteristics to which static testing is commonly applied are reliability, installability and portability.

Techniques

These techniques are used for both evaluation and static testing:
- *Reviews*[1]: A group of people examining and reviewing a document. There are many different types of reviews, including peer reviews, walkthroughs, (Fagan) inspections and technical reviews. The most distinctive characteristic is the review's purpose, such as determining the quality of a document, reaching consensus on the solution, or searching for improvement opportunities. Other identifying characteristics of a review type are the role of the document author, the use of a moderator, the group composition (peers, users, management etc.) and the degree of formality.
- *Static analysis:* A document, like source code or a formally structured design document, that is analyzed using a tool. A compiler is a well known static analyzer (for source code).
- *Checklists:* A structured list to assure that all important items are checked, commonly used in reviews. If a checklist is not used, there is a risk that a document is merely checked for spelling. The checklist content can be agreed upon in an early phase, clarifying upfront expectations and possible differences in reviews.

Evaluations prove again and again to be the most effective and efficient way to find defects.

The most obvious value of the test team actively participating in evaluations is that issues can be identified earlier and cheaper than when they are detected during testing or in field use. Evaluation can be easily undertaken because there are no programs to run and no test environments to organize.

The cost to find and fix a defect using a well-conducted review may be ten to a hundred times less than if the same defect is found by test execution or in the field.

---

[1] For more information on reviews please refer to TMap NEXT [17] or the IEEE Standard for Software Reviews (IEEE Std. 1028).

7.10 BDTPI can be used for evaluation

> **Example - Benefits of evaluation**
> A supplier of packages has achieved a return-on-investment of 1000% through early evaluation of the designs. As a result €21.4 million is saved annually on project costs, and the average time-to-market has been reduced by 1.8 months.
> A large computer manufacturer saves 20 hours of test effort and 82 hours of rework for every hour spent on inspections.

The key evaluation activity for a test team is the testability review, also called the inspection of the test basis. This is a detailed check of the test basis on testability - the ease and speed with which characteristics of the system can be tested (following each adjustment).

It is good practice to use checklists for this review; one checklist for a general evaluation of the test basis, and one specifically for the test design technique that will be used for test case design.

The testability review is important for three reasons. To:
- Check the testability of the test basis (as a basis for the test case design).
- Find early defects (like inconsistencies) in the test basis.
- Get familiar with the test basis.

> **In more detail - No evaluation, but still a testability review ...**
> It is important to bear in mind that systems and products, intermediary or not, can be judged on a number of quality characteristics like functionality, performance, security, etc. Testability is just one of those characteristics. When a project manager organizes an evaluation, he or she defines what the participants should pay attention to or what not. Testability can be in or outside the scope, so a testability review may or may not be performed.
> When there is no evaluation, the test manager will probably take action to assess the quality of the test basis, as part of carrying out best testing practices. This action is very likely to be called a 'testability review'!

Evaluation is also a good means of improving the quality of the testware. Here, the intermediary product is not created by another process (as it is with the test basis), but by testing itself. An example of evaluating testware to improve the test process quality is described as follows:
- *Perform a review and use a checklist:* For example through a peer review of the test case design, or by organizing a walkthrough session of the test plan, and so creating a common understanding of the test approach.

7.10.2 Evaluation and test process improvement

Stakeholder commitment
The initiative for organizing review sessions of the test basis and other intermediary products should be taken by stakeholders (as they are responsible for the test basis and most other intermediary products). The

test team should be invited to participate in these reviews. At best evaluation is part of the test assignment.

Test strategy
Evaluation should be included in the test strategy (the evaluation strategy). Not all (parts of) intermediary products are evaluated equally and the different levels of evaluation are based on risk potential. In re-evaluations, a strategic decision is taken on the choice between 'evaluate solutions only' and 'a complete re-evaluation'. For variation in the thoroughness of evaluation different evaluation techniques can be selected for specific intermediary products. Discuss the different intermediary products and quality characteristics with the principal stakeholder and try to find out their relative importance.
A problem with evaluations with a high degree of formality is that re-evaluations are often regarded as being too expensive. To prevent that no rework is done, it is better to have the re-evaluation carried out in a simplified way. If there is only one technique available, try to put in more or less depth by means of simple variations, like involving or not involving certain people and by time boxing.

Defect management
Make sure that the reported defects from the evaluations are managed. The solution of important defects should be checked.

Methodology practice
Make various evaluation techniques available. Each technique consists in general of the following phases: plan, assessment, rework and check.
Checklists can be applied as an evaluation technique. Make testers aware of the objectivity and relative completeness of checklists as a means of substantiating a judgment (compared to just indicating "the intermediary product is not easily understandable"). Communicate the checklists used to relevant stakeholders beforehand. Have the principal stakeholder approve the checklists to avoid discussions afterwards.

Test case design
Make testers aware of the importance of a testability review of the test basis. Make use of checklists for the general evaluation of the test basis as well as a checklist for each test design technique used. Not every test design technique is suitable for a given test basis. Make the results of the review available within the test team.

7.11 BDTPI can be used for integration

A complete system is no longer a matter of an owner, a supplier, some users and a simple configuration. IT products have become more and

7.11 BDTPI can be used for integration

more complex, not only through an increasing complexity of their functionality but also through the growing integration of programs and systems. Moreover, there are challenges in the control and management of different and, in some cases, dozens of suppliers, numerous users, back-end and front-end systems and a variety of other parties involved - both inside and outside the company.

Using the term integration, we mean the integration, assembly or combination of two or more identifiable end-products. Such an end-product can be a component, a subsystem or even a complete system. Integration testing deals with the testing of such combined components. For testing the integration of complete systems often the term end-to-end-testing is used, for example as described in the book "End-to-end testing with TMap NEXT®" [23]. In the remainder of this section we will use the generic term integration testing.

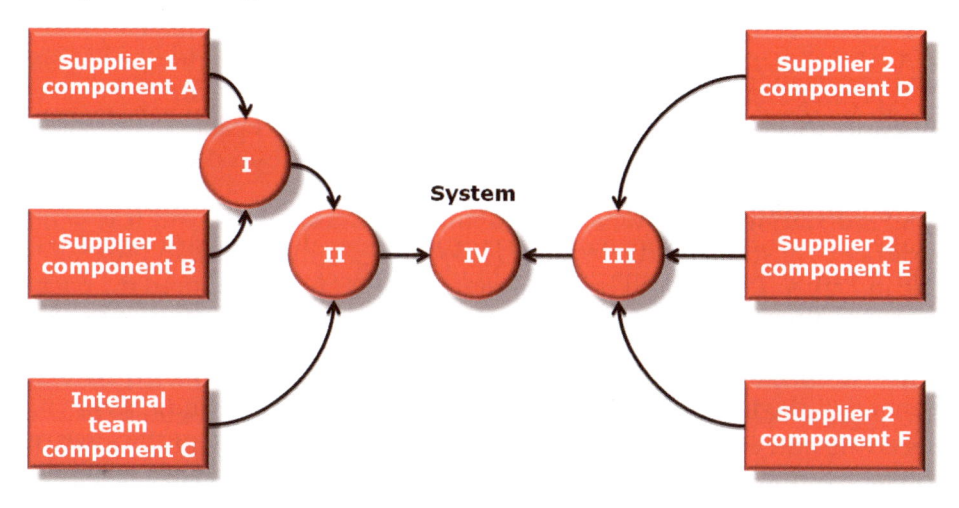

Figure 7.4: An example of the integration of various components.

Figure 7.4 illustrates a simplified integration of different components into one system, showing:
- 6 components (A to F)
- 4 integration steps (I to IV)
- 3 teams: 2 external supplier teams and an internal team.

Every integration step must be organized and planned. For almost every integration step, there is more than one internal or external party involved. One of the integration issues is to decide what functionality should be available in which component. A certain minimum functionality per component is necessary so that it is possible to integrate each component with other (assembled) components.

After that, integration is carried out according to a planned sequence or strategy. As Figure 7.4 shows, variances are possible, as both integration steps I and III can be performed first or even in parallel.

Another integration strategy could be a 'big bang' approach in which all the components are brought together at the same time in one single full-scale integration step.

7.11.1 Integration and testing

Integration testing has the following objectives:
- Verify that one or more components are ready (and if necessary tested) for assembly. This verification is performed as an entry criterion for the integration test;
- Verify that the assembly of components (hardware and/or software) does not result in degradation of functionality of the assembled parts;
- Verify that the interface and communication between the assembled (hardware and/or software) components work as designed;
- Verify that the integration as a whole is stable and reliable;
- Validate that the integrated system provides the desired functionality.

The integration strategy defines the integration sequence and it is good practice to ensure that the strategy is based on product risks. In the example in Figure 7.4, it could be that Component A and B are standard packages and their assembly is proven quality in practice. In that case, testing the integration may not be necessary at all.

To increase the flexibility of the integration strategy, stubs and drivers can be used, which are placeholders for 'not ready' units. A stub is at the receiving end of the interface and a driver at the sending end. The disadvantage is that additional effort is needed to create (and maybe even test) these stubs and drivers, and the integration step must be repeated after the unit is delivered. The advantage is the improved flexibility: integration testing can be executed while the components needed for integration are still being developed.

Some well-known integration strategies are:
- *Big bang:* Units A to F are integrated all at the same time. No stubs or drivers are used as placeholder for units.
- *Top-down:* This assumes Units A and B drive or control Unit C. As long as Unit C cannot be provided, it is replaced by a stub.
- *Bottom-up:* This assumes Units A and B are driven or controlled by Unit C. As long as Unit C cannot be provided, it is replaced by a driver.

Having defined a delivery sequence based on product risks, the timely delivery of components becomes very important. A failing component can delay the whole integration process and with that, the integration testing. This means that good co-ordination between all involved parties is especially important. Typical defects found in integration testing relate to communication and interfaces between units, its correct interpretation and implementation.

7.11.2 Integration and test process improvement

When using Business Driven TPI in the context of integration testing, the following Key areas have a slightly different focus and need special attention:

Test strategy
The test strategy follows the integration strategy. There should be a difference in the depth of the integration tests depending on the (component) risks. Not all integrated components are tested to the same degree of thoroughness.
Entry criteria for the parts are defined and used before parts are admitted to the integration test; examples include percentage of achieved test coverage and/or the amount of unsolved defects. Regression testing is a specific point of interest for the strategy in this context.
The sequence of delivery should be co-ordinated with all parties. The number and sequence of integration steps are based on estimated risks, technical constraints and the impact of changes.

Defect management
All delivering parties 'synchronize' their defect information. Especially with external suppliers involved it is very likely that several defect management tools are in order. Unambiguous references to the same defect in one of the other defect management systems is a 'must' for smooth defect management. The defect procedure should also include explicit agreement and alignment on 'coded entries': is a 'priority-1' defect a defect with the highest or lowest priority? Or is it neither, since priority-0 also exists? And should a blocking defect be solved within 2, 4, 8 hours?

Testware management
The sequence of delivery from supplier(s) to testing needs to be defined and documented.
Transfer to and from the test team of components and documents should take place according to agreed procedures. The elements comprising a transfer should be made clear in the form of a delivery report. This should describe which parts and versions of the test object, which version of the test basis, (un)solved defects, configurations, etc.

Tester professionalism
The role of an integrator should be covered within the test project. An integrator is responsible for integrating the separate parts into an assem-

7 The BDTPI Model can be used in any situation

bled system including integration testing, and will give more focus to, and take control over, the integration process.

Test case design
The test cases used for component testing may be used for the integration test as well.

Test environment
The test environment needs to support the frequent installing and de-installing of components, stubs and drivers.

8 The BDTPI Model has proven its value in practice

This chapter describes a case that explains how Business Driven TPI (BDTPI) was used successfully in practice. This case combines experiences from several real-world cases. As a result, the case includes more details and is more complex than one would expect when using BDTPI in real life. The case is written from the perspective of two external BDTPI assessors. This case follows the generic improvement process as described in chapter 5.

8.1 Generate awareness

The organization in this case is a large international bank. It is based in the UK and has offices in USA, Ireland, Germany and France. Its IT operations are centralized in the UK, but split up in the different business units. These business units are:
- CNS
- MKT
- ONI
- PAY

The different, relatively isolated, business units and their IT counterparts have developed their own ways of software development and testing over the years. The different test approaches used to be no problem, until more and more projects across the different business units took place. At the same time, the time-to-market for IT support was insufficient, which jeopardized the competitive edge of the company. The common understanding of IT management was that testing was one of the major delaying factors.

Recently, a central test organization was established that provides all test projects with test environments, test method support and related services.

8.2 Determine goals, scope and approach

A test process improvement initiative was started to reduce the time-to-market by cutting the time testing is on the critical path of development projects, as well as to unify the way the different test processes could be controlled from a business perspective.

8 The BDTPI Model has proven its value in practice

> **In more detail - The assignment**
> The aim of the project is to establish a planning and control process that enables the pro-active steering on timely delivery of (joint) releases, realized by the business units.
>
> This translates into the following assignment:
> 1. Implement one integrated and consolidated steering and reporting mechanism that covers all individual test reporting.
> 2. Reduce testing lead-time ratio by 50%.
>
> Subjects to be covered by the consolidated reports are:
> 1. Planned/forecasted/actual end date
> 2. Planned/forecasted/actual budget
> 3. Risks plus mitigating measures.
>
> The norm and the way of measuring testing lead-time ratio are defined as follows:
> - Test lead-time ratio = test lead-time / overall project lead-time
> - Overall project lead-time = implementation date - date of approval of project initiation document
> - Test lead-time = end date User Acceptance Test - start date System Test
>
> Project data from the project support database for all projects with project initiation document approval date after January 1st, 2006 and implementation date before April 1st, 2009 serves as the base line for these metrics.
>
> All high level tests (system test, system integration test, acceptance test) are in scope of the assessment. Development tests at CNS are in scope as well. All other development tests are out of scope.

As a first step of the test process improvement initiative, an analysis was made of how testing was done in the four different business units. After that, practical improvement goals for the test process were defined, followed by a roadmap to reach these goals. After the assessment, the roadmap was used as a foundation for a test process improvement project. The test processes of all business units were in scope of the assessment. Each business unit provided one representative project for the assessment as a reference of the current situation.

The principal stakeholder was the manager of the international Marketing & Sales department. International projects were initiated by this department and overall day to day management of these project are in the hands of the members of a small unit of program managers. One of these program managers had accepted the assignment to improve the results of international projects and acted as the principal for the Test Process Improvement initiative. In addition, the steering committee comprised the head of corporate IT and the senior managers from each business unit.

All test managers and testers in the different business units would be affected by the results of the test process improvement initiative. They were involved in the project in the form of a reference group where the results of the test process assessment would be discussed and by whom improvement steps would be implemented.

8.3 Assess the current situation

The maturity of the existing test processes was assessed by verifying which of the Checkpoints that the BDTPI model provides, were fulfilled by the processes. When you are directly involved in the test process and are familiar with the BDTPI model, it is not hard to perform a self-assessment. If you're not familiar with the BDTPI model, it is recommended to have an external BDTPI expert assess your test process.

8.3.1 Interviews and document study provide the information needed about the test process

As external assessors, we were not familiar with the test processes we were supposed to evaluate. In order to find the information needed to decide which Checkpoints were fulfilled, we interviewed the persons who were involved in the test processes, and analyzed example documents. We interviewed multiple persons who were somehow involved in the test processes, not only since one person probably won't know every detail, but also to collect different perspectives and insights.

For the CNS business unit, the following roles were interviewed:
- Principal stakeholder (for getting information about Stakeholder Relations)
- Project manager (for getting information about Stakeholder Relations)
- Test manager (for getting information about Test Management)
- Tester (for getting information about Test Profession)
- Lead developer (for getting information about Stakeholder Relations and Test Profession for development tests)

For the MKT, ONI and PAY business units, the following roles were interviewed:
- Project manager (for getting information about Stakeholder Relations)
- Test manager (for getting information about Test Management)
- Tester (for getting information about Test Profession)

For the test organization, the following roles were interviewed:
- Test method responsible (for getting information about methodology practice)

8 The BDTPI Model has proven its value in practice

- Test environment responsible (for getting information about test environments).

Not all roles could provide enough information about each Key area, so in order to get answers about a specific Key area, not all roles are equally relevant. The BDTPI model already categorizes the Key areas in Stakeholder Relations, Test Management and Test Profession. The Key areas in the Stakeholder Relations category are typically relevant when interviewing principal stakeholders. Likewise, interviews of test managers should primarily focus on the Key areas in the Test Management category and the Key areas in the Test Profession category should be the primary focus when interviewing testers and test engineers.

Based on this categorization, we made an overview of which Key areas were relevant for each role.

Key area	Category	Test manager	Tester	Project manager	Principal stakeholder	Lead developer
Stakeholder commitment	SR	+		++	++	++
Degree of involvement	SR	+		++	++	++
Test strategy	SR	+		++	++	++
Test organization	SR	++		+	+	
Communication	SR	+		++	++	
Reporting	SR	+		++	++	
Test process management	TM	++	+	+		
Estimating and planning	TM	++	+	+		
Metrics	TM	++	+	+	+	
Defect management	TM	++	+	+		+
Testware management	TM	++	+	+		+
Methodology practice	TP	+	++			++
Tester professionalism	TP	+	++			++
Test case design	TP	+	++			++
Test tools	TP	+	++			++
Test environment	TP	+	++			++

Table 8.1: The importance of each Key area for the roles to be interviewed.

8.3 Assess the current situation

The test manager role is by nature highly relevant for all Key areas. However, it is hardly realistic to discuss all Key areas sufficiently in one interview. For this reason, we focused on obtaining the relevant information from interviews with other roles as much as possible. This way, we 'offloaded' the interview with the test managers as much as possible and only concentrated on information that we could not obtain in other interviews. For the lead developer, the Key areas in the Test Profession category were interesting specifically for the development tests.

Preparing the interviews was done by selecting the relevant Key areas for the role to be interviewed. We avoided using the Checkpoints as direct questions. Asking such questions directly would give unreliable answers in practice, since the essence of the Checkpoint is often not entirely understood by the persons interviewed. Also, it is too easy to just say "Yes" than having to admit the real answer would be "No."

Instead, we used a different approach: for Key areas that were moderately relevant for the role to be interviewed, we turned the statements for those Key areas into questions. For Key areas that were highly relevant, we turned the statements for the Controlled, Efficient and Optimizing levels into questions as well. This way, we assembled question lists for each role to be interviewed.

> **Example - Deriving interview questions from statements**
> The main statement for the Test case design Key area is: "Test case design directs test execution to search for defects according to the test strategy." A suitable question could be "How do you prepare for test execution so that you find defects according to the test strategy?" This question could be used for interviews were this Key area is considered moderately relevant.
> For Controlled, the statement is "The test cases make test execution repeatable and person independent." A suitable question could be "How do you ensure that the test execution is repeatable and person independent?" This question could be used for interviews were this Key area is considered highly relevant.
> For Efficient, the statement is "Designing test cases that focus on achieving a specific coverage provides a justified elaboration of the test strategy". A suitable question could be "How do you ensure that your test cases provide a variation of test coverage according the test strategy?" This question could be used for interviews were this Key area is considered highly relevant.
> For Optimizing, the statement is "Evaluation of test cases, test design techniques and defects increase test effectiveness." A suitable question could be "How do you see to that the test cases, test design techniques and defects increase test effectiveness?" This question could be used for interviews were this Key area is considered highly relevant.

It happened that the questions for Efficient and especially Optimizing were not understood by the person interviewed. If this person should have known (based on his role) and we got the impression that the test

8 The BDTPI Model has proven its value in practice

process was not Controlled anyway, we considered this as a symptom that the test process under investigation was not mature enough. In such case, we did not dig deeper into the relevant Key area, at least in that interview.

For each business unit, we analyzed the following documents for crosschecking with the answers we received from the interviews:
- Project plan
- Master test plan (including test strategy, per test level and overall)
- Test cases (together with related test basis, examples)
- Defect reports (examples)
- Progress reports (examples)
- Test reports (per test level and overall)
- Minutes of meeting (examples)

Based on the interviews and the document study, we made and collected notes per business unit and per Key area, across all roles. Based on these notes, we could relatively easily fill in the Checkpoints for each Key area.

8.3.2 The results are shown in the Test maturity matrix

The 'scores' of the individual test processes were shown in a Test maturity matrix for the test process of each business units. Additionally, a Checkpoint coverage score was provided, broken down in Controlled, Efficient and Optimizing, as well as the three Key area categories.

The Checkpoints also provide an excellent way to compare the different test processes. A 'worst-case' matrix was drafted that shows which Checkpoints all projects fulfilled. This matrix shows that any new test process would at least fulfill these Checkpoints. At the same time, a 'best-case' matrix was drafted that shows how many skills and experience is available in the entire organization. By sharing these skills across the business units and without having to enhance the skills in the organization, all business units could reach this score.

The Test maturity matrix (see figure on next page), most important issues and checkpoint coverage figures for the CNS business unit are shown here as an example. Similar reporting was done for the other business units.

In general, the test process was controlled but with a few issues. The most important issues were:
- Limited degree of involvement: a test manager was assigned to the project at start up time and he participated in the kick-off meeting where the overall approach was discussed. However, he was not further involved until the systems were delivered for testing, due to insufficient

8.3 Assess the current situation

	Initial				Controlled				Efficient				Optimizing		
1 Stakeholder commitment		1	2	3	4	1		2		3	1		2		3
2 Degree of involvement		1	2	3	4	1		2		3	1			2	
3 Test strategy		1	2	3	4	1		2		3	1			2	
4 Test organization			1	2	3	4	1		2		3	4	1	2	3
5 Communication		1	2	3	4	1		2		3	1			2	
6 Reporting		1		2		3	1		2		3	1		2	
7 Test process management		1	2	3	4	1		2		3	1			2	
8 Estimating and planning		1	2	3	4	1	2		3		4	1	2		3
9 Metrics			1		2		3	1	2		3	4	1		2
10 Defect management		1	2	3	4	1	2		3		4	1	2		3
11 Testware management		1	2	3	4	1		2		3	1	2		3	
12 Methodology practice		1		2		3	1	2		3		4	1		2
13 Tester professionalism		1	2	3	4	1	2		3		4	1	2		3
14 Test case design			1		2		3	1	2		3	4	1	2	3
15 Test tools		1		2		3	1	2		3		4	1	2	3
16 Test environment		1	2	3	4	1		2		3		4	1	2	3

Figure 8.1: Test maturity matrix for the test process within the CNS business unit.

time: the test manager was also responsible for two other test processes at the same time.

- Communication in the project was sufficient but informal. While everyone in the test team and the stakeholders were informed, the test team did not register minutes of meetings and could not trace back to decisions made in the past. The test team did provide insight into the product quality, but not about the process quality or project risks.
- Tester professionalism was limited: the testers were not sufficiently familiar with the method they applied. In the selection of testers for this project, testing skills were not sufficiently considered.
- The test environment was shared with other projects, which disturbed the test execution. Also, planned changes in the test environment had to be adjusted with other projects, which increased the lead-time for test execution.

Total Checkpoint coverage for Controlled (of 59)	44	75%
Checkpoint coverage for Controlled, Stakeholder Relations (of 23)	13	57%
Checkpoint coverage for Controlled, Test Management (of 19)	19	100%
Checkpoint coverage for Controlled, Test Profession (of 17)	12	71%
Total Checkpoint coverage for Efficient (of 57)	7	12%
Checkpoint coverage for Efficient, Stakeholder Relations (of 19)	3	16%
Checkpoint coverage for Efficient, Test Management (of 18)	4	22%
Checkpoint coverage for Efficient, Test Profession (of 20)	0	0%

Table 8.2: Coverage figures for the test process at the CNS business unit.

8 The BDTPI Model has proven its value in practice

Worst-case and best-case

The worst-case picture shows all Checkpoints that were fulfilled by all test processes. It shows the maturity of the organization as a whole and was mainly useful to demonstrate in which areas improvement was most needed (in relation to the improvement goals that were set).

The best-case picture shows all Checkpoints that are fulfilled by at least one of the processes. It shows what best practices are available within the organization so that if an improvement action is needed relevant experiences can easily be obtained.

Both best-case and worst-case are shown in the same figure.

Figure 8.2: Test maturity matrix for worst-case situation (red) and best-case (grey).

Total Checkpoint coverage for Controlled (of 59)	**19**	**32%**
Checkpoint coverage for Controlled, Stakeholder Relations (of 23)	5	22%
Checkpoint coverage for Controlled, Test Management (of 19)	6	32%
Checkpoint coverage for Controlled, Test Profession (of 17)	8	47%
Total Checkpoint coverage for Efficient (of 57)	**0**	**0%**
Checkpoint coverage for Efficient, Stakeholder Relations (of 19)	0	0%
Checkpoint coverage for Efficient, Test Management (of 18)	0	0%
Checkpoint coverage for Efficient, Test Profession (of 20)	0	0%

Table 8.3: Coverage figures for the worst-case situation.

Total Checkpoint coverage for Controlled (of 59)	**53**	**90%**
Checkpoint coverage for Controlled, Stakeholder Relations (of 23)	19	83%
Checkpoint coverage for Controlled, Test Management (of 19)	19	100%
Checkpoint coverage for Controlled, Test Profession (of 17)	15	88%
Total Checkpoint coverage for Efficient (of 57)	**10**	**18%**
Checkpoint coverage for Efficient, Stakeholder Relations (of 19)	5	26%
Checkpoint coverage for Efficient, Test Management (of 18)	5	28%
Checkpoint coverage for Efficient, Test Profession (of 20)	0	0%

Table 8.4: Coverage figures for the best-case situation.

8.4 Define improvements

When we discussed the findings of the current situation with the principal stakeholder, his initial response was that he wanted to improve all aspects of the test process: improve the quality of testing, reduce the time needed for testing and reduce the costs for testing. If no specific business driver is identified, or multiple business drivers together call for improving the test process, the base Clusters of the BDTPI model can be used. This clustering can be followed until the test process has reached a certain maturity level, like a controlled maturity level.

After further discussion with the principal stakeholder, the time driver was still considered dominant. For this reason, we applied the business-driven aspects of BDTPI. With the principal stakeholder, we agreed on prioritizing the Key areas as follows:
- *High:* Stakeholder commitment, Test strategy, Reporting, Test tools and Test environment.
- *Neutral:* Degree of involvement, Communication, Test process management, Estimating and planning, Metrics and Tester professionalism.
- *Low:* Test organization, Defect management, Testware management, Methodology practice and Test case design.

Note that we did not follow the prioritization as suggested in section 6.6.3 entirely. That prioritization is based on reduction of lead-time only and it would partially contradict with our goal of aligning the test processes and establishing the test policy. The principal stakeholder considered this customized prioritization more suitable to support both goals.

8 The BDTPI Model has proven its value in practice

Regarding the alignment of test processes from the different business units, the principal stakeholder defined the following goals:
1. An overall test policy was to be defined, that would be applicable for all business units. This test policy should address the following Key areas: Stakeholder commitment, Test strategy, Reporting, Test process management, Metrics and Methodology practice.
2. For each business unit, a test method specific for that business unit would be defined (or adapted). These methods would extend the test policy and would be applied by all test processes in the business units. These methods would cover all Key areas that are not covered by the test policy.
3. The maturity of all business unit specific test methods would be aligned (and kept aligned) in terms of Checkpoints to be fulfilled.

8.5 Make a plan of action

Based on the prioritization of Key areas, we created the following Clusters:

	Initial	Controlled				Efficient				Optimizing		
1 Stakeholder commitment		A	A	A	B	E	G	G	J	L	L
2 Degree of involvement		A	B	C	E	H	H	J	L		L
3 Test strategy		A	A	A	D	E	E	G	J		K
4 Test organization		B	E	E	F	J	J	K	K	L	M	M
5 Communication		B	C	C	D	F	F		J	M		M
6 Reporting		A		C	C	G	H		J	K		M
7 Test process management		A	A	B	B	G	H		J	K		M
8 Estimating and planning		B	B	C	C	G	H	I	I	K	L	L
9 Metrics		C		C		D	G	H	H	I	K		K
10 Defect management		B	B	C	E	G	G	I	K	L	M	M
11 Testware management		C	C	E	F	J		J	K	M	M	M
12 Methodology practice		D		E	F	G	I	K	K	M		M
13 Tester professionalism		D	D	E	E	G	G	I	I	K	K	M
14 Test case design		B	B		F	G	J	J	K	L	L	M
15 Test tools		D		D	D	E	F	F	H	K	L	L
16 Test environment		B	C	C	D	F	G	I	I	K	L	L

Figure 8.3: The specific Clusters used for improving the test process.

We built a roadmap by defining improvement stages (one stage for each Cluster A to M). In each stage, all missing Checkpoints belonging to the respective Cluster were to be improved. The BDTPI model provides improvement suggestions for this.

Each stage in the roadmap had two different approaches that were applied in parallel. The first approach was to establish a test policy. Checkpoints of Key areas that are included in the test policy were aligned and improved in workshops where stakeholders from all business units partici-

8.5 Make a plan of action

pated. We made agreements of how exactly these Checkpoints were to be improved in a uniform way.

The second approach was to align the business unit specific test methods with the test policy. For each business unit, an improvement path was defined that followed the stages of the roadmap. The test methods were aligned with the test policy and for Key areas that were not part of the test policy, improvement actions were defined to exchange experience for the remaining Key areas. This way, the business units could learn from each other's strengths, as well as adopt skills from external sources.

For each stage, improvement actions were defined for:
- Definition of the test policy and specific test methods, where the focus was on describing the improvements of the policy and methods (like enhancing the test method, instructions and guidelines)
- Implementation of the test policy and specific test methods, where the focus was on seeing to that the defined process could be used (like performing workshops and trainings, as well as defining templates)
- Governance of the test policy and specific test methods, where the focus was on verifying that the test method would be used as intended (like performing inspections, reviews and audits, as well as following up on compliance issues).

Tools for Implementation (like training materials) and Governance (like checklists) were to be developed together with the Definition activities, in parallel with roll-out in pilot projects in the respective stage. Business unit-wide implementation and governance could be rolled out in the stage after that.

In each stage, the time that testing would be on the critical path of the projects was measured and compared with the base line. This way, a decision could be made to which extent the business goal was met and if further test process improvement in the next stage would be necessary.

Initially, we had reported the Checkpoint coverage, broken down by Stakeholder relations, Test management and Test profession. Now that the Key areas were reprioritized, we felt that this was not meaningful anymore. Instead, we categorized the Key areas by priority and broke down the Checkpoint coverage accordingly.

The coverage figures were used as a baseline for the CNS business unit. Note that the total coverage figures for Controlled, Efficient and Optimizing, are the same as shown in the previous section. For the other business units, similar figures were calculated.

CNS business unit

Total Checkpoint coverage for Controlled (of 59)	44	75%
Checkpoint coverage for Controlled, Stakeholder Relations (of 18)	14	78%
Checkpoint coverage for Controlled, Test Management (of 23)	19	100%
Checkpoint coverage for Controlled, Test Profession (of 18)	12	71%
Total Checkpoint coverage for Efficient (of 57)	7	12%
Checkpoint coverage for Efficient, Stakeholder Relations (of 17)	0	0%
Checkpoint coverage for Efficient, Test Management (of 21)	7	33%
Checkpoint coverage for Efficient, Test Profession (of 19)	0	0%

Table 8.5: Baseline for coverage at the CNS business unit.

The organization already collected metrics from which we could calculate the test lead-time per project. We could calculate the same metric per business unit (average of all projects in that business unit over the last six months) and organization-wide (average of all business units over the last six months).

During the improvement project, we tracked these figures per business unit and organization-wide. The figures for the baseline and target for Test lead-time were:

Business unit	Baseline	Target
CNS	23%	12%
MKT	34%	17%
ONI	27%	14%
PAY	41%	21%
Organization	31%	16%

Table 8.6: Baseline for Test lead-time for the different business units and organization.

8.6 Implement actions

The exact actions to implement have a large dependency on the test method which is applied in the organization. Your organization will probably work according to a different test method than the organization in this case. Therefore we do not go in-depth on the actions implemented.

Some examples of the essence of actions that were implemented in our project are:
- Plan the test process more tightly, so that preparation and specification activities were taken off the critical path of the overall project.
- Specify and order test environments and changes in test environments in an early stage, reducing idle time before and during test execution.
- Increase stakeholder involvement in product risk analysis and test strategy to ensure that only important tests will be performed.
- Perform workshops, trainings and presentations to educate all testers and stakeholders involved about the test policy and business unit specific test processes (to the level that's relevant for them).
- Design better -physical- test cases, to accelerate test execution (which is, by its nature, always on the critical path).

8.7 Evaluate and redirect

During the improvement project, we measured and reported the following:

In each test process we measured the checklist coverage, categorized in High, Neutral and Low importance Key areas like we reported in tables 8 to 11. We used quick scans, i.e. small-scale assessments for this where we performed short interviews with the respective test managers, who backed up his answers by providing example documentation. The Checkpoints for the respective Clusters were in scope of the interviews. We considered this sufficiently detailed for this kind of assessment, as the test managers were already familiar with the test process improvement initiative.

The resulting values were reported by each test process as part of the test process evaluation.

As part of the improvement project, we aggregated these values across the test processes and reported the average checklist coverage per business unit, as well as average checklist coverage organization-wide.

Checkpoint coverage	CNS	MKT	ONI	PAY	Organization
Controlled, total	75%	54%	44%	69%	61%
Controlled, high	78%	44%	33%	61%	54%
Controlled, neutral	65%	43%	78%	74%	65%
Controlled, low	83%	78%	67%	72%	75%
Efficient, total	12%	2%	0%	5%	5%
Efficient, high	0%	0%	0%	6%	2%
Efficient, neutral	33%	5%	0%	10%	12%
Efficient, low	0%	0%	0%	0%	0%

Table 8.7: Baseline of all Checkpoint coverage figures per business unit and organization.

8 The BDTPI Model has proven its value in practice

In each test process, we also measured the amount of days that test execution was on the critical path of the project, as a percentage of the total lead-time of the project. In the improvement project, we aggregated these values as well, and reported the average values per business unit, and organization-wide. An example can be found in table 8.8.

Business unit	Baseline	Current	Target
CNS	23%	20%	12%
MKT	34%	28%	17%
ONI	27%	22%	14%
PAY	41%	35%	21%
Organization	31%	26%	16%

Table 8.8: All Test lead-time figures per business unit and organization.

After six months in the improvement project, we had improved the test process to Cluster F. The test policy and specific test methods were ready, but the test lead-time for the organization was reduced with around 30% rather than the goal of 50%. The CNS and PAY business units did not reach their goals, since they could not get sufficient grip on the test environments.

Based on the costs that further overall test process improvement would require, the principal stakeholder made the decision that the test process improvement initiative was ready: it would not be cost-effective to continue improving in the way we were doing.

For the CNS and PAY business units, an extra focused effort would be made to improve the test environments, so they would reach their goals after all. The test process improvement initiative was hereby discharged. All-in-all the principal stakeholder, as well as almost all other people involved, were enthusiastic about the achievements of the Test Process Improvement initiative that enabled them to reduce the lead-time of their projects and at the same time improve the testing which enabled the developers to deliver higher quality systems.

Appendices

A Appendix: Maturity of the use of test tools

A.1 Maturity in the use of test tools

The Key area Test tools describes the maturity of the test process with respect to the use of tools that support this process. These tools can be any type of tool: test tools specifically built for testing purposes; other tools that support the tester in preparing and executing tests; or management tools that support the test manager in planning and controlling the processes. All these separate types of tools have different objectives and therefore differ in the way they support the test process. In other words, each type of tool has a different contribution to the business case of testing.

Because the maturity level for Test tools is independent of the tools that are actually used, this maturity level will always be a generalization. First of all, the maturity level for Test tools applies to all tools that are being used and therefore does not distinguish the maturity in the use of the individual tools. For example, if a tool for automated test execution and a test management tool are both used, a mature way of using the automated test execution tool does not automatically mean that the test management tool is also used in a mature way. Secondly, it does not take into account the different objectives of the various types of tools. A test management tool for instance should be used to maximize insight into quality and progress, while a tool for automated test execution is used to minimize the effort and lead time for test execution.

In order to deal with the different types of tools used, tool-specific maturity stages are used in addition to maturity levels. These maturity stages allow for more specific assessment and give more particular guidance for improving the way a tool is used. Tool-specific maturity stages take into account both the objectives of a tool and how the use of a tool should be incorporated in the test process. The implication is that improvements in tool usage are not only concerned with how to improve the way the tools support the test process, but also with how to improve the test process to maximize the effect of using the tools.

A.1.1 Tool-specific maturity stages

The tool-specific maturity stages are based on the way a tool can contribute to the different aspects of the business case for testing: the use of a tool is considered to be more mature when it contributes to more aspects. A specific tool can contribute to aspects relating to its objectives and capabilities, therefore more general maturity stages are used. These maturity stages describe the focus of the use of the tool, so that a broader focus implies a more mature usage of the tool.

- *Tool-focused maturity*
  The use of a tool is considered tool-focused when it is based on the functionality it provides. The tool is seen as a means of supporting or improving specific activities, but its impact on other activities within the test process is not considered.
- *Process-focused maturity*
  When the effect of the use of a tool on all relevant activities within the test process and the effect of other activities on the user of the tool are considered, the maturity is process-focused. In this stage, the use of the tool becomes more integral to the test process, thus increasing its contribution to the business case of testing.
- *Goal-focused maturity*
  When the use of a tool is aimed at maximizing its contribution to the business case of testing, the maturity is goal-focused. In this stage, the tool is considered a strategic means of reaching specific test goals.

A.1.2 Application of the tool-specific maturity stages

Because a higher tool-specific maturity means that the use of the tool contributes to more aspects of the business case of testing, improving tool-specific maturity implies Business Driven Test Process Improvement. But the only direct relationship between the general BDTPI maturity levels and the tool-specific maturity stages is the relationship between the goal-focused stage and the Optimizing level. The growth to a goal-focused maturity equals the growth to an Optimizing level in the Key area Test tools. This applies to any tool introduced on the basis of a positive business case for use during testing.

There is no direct relationship between the individual tools that are used and the maturity for Test tools; there is no requirement for a specific type of tool to be used in order to reach a higher maturity. This is due to the fact that the reason a tool is not used can be influenced by factors other than the test maturity itself. The application being tested can have a Graphical User Interface (GUI) that is not suitable for the use of automated test execution tools; the volume of regression tests can be too small to be efficiently automated; the organization may not be large enough to implement an advanced test management tool; or there may be no need to do performance testing. Having evaluated these factors is maturity in itself, so not having a tool might be more mature than having one!

The tool-specific maturity stages apply to the use of the tools, not to their implementation. In the lifecycle model for tool implementation, maturity assessment and improvement become regular activities during the Operation phase, illustrated below in Figure A.1.

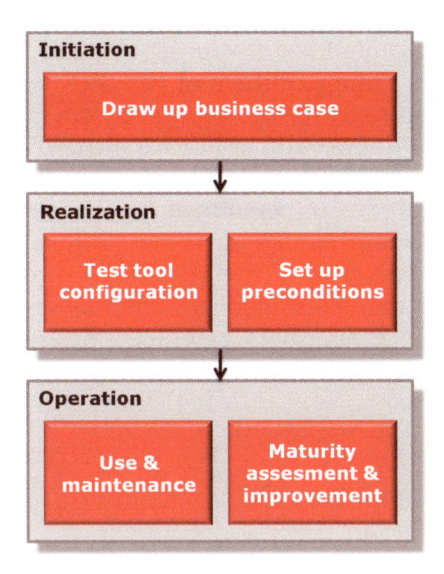

Figure A.1: Lifecycle model for tool implementation.

A.1.3 Types of tools

The tool-specific maturity stages apply especially to the test tools that have been purposely developed for testing. In the following section, the maturity stages of three types of test tools are considered:
- Test management tools
- Automated test execution tools
- Performance test tools

These types of test tools have been chosen because they are the most commonly used, but the tool-specific maturity stages are not limited to these three types of tools. The tool-specific maturity stages can also be extended to other types of tools.

In determining the tool-specific maturity there is no difference between commercially available tools, open-source/freeware tools or internally developed tools. The aspects of costs related to acquisition and maintenance are part of the individual business cases for the tools and have no impact on the tool-specific maturity.

A.2 Test management tools

Test management tools are applications for storing and managing tests, test results and defects. These are provided either in composite or separate applications for defect management and testware management.

A Appendix: Maturity of the use of test tools

By nature, test management tools are product-centered; their primary functionality is to store the products of the activities of a tester. When relating these products to the test process, they are mainly produced during the Specification and Execution phases. One of the big advantages of a test management tool is its use in the Control phase, where its reporting capabilities support monitoring quality and progress.

While the support of a test management tool in the Control phase applies to a single project, it can also provide metrics over multiple projects. This is a strong argument to use a test management tool as widely as possible.

Figure A.2 below depicts the main products of the test process that are covered by test management tools and indicates possible relationships with other types of tools.

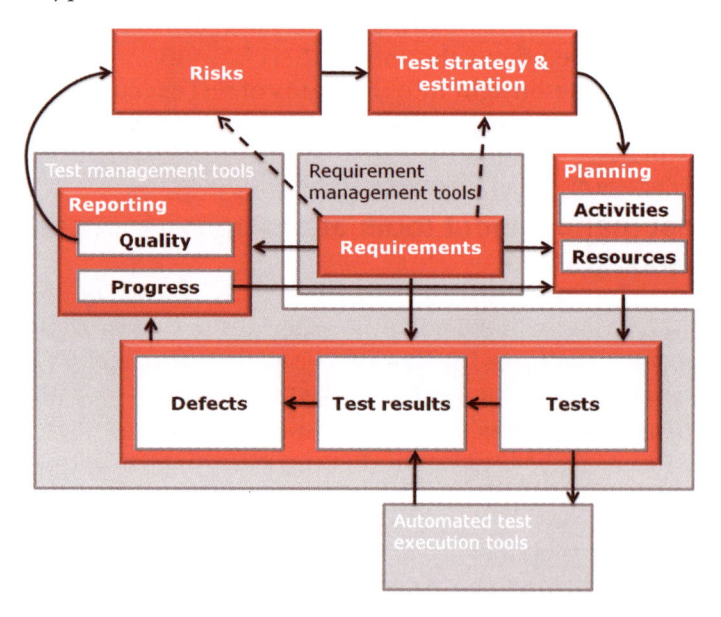

Figure A.2: Products of the test process that are covered by test management tools.

The coverage of test products in Figure 2 represents test management tools as defined in this appendix. This definition is based on the typical use of test management. It is noted that the ideal test management tool should also include support for risk management, test strategy, estimation and resource planning.

Because of their inherent purpose, using test management tools is very beneficial for the maturity of the Key areas Testware management, Defect management and Reporting. They also play a key role in producing metrics, making a test management tool an Enabler for the Key area Metrics.

A.2.1 Test management tools at a tool-focused maturity stage

The use of a test management tool is considered tool-focused when it is primarily used as storage of the products of the tester; either only defects or defects as well as tests and test results. This does not mean that at this stage there are no processes concerning these products, but that these processes focus only on the administration and maintenance of the products. For example, when there is a defect procedure in place, even if it is supported by a workflow within the tool, this still only focuses on the defect itself.

At this stage the test management tool already provides substantial benefits, mainly because it provides a single source of information and any information retrieved from the tool is therefore up-to-date. Because of this, the tool provides insight into the status of test execution and defects, and therefore importantly contributes to the 'Risk' aspect of the business case for testing.

A.2.2 Test management tools at a process-focused maturity stage

At the process-focused maturity stage, a test management tool is not only used for storing the products, but also as a source for both quality and progress reporting. The reports produced with the test management tool include statuses and priorities for test specification, test execution and defects. At this stage, it is essential that the reporting is used as input for control; scheduling of next steps is also based on information reported with the tool.

Because at this stage a test management tool has an important role in exerting control, its use has a direct influence on the timely completion of a test project, making the tool also contribute to the 'Time' aspect of the business case for testing.

A.2.3 Test management tools at a goal-focused maturity stage

The test management tool at the goal-focused maturity stage is used to provide insight into the coverage of requirements and risks. This applies to both the execution and specification phases.

When this is achieved, the test management tool is used to determine if specific test goals have been achieved. In this case, reporting focuses not on numbers of test cases or defects, but on the coverage and coverage status of test goals, risks and/or requirements. It is much more powerful to be able to report that "we have tested X requirements and found blocking

A Appendix: Maturity of the use of test tools

defects for Y of them" than to report "we have executed Z test cases and found Q blocking defects".
Because at this stage the tool's information is related to the test goals, the tool also contributes to the 'Result' aspect of the business case for testing.

A.3 Automated test execution tools

Automated test execution tools automatically execute functional tests. The most common tools in this category are Record & Playback test tools that have the capability to interact with objects on the GUI of an application. This interaction not only consists of entering test data, but also retrieving data, so that checks can be performed.
The most common reason for using a Record & Playback test tool is to reduce costs. This type of tool will indeed reduce costs for test execution, but there is more involved in the use of a Record & Playback test tool than test execution alone. Whether the use of such a tool actually reduces costs depends on the costs for implementation and maintenance and the savings while using the automated tests. The costs for maintenance are recurring and depend on the frequency of changes in the application that is tested. The savings are also recurring, but depend on the frequency of use of the automated tests. Each of these aspects has a relationship with the complexity of the application, the ability of the tool to interact with the GUI of the application, and the volume of tests to be automated.
The reduction of costs should be considered in the business case for implementing a Record & Playback test tool. However, if the tool does not contribute to the 'Costs' aspect it could be still considered worthwhile because of its contribution to other aspects, such as 'Time' and 'Result'.
For the maturity stages for this type of test tool, the Costs aspect is disregarded because it is only indirectly influenced by the maturity of the use of the tool. There is, however, a relationship between the implemented technical solution and the costs of maintenance. There are three technical solutions for using these tools:

- *Record & Playback*
  Individual test cases are recorded with the tool with the intention to automatically execute them exactly the same as they are recorded. When the application and test cases change, maintenance must be carried out on large groups of toolscripts, making this an expensive activity.
- *Data Driven*
  Toolscripts are recorded, but test data is retrieved from external data sources like files or a database. During test execution, a toolscript is repeated for different sets of test data. This reduces the number of toolscripts and shifts the maintenance of test data to the external data sources, making it a more maintenance-friendly technical solution.

- *Keyword Driven*
  The automated test is driven from external data sources, which contain not only the test data, but also keywords that state which test action to execute. In the tool, a processor is built that interprets the keywords and calls the appropriate functions with the accompanying test data. This creates a modular set-up of the technical solution and the maintenance of test cases is shifted to the external data sources, resulting in the most maintenance-friendly technical solution.

By implementing the right technical solution, the costs of maintenance can be reduced. But so can the lead time for maintenance. Having a short lead time for maintenance is essential to be able to execute the automated tests as soon as possible after a new release of an application has been delivered.

Because automated test execution depends heavily on the ability to trace and maintain test cases, the use of these tools strongly relies on the maturity of the Testware management key area.

A.3.1 Automated test execution tools at a tool-focused maturity stage

At a tool-focused maturity stage, the maintenance and use of automated tests is treated as a separate process, one that supports the test process, but is executed in parallel.

At this stage, maintenance typically commences when the Execution phase has already started. The actual trigger for doing maintenance is having to execute the automated tests. Any need for adjustments to the automated tests is uncovered when running them.

As a result, maintenance of the automated tests becomes a time-consuming activity that prevents the running of the automated tests on time. So while the actual time spent on execution of the test cases is reduced, the automated tests do not provide a reduction in lead time. Because of that, the tool at this stage does not contribute to the 'Time' aspect of the business case for testing.

Because the tool is used to execute tests that would otherwise not have been executed, it increases test coverage and therefore contributes to the 'Risk' aspect of the business case for testing.

A.3.2 Automated test execution tools at a process-focused maturity stage

When the maintenance of automated tests has already been addressed during the Preparation and Specification phases of the test process, the use of Automated test execution tools is considered to be process-focused.

A Appendix: Maturity of the use of test tools

During the Preparation phase, the first information is gathered to determine the impact of the changes in the application and tests cases on the automated tests. In the Specification phase, the test cases are maintained and a start is made to maintain the technical solution. The majority of the maintenance is done during the Execution phase because, in most cases, the availability of the new release of the application is required to do this. But, because of early involvement, this is accelerated, ensuring the availability of correctly-running automated tests as soon as possible.

The process-focused stage for Automated test execution tools shows an early availability of automated tests. This means that the automated tests will result in a reduction in lead time, making it contribute to the 'Time' aspect of the business case for testing, in addition to the 'Risk' aspect.

A.3.3 Automated test execution tools at a goal-focused maturity stage

The use of Automated test execution tools is goal-focused when the maintenance and use is integrated into the planning and estimation of the entire test process and is part of the progress and quality reporting. In other words, automated tests are fully incorporated into Planning and Control.

When automated tests are considered during the Planning phase, their contribution to the test goals is taken into account. Additionally, the successful running of automated tests becomes a means of achieving those test goals. Therefore, Automated test execution tools contribute to the 'Result' aspect of the business case for testing at this maturity stage in addition to the 'Risk' and 'Time' aspects.

A.4 Performance test tools

Performance test tools simulate large numbers of simultaneous users of an application, in order to test the performance of the application under load or stress.

This type of tool typically bypasses the GUI and interacts with the application on the network protocol level, by sending network calls to the server and retrieving the corresponding response. This allows for a large number of users to be simulated on a single machine. Typical measurements provided during testing are response times, the time it takes between the call to be sent and the response to return, and resource usage on the infrastructure during testing. These measurements are gathered during test execution to determine if they meet the requirements.

For applications that have online user interaction and many simultaneous users, using a performance test tool is the only way to execute a performance test. The tool thus becomes a prerequisite to producing a result.

However, using such a tool does not automatically mean that the results are meaningful. Producing a meaningful result requires special attention. One of the main influences on the significance of the results is the test environment. This should be representative of the production environment in terms of hardware resources as well as volumes of data in the databases. This results in a relationship between the use of this type of tool and the maturity level of the Key area 'Test Environments'.

The other main influence is the performance test that is executed. The applied load should be comparable to the load that will occur in the production situation. The quality of the executed performance test is part of the maturity stage of the use of Performance test tools.

Performance testing by itself is an expensive type of testing, mostly because of the prerequisites of the test environment. It can also be time-consuming due to setting up the test environment, preparing the tool scripts and test data, and analyzing the test results. Furthermore, performance testing is most meaningful when the application has passed the functional testing, making it one of the lasts tests to be executed. Any delay resulting from previous tests has an impact on the success of performance testing. This means that there is a strong relationship with the maturity of the area Test strategy - the ability to translate the importance of the quality characteristic 'Performance' to the right emphasis on performance testing.

A.4.1 Performance test tools at a tool-focused maturity stage

When the main focus of a performance test is getting a Performance test tool to work, the maturity of its use is tool-focused. Because of the way these tools work, a thorough technical understanding of both the tool, as well as the application, is needed to be able to create working toolscripts. This often leads to the situation where this becomes the primary target, rather than focusing on executing a meaningful test. Similarly, there is little or no attention to what should be measured in order to validate if the performance requirements are being met. The test results then provide great amounts of data with little actual information about the actual performance in relation to the required performance.

When the focus lies too much on the tool and the test does not provide meaningful results, the use of a performance test tool does not really contribute to the business case of testing.

A.4.2 Performance test tools at a process-focused maturity stage

The use of a Performance test tool is process-focused when, prior to starting to use the tool, the test organization has specified the following; how the performance test must be executed in order to be meaningful, and what should be measured in order to demonstrate that the application has met its performance requirements.

Typically, at this maturity stage, the specification of the performance tests is based on the defined performance requirements. This does not automatically mean that all performance risks are covered; performance requirements tend to be incomplete and they do not take into account the technical architecture of the application, which may introduce specific performance risks.

At this stage of maturity, the performance test tool contributes to the 'Results' aspect of the business case of testing because the tests prove that the performance requirements have (or have not) been met. This does not mean that the tool does not contribute to the 'Risk' aspect, but its contribution to this aspect is limited because the performance test will only cover the risks that are covered by the requirements.

A.4.3 Performance test tools at a goal-focused maturity stage

At the goal-focused maturity stage, the performance tests are planned by specifying test goals that are based on performance risks. These risks can affect:

- the business; inadequate performance results in damage to business operations,
- the user perception; inadequate performance results in unsatisfied or unproductive users; or
- the technical operation of the application; there are components in the architecture that, if they cannot handle the load, will influence performance or even availability in a significant way.

By identifying performance risks from all these three points of view, the associated test goals will give greater coverage than by focusing on requirements alone.

Planning the actual performance tests involves considering the identified performance risks against the time and costs involved in testing them. This maturity stage of performance testing ensures that there is an adequate coverage of the performance risks. Reporting on performance tests involves the results of the executed performance tests, but also reporting on the performance risks that have not been covered by executing a performance test.

Because, at this stage, the use of a performance test tool is based on performance risks, it contributes to the 'Risks' aspect of the business case of performance testing, in addition to the 'Results' aspect. This implies that in a risked-based testing approach, only a goal-focused use of a performance test tool produces a valuable performance test.

B Appendix: Creating new Clusters

B.1 Introduction

To improve the test process and take it to a higher level of maturity it is necessary to implement improvement measures. The measures you need to take do not only depend on the current state of maturity, but also depend on the improvement goals that need to be reached. To support the improvement process the Business Driven TPI model provides a step by step approach, where each step is described in a Cluster. A Cluster combines a limited set of Key areas and a limited number of Checkpoints belonging to that Key area.

As described in Chapter 6 the goals for improvement can be various and they affect the composition of the Clusters. Specific business drivers, or in some situations improvement drivers from within the test process itself, implicate a rearrangement of the Key areas into different categories of priority. With that there will be a necessary shift in the improvement measures and activities. This appendix describes how to create new Clusters. The starting point for this are the base Clusters as described in Chapter 3.

B.2 Cost reduction as an example

For a better understanding the business driver 'cost reduction' is worked out as an example in this appendix.

Note that the preceding steps, described in Chapter 6, already have been taken. These steps are:

1. The business driver has been defined. In our cost reduction example: "Provide a good return on (IT enabled) business investments".
2. The related IT goal has been defined: In our example: "Improve IT's cost efficiency".
3. For Test Process Improvement this means: "Reduce the cost of testing".
4. The Key areas have been categorized into categories that support the improvement goals to a High, Neutral or Low degree, leading to the following categories:

B Appendix: Creating new Clusters

High	Neutral	Low
Degree of involvement	Communication	Stakeholder commitment
Test strategy	Test process management	Reporting
Test organization	Estimating & planning	Metrics
Defect management	Testware management	Test environment
Test tools	Methodology practice	
	Tester professionalism	
	Test case design	

Important: The above described categories and their Key areas may not be applicable to your specific situation. It is always necessary to judge and use the tables consciously and adapt where applicable.

B.3 Re-clustering

The categorized Key areas and their Checkpoints need to be worked out in new Clusters. The basis for the new Clusters is the base Cluster arrangement in Chapter 3. The Clusters are named A, B, C etc. The first step to grow from Initial to Controlled maturity is Cluster A.

	Initial	Controlled			Efficient			Optimizing		
1 Stakeholder commitment	A	B	B	C	F	H	H	K	M	M
2 Degree of involvement	A	B	C	E	H	H	J	L		L
3 Test strategy	A	A	B	E	F	F	H	K		L
4 Test organization	A	D	D	E	I	I	J	J	K	L	L
5 Communication	B	C	C	D	F	F	J	M		M
6 Reporting	A		C		C	F	G	G	K		K
7 Test process management	A	A	B	B	G	H	J	K		M
8 Estimating and planning	B	B	C	C	G	H	I	I	K	L	L
9 Metrics	C		C		D	G	H	H	I	K		K
10 Defect management	A	A	B	D	F	F	H	J	K	L	L
11 Testware management	B	B	D	E	I		I	J	L	L	L
12 Methodology practice	C		D		E	F	H	J	J	M		M
13 Tester professionalism	D	D	E	E	G	G	I	I	K	K	M
14 Test case design	A		A		E	F	I	I	J	K	K	M
15 Test tools	E		E		E	F	G	G	I	L	M	M
16 Test environment	C	D	D	E	G	H	J	J	L	M	M

Figure B.1: Base Clusters of Key areas and Checkpoints.

The base Clusters show that all Checkpoints belong to a specific Cluster. For example: in the Stakeholder commitment Key area, one Checkpoint at the Controlled level belongs to Cluster A, two Checkpoints at the level Controlled belong to Cluster B and one Checkpoint belongs to Cluster C.

B.3.1 Categorized Key areas

In our example, the categories (High, Neutral and Low) for the business driver 'cost reduction' are illustrated in the Test maturity matrix below):

	H	N	L	Initial	Controlled			Efficient			Optimizing		
1 Stakeholder commitment			x		A	B	B	C	F	H	H	K	M	M
2 Degree of involvement	x				A	B	C	E	H	H	J	L		L
3 Test strategy	x				A	A	B	E	F	F	H	K		L
4 Test organization	x				A	D	D	E	I	I	J	J	K	L	L
5 Communication		x			B	C	C	D	F	F	J	M		M
6 Reporting			x		A		C		C	F	G	G	K		K
7 Test process management	x				A	A	B	B	G		H	J	K		M
8 Estimating and planning	x				B	B	C	C	G	H	I	I	K	L	L
9 Metrics			x		C		C		D	G	H	H	I	K		K
10 Defect management	x				A	A	B	D	F	F	H	J	K	L	L
11 Testware management		x			B	B	D	E	I		I	J	L	L	L
12 Methodology practice		x			C		D		E	F	H	J	J	M		M
13 Tester professionalism		x			D	D	E	E	G	G	I	I	K	K	M
14 Test case design		x			A		A		E	F	I	I	J	K	K	M
15 Test tools	x				E	E	E	E	F	G	G	I	L	M	M
16 Test environment			x		C	D	D	E	G	H	J	J	L	M	M

Figure B.2: Categorized Key areas for the business-driver 'cost reduction'.

B.3.2 Shift Checkpoints to new Clusters

Following the defined categories, the next step is to shift the Key areas and Checkpoints:
- Key areas and Checkpoints with 'H' (High) will shift to a Cluster with a preceding letter of the alphabet: Checkpoints in Cluster A will stay where they are, Checkpoints in Cluster B will shift to Cluster A, Checkpoints in Cluster C will shift to Cluster B etc.
- Key areas and Checkpoints in the 'N' (Neutral) category will **not** shift from Clusters.
- Key areas and Checkpoints in the 'L' (Low) category will shift to a Cluster with the next letter in the alphabet: Checkpoints in Cluster A will shift to Cluster B, Checkpoints from Cluster B will shift to Cluster C, Checkpoints in Cluster C will shift to Cluster D etc. Checkpoints in Cluster M will remain in this Cluster.

B Appendix: Creating new Clusters

This leads to a new arrangement of Clusters in the Test maturity matrix:

	H	N	L	Initial	Controlled				Efficient			Optimizing		
1 Stakeholder commitment		x			B	C	C	D	G	I	I	L	M	M
2 Degree of involvement	x				A	A	B	D	G	G	I	K		K
3 Test strategy	x				A	A	A	D	E	E	G	J		K
4 Test organization	x				A	C	C	D	H	H	I	J	K	K
5 Communication		x			B	C	C	D	F	F	J	M		M
6 Reporting			x		B		D	D	G	H	H	L		L
7 Test process management	x				A	A	B	B	G	H	J	K		M
8 Estimating and planning	x				B	B	C	C	G	H	I	K	L	L
9 Metrics		x			D		D	E	H	I	I	J	L	L
10 Defect management	x				A	A	A	C	E	E	G	I	J	K	K
11 Testware management	x				B	B	D	E	I	I	J	L	L	L
12 Methodology practice	x				C		D	E	F	H	J	J	M		M
13 Tester professionalism	x				D	D	E	E	G	G	I	I	K	K	M
14 Test case design	x				A	A		E	F	I	I	J	K	K	M
15 Test tools	x				D		D	D	E	F	F	H	K	L	L
16 Test environment			x		D	E	E	F	H	I	K	K	M	M	M

Figure B.3: Categorized Key areas and new Clusters.

Note that after re-arranging the Checkpoints the Key area 'Stakeholder commitment' (as an example) has no Checkpoints in Cluster A, because of its lower priority. In practice this means that improvement of this Key area starts after the improvements of the Key areas belonging to Cluster A.

B.3.3 Taking dependencies into account

The base Cluster arrangement takes dependencies between Key areas and Checkpoints into account. A Checkpoint that is a prerequisite for another Checkpoint to be met, has been positioned in an earlier or the same Cluster. This interdependency between Checkpoints may be violated as a result of shifting Checkpoints to other Clusters. When this is the case, the dependency must be reinstated, by shifting a Checkpoint once more. In principal, Checkpoints that are a prerequisite for another Checkpoint but ended up in a Cluster with a priority which is too low, are shifted to the left to the first Cluster in which it satisfies the dependency.

In this section the short notation [Key area].[Maturity level].[Checkpoint] is used to refer to individual Checkpoints. The Maturity level is indicated by a "C" for the Controlled level, an "E" for the Efficient level and an "O" for the Optimizing level.

> **Example - Short Checkpoint notation**
> The Checkpoint 7.C.3 refers to the third Checkpoint at the Controlled level of the seventh Key area in the Test maturity matrix. This is the "Each test activity is monitored and when necessary adjustments are initiated" Checkpoint of the Test process management Key area.

B.3 Re-clustering

The following base cluster Checkpoint dependencies need to be maintained:

… is a prerequisite for …		Rationale:
1.C.1	2.C.1	1.C.1 addresses the identification of the principal stakeholder.
		2.C.1 states that the test assignment is negotiated with the principal stakeholder.
1.C.1	3.C.1	3.C.1 states that the principal stakeholder agrees with the test strategy.
1.C.1	7.C.2	7.C.2 states that the test plan is agreed with the principal stakeholder.
2.C.1	7.C.1	2.C.1 addresses some elements that need to be included in the test plan mentioned in 7.C.1.
8.C.2	7.C.3	8.C.2 identifies test activities, 7.C.3 states that test activities need to be monitored.
1.E.1	3.E.1	1.E.1 addresses identifying the stakeholders, 3.E.1 assumes they are known.

Please note that the table above does not contain all dependencies within the base Cluster arrangement. It contains only those hat can be violated by shifting Checkpoints. Two types of dependencies can be disregarded since they can never be violated by creating new Clusters.
1. In several Key areas an implicit dependency exists within a Maturity level. For instance, in the Controlled level of Test process management Checkpoint 7.C.2 ("The test plan is agreed with the principal stakeholder") in Cluster A of the base Cluster arrangement is a prerequisite for 7.C.4 ("The test plan is agreed with the relevant stakeholders") in Cluster B. Since they are Checkpoints of the same Key area they can never occur in a different order. This is also the case for 2 Checkpoints of a Key area in the same Cluster. They will stay in the same Cluster.
2. Another type of a dependency that can not be affected by shifting Checkpoints is Checkpoints with 'a Cluster in between'. For example, Checkpoint 3.C.2 ("The test strategy is based on a product risk analysis") in Cluster A can never be shifted past Checkpoint 1.C.4 ("The principal stakeholder is responsible for a documented product risk analysis (the input for the test strategy)") in Cluster C.

B Appendix: Creating new Clusters

This leads to the following arrangement of Checkpoints over the Clusters:

	H	N	L	Initial		Controlled			Efficient				Optimizing	
1 Stakeholder commitment		x		A	C	C	D	E	I	I	L	M	M
2 Degree of involvement	x			A	A	B	D	G	G	I	K		K
3 Test strategy	x			A	A	A	D	E	E	G	J		K
4 Test organization	x			A	C	C	D	H	H	I	I	J	K	K
5 Communication		x		B	C	C	D	F	F	J	M		M
6 Reporting			x	B		D	D	G	H	H	L		L
7 Test process management		x		A	A	B	B	G	H	J	K		M
8 Estimating and planning		x		B	B	C	C	G	H	I	I	K	L	L
9 Metrics			x	D		D	E	H	I	I	J	L		L
10 Defect management	x			A	A	A	C	E	E	G	I	J	K	K
11 Testware management		x		B	B	D	E	I		I	J	L	L	L
12 Methodology practice		x		C		D	E	F	H	J	J	M		M
13 Tester professionalism		x		D	D	E	E	G	G	I	I	K	K	M
14 Test case design		x		A		A	E	F	I	I	J	K	K	M
15 Test tools	x				D		D	D	E	F	F	H	K	L	L
16 Test environment			x	D	E	E	F	H	I	K	K	M	M	M

Figure B.4: Final Clusters for the business driver 'cost reduction'.

Checkpoint 1.C.1 has moved from Cluster B back to Cluster A again, and Checkpoint 1.E.1 shifts two Clusters to the left to remain in the same Cluster as Checkpoint 3.E.1.

B.3.4 Balancing the Clusters

After the Checkpoints have been shifted from one Cluster to another, the final step is to balance the Clusters. In our example for Cost driven improvement the new Clusters contain the following Checkpoints:

B.3 Re-clustering

| | Checkpoints / Cluster ||||
	C	E	O	Total
Cluster A	14	0	0	14
Cluster B	9	0	0	9
Cluster C	10	0	0	10
Cluster D	17	0	0	17
Cluster E	8	6	0	14
Cluster F	1	6	0	7
Cluster G	0	9	0	9
Cluster H	0	10	0	10
Cluster I	0	17	0	17
Cluster J	0	7	3	10
Cluster K	0	2	14	16
Cluster L	0	0	12	12
Cluster M	0	0	12	12

Figure B.5: Number of Checkpoints within the new Clusters.

In this new situation Cluster A contains 14 Checkpoints, Cluster B has 9 Checkpoints etc. Cluster E (and others) has Checkpoints from different levels of maturity: 8 from the Controlled level and 6 from Efficient level. This is caused by the fact that a further step in improvement (in our cost driven example: making the test process more and more 'cheaper') may also require Checkpoints from other levels of maturity.

Clusters D contains relatively many Checkpoints, as do Cluster I and K, Cluster F contains few Checkpoints. Depending on the specific situation in the assessed organization or project, consider to shift Checkpoints in such a manner that the number of Checkpoints per Cluster gets spread evenly across the Clusters.

C Appendix: Backwards compatibility

C.1 Introduction

In the past decade many organizations have used the TPI model [16] to improve their test process or to gain a clearer view on their current test activities and maturity. Although the Business Driven TPI model has been changed on some aspects, it is still possible to use the results of former assessments and improvement processes and proceed with Business Driven TPI. For instance, you may want to analyze trends in maturity growth or you want to perform a re-assessment after you have done one or more assessments with the original TPI model.

C.2 Transform assessment information to the BDTPI model

If the original TPI model has been used and information from an assessment is still available it is advisable to use this data to compose a new Business Driven TPI matrix. However: some of the Key areas and Checkpoints are new or have changed in such a way that relevant information may not be available. In that case, perform a quick assessment (just a few interviews, aimed at specific questions and study a few documents) to obtain answers to the missing questions. The new Test maturity matrix can then be the starting point for a re-assessment, performed entirely with the Business Driven TPI Key areas and Checkpoints.

C.3 Transform the original TPI matrix into the Business Driven TPI matrix

Compared to the situation described above it is more likely that the detailed information is not available anymore, but there still are reports containing a TPI Test maturity matrix, illustrating the levels of maturity. In that case you may want to use these matrices to spot trends in maturity growth. The following steps will guide you through this conversion.

C.3.1 Groups of Key areas

In Chapter 3.2 we explained that the Key areas in Business Driven TPI are grouped according to their importance for:

C Appendix: Backwards compatibility

Group	Key areas
Stakeholder Relations	1 Stakeholder commitment 2 Degree of involvement 3 Test strategy 4 Test organization 5 Communication 6 Reporting
Test Management	7 Test process management 8 Estimating and planning 9 Metrics 10 Defect management 11 Testware management
Test Profession	12 Methodology practice 13 Tester professionalism 14 Test case design 15 Test tools 16 Test environment

Table C.1: Grouping of Key areas.

We use this grouping of the Test maturity matrix to be able to make a smooth translation between the original TPI model and Business Driven TPI. This is not the level of detail you need to pinpoint adequate or specific improvement measures, but it will help to spot trends and provide stakeholders with management information. It will show how the maturity of the test process has developed. It also shows where, on these group levels, improvement measures are necessary to reach required goals.

C.3.2 Two examples of TPI maturity

To explain the conversion method we use two examples of a Test maturity matrix that was produced in an assessment using the original TPI model as the start of an improvement project.

Example A comes from a rather immature test process. The Key areas Moment of involvement, Metrics and Defect management are at a Controlled level. The other Key areas still need improvement to take the process to the Controlled level.

C.3 Transform the original TPI matrix into the Business Driven TPI matrix

Key area	0	1	2	3	4	5	6	7	8	9	10	11	12	13
		\multicolumn{5}{c	}{Controlled}	\multicolumn{4}{c	}{Efficient}	\multicolumn{3}{c	}{Optimizing}
1 Test strategy		A					B				C		D	
2 Life-cycle model		A			B									
3 Moment of involvement			A				B				C		D	
4 Estimating and planning				A							B			
5 Test specification techniques		A	B											
6 Static test techniques					A		B							
7 Metrics						A			B			C		D
8 Test tools					A			B			C			
9 Test environment			A					B						C
10 Office environment			A											
11 Commitment and motivation		A				B						C		
12 Test functions and training			A				B			C				
13 Scope of methodology				A							B			C
14 Communication			A	B								C		
15 Reporting		A		B			C						D	
16 Defect management		A				B		C						
17 Testware management			A			B				C				D
18 Test process management		A	B									C		
19 Evaluation							A			B				
20 Low-level testing					A		B		C					

Figure C.1: Test process at a low level of maturity.

The other example comes from a test process that has reached the Controlled level. All the A's of the matrix are fulfilled and a majority of the B's as well. This Test maturity matrix shows that the test process has the right instruments to manage and steer the process and keep it under control.

Key area	0	1	2	3	4	5	6	7	8	9	10	11	12	13
		\multicolumn{5}{c	}{Controlled}	\multicolumn{4}{c	}{Efficient}	\multicolumn{3}{c	}{Optimizing}
1 Test strategy		A					B				C		D	
2 Life-cycle model		A			B									
3 Moment of involvement			A				B				C		D	
4 Estimating and planning				A							B			
5 Test specification techniques		A	B											
6 Static test techniques					A		B							
7 Metrics						A			B			C		D
8 Test tools					A			B			C			
9 Test environment				A				B						C
10 Office environment				A										
11 Commitment and motivation		A				B						C		
12 Test functions and training				A			B			C				
13 Scope of methodology				A							B			C
14 Communication			A	B								C		
15 Reporting		A		B			C						D	
16 Defect management		A				B		C						
17 Testware management			A			B				C				D
18 Test process management		A	B									C		
19 Evaluation							A			B				
20 Low-level testing						A	B		C					

Figure C.2: Test process at a Controlled level.

C Appendix: Backwards compatibility

We will use the Levels indicated by A, B, C and D to transform both matrices into a Business Driven TPI matrix.

C.3.3 Working with the conversion table

The Levels A, B, C and D are transformed to the Business Driven TPI Maturity levels by using the next conversion table.

	I Key area	II	III A	III B	III C	III D		IV A	IV B	IV C	IV D
1	Test strategy	SR	C	E	E	O		4	4	6	6
2	Life-cycle model	TM	C	E				4	3		
3	Moment of involvement	SR	C	E	E	E		1	1	1	1
4	Estimating and planning	TM	C	E				2	2		
5	Test specification techniques	TP	C	E				2	3		
6	Static test techniques	SR	E	E				2	1		
7	Metrics	TM	C	E	E	O		3	2	2	2
8	Test tools	TP	C	E	O			3	6	5	
9	Test environment	TP	C	C	E			5	3	1	
10	Office environment	TP	C					2			
11	Commitment and motivation	SR	E	E	O			3	6	4	
11	Commitment and motivation	TP	C		O			3		3	
12	Test functions and training	SR	C	E	N/A			2	6	-	
12	Test functions and training	TM		C	N/A				1	-	
12	Test functions and training	TP	C	C	N/A			2	1	-	
13	Scope of methodology	TP	C	E	O			3	3	2	
14	Communication	SR	C	E				3	7		
14	Communication	TP			O					2	
15	Reporting	SR	C	C	E	O		1	2	4	1
16	Defect management	TM	C	E	E			2	3	2	
17	Testware management	SR		E					1		
17	Testware management	TM	C	E	O	E		3	2	2	2
18	Test process management	TM	C	C				1	4		
18	Test process management	TP			E					3	
19	Evaluation	X	N/A	N/A				-	-		
20	Low-level testing	X	N/A	N/A	N/A			-	-	-	

Figure C.3: Conversion table, from TPI to BDTPI.

The columns of the table are used as follows:
I   The first column contains the Key areas of the original TPI model. Some Checkpoints from a certain Key area cannot be associated with only one single group, so they are split up. Example: Commitment and motivation has elements from Stakeholder relations (the 'commitment' checkpoints) and from Test profession (the 'motivation' checkpoints).

C.3 Transform the original TPI matrix into the Business Driven TPI matrix

II The second column shows the groups of Business Driven TPI:
SR: Stakeholder Relations
TM: Test Management
TP: Test Profession
Each Key area of the original TPI model has a relationship with one of the groups. Note that the Key areas Evaluation and Low level testing do not relate to any group of Business Driven TPI. Their Checkpoints were, where relevant, placed under another Key area in Business Driven TPI (see also sections 7.9 and 7.10).

III The letters A, B, C and D (in the top row) relate to the Levels of the orginal TPI model. The letters C, E and O stand for Controlled, Efficient and Optimizing from the Business Driven TPI model. Each Maturity level can be converted to a group.
Examples:
Test strategy Maturity level A (original TPI model) converts to group Stakeholder relations Maturity level Controlled (C)
Commitment and motivation (the 'motivation' checkpoints) Maturity level A is converted to group Test profession Maturity level Controlled (C).

IV The last column shows the number of Checkpoints belonging to a specific level of maturity (A, B, C or D) and the related Business Driven Maturity level (C, E or O). Each Checkpoint is categorized under one of the Maturity levels of Business Driven TPI.
Example:
Test functions and training has 2 Level A Checkpoints (original TPI model) under Stakeholder relations Maturity level Controlled, 6 level B Checkpoints (original TPI model) under Stakeholder relations Maturity level Efficient, 1 Level B Checkpoint (former TPI model) under Test management Maturity level Controlled and 1 level B Checkpoint (original TPI model) under Test profession Maturity level Controlled.

Note: In this conversion table each Checkpoint has been weighed against its significant conversion from the original TPI model to the Business Driven TPI model. It is possible to convert all matrices manually using the conversion table as shown, but in that case all Checkpoints should be (re)considered. Therefore we provide a tool to support this conversion. The tool is available on the TPI NEXT website (www.tpinext.com).

C.3.4 After conversion

The two examples from the previous section have been transformed into a new Business Driven TPI Test maturity matrix, showing the maturity on the level of the combined Key areas.
Example A, indicating a relatively low level of test process maturity, shows the following maturity in the Business Driven TPI model:

C Appendix: Backwards compatibility

			Initial	Controlled	Efficient	Optimizing
Stakeholder Relations	1	Stakeholder commitment		38%	7%	0%
	2	Degree of involvement				
	3	Test strategy				
	4	Test organization				
	5	Communication				
	6	Reporting				
Test Management	7	Test process management		50%	17%	0%
	8	Estimating and planning				
	9	Metrics				
	10	Defect management				
	11	Testware management				
Test Profession	12	Methodology practice		8%	0%	0%
	13	Tester professionalism				
	14	Test case design				
	15	Test tools				
	16	Test environment				

Figure C.4: Converted matrix to Business Driven TPI, low level of maturity.

The percentages indicate which part of the Maturity level is covered by checks from the original TPI model. The Test management Key areas are relatively well under control, the Test profession Key areas still need a lot of improvement to take them to the Controlled level.

Example B showed a test process well under control and making progress towards the Efficient level. After conversion the matrix looks like this:

			Initial	Controlled	Efficient	Optimizing
Stakeholder Relations	1	Stakeholder commitment		100%	74%	0%
	2	Degree of involvement				
	3	Test strategy				
	4	Test organization				
	5	Communication				
	6	Reporting				
Test Management	7	Test process management		100%	44%	0%
	8	Estimating and planning				
	9	Metrics				
	10	Defect management				
	11	Testware management				
Test Profession	12	Methodology practice		100%	38%	0%
	13	Tester professionalism				
	14	Test case design				
	15	Test tools				
	16	Test environment				

Figure C.5: Converted matrix to Business Driven TPI, Controlled level of maturity.

Both the former and the converted matrix indicate a Controlled level of maturity and also a quite high percentage of efficiency. The high score of Moment of involvement in the original TPI matrix at the Optimizing level contributes to the high score of Stakeholder relations in the new matrix. When a new assessment is performed with Business Driven TPI, the results of that assessment can be compared with this converted matrix to show progress.

Glossary

Acceptance test
A test executed by the user(s) and manager(s) in an environment simulating the operational environment to the greatest possible extent, that should demonstrate that the developed system meets the functional and quality requirements.

Base Cluster arrangement
See: Base Clusters.

Base Clusters
The base Clusters provide an improvement path (of 13 Clusters) from the Initial level up to fully Optimizing in which no single business driver is relevant or leading: the improvement of the test process is regarded as a general improvement process.

BDTM
Business Driven Test Management is aimed at enabling the client to manage the test process on rational and economic grounds. Important BDTM aspects are: result, risk, time and cost.

BDTPI
Business Driven Test Process Improvement, see TPI NEXT.

Business case
Provides the economic justification for the project and answers the questions: why do we do this project, which investments are needed, what does the client wish to achieve with the result?

Business-driven Clusters
The business-driven Clusters are an adapted version of the base Clusters to suit a specific business situation or particular business driver. By first acknowledging which Key areas are more or less relevant to the required bias (e.g. cost, time, quality as a business driver), and secondly by determining how this influences the distribution of the Checkpoints over the Clusters, new Clusters are specified attuned to a specific business driver. In this situation a Cluster may exceed the borders of a Maturity level and contain Checkpoints of multiple Maturity levels. Business-driven Clusters do not change the position of individual Checkpoints in the Test maturity matrix as the position of Checkpoints is fixed.

Glossary

Business driver
A management directive, usually a direct derivative of the organization's vision and/or business strategy, which desires specific outcomes of the organization at an operational level. It is a reason, motivator or challenge for test process improvement, commonly indicated as (a combination of) result, risk, time and cost.

Checkpoint
A Checkpoint is the measuring unit of the (TPI) model. A Checkpoint is phrased as a statement that can be confirmed with a 'yes' or a 'no'. Fulfilling a Checkpoint means that the answer for a specific test process is 'yes', with sufficient proof available to substantiate it. A Checkpoint always relates to one Key area and one Maturity level.

Cluster
A Cluster is a group of Checkpoints from multiple Key areas that function as one improvement step. Clusters are used for the purpose of increasing the maturity of the test process. Each Cluster is identified by an alphabetic letter that identifies its position in the improvement path, where Cluster 'A' is the first improvement step.

Clustering
Partitioning of the TPI Matrix into ordered Clusters, representing an improvement path.

CMMI
Capability Maturity Model Integration (CMMI) is a process improvement approach that provides organizations with the essential elements of effective processes that ultimately improve their performance (see www.sei.cmu.edu/cmmi).

Controlled level
The second level of maturity (after Initial) in the TPI model. It can be expressed as "doing the right things".

Coverage
The ratio between that which can be tested and that which is tested with the test set.

Defect
Any kind of difference between the actual behavior of the test object and the expected behavior.

Defect management
The process of recognizing, investigating, taking action and disposing of defects. It involves recording defects, classifying them and identifying the impact.

Dynamic testing
Testing by execution of the test object and/or the running of software.

Effectiveness
The degree to which the information system meets the demands of the organization and the profile of the end users for whom it is intended, as well as the degree to which the information system contributes to the achievement of business goals.

Efficiency
The relationship between the performance level of the system (expressed in the transaction volume and overall speed) and the amount of resources (CPU cycles, I/O time, memory and network capacity, etc.) that are used.

Efficient level
The third level of maturity (after Initial and Controlled) in the TPI model. It can be expressed as "Doing things the right way".

Enabler
Enablers in the Business Driven TPI model connect Key areas with aspects of the Software Development Life Cycle (SDLC) in order to keep test process improvements aligned with other processes from the SDLC.

End-to-end test
The dynamic test intended to demonstrate that the consecutive series of systems supports the (business) process according to specifications.

Error
Human mistake; this action takes place prior to any defects/faults and/or failures.

Evaluation
Evaluation is assessing the intermediary products in the system development process.

Exploratory Testing
The simultaneous learning, designing and executing of tests, in other words every form of testing in which the tester designs his tests during test execution and the information obtained is reused to design new and improved test cases.

Glossary

Failure
The result or manifestation of one or more defects/faults. When the system is performing differently from the required behavior, from a viewpoint outside the system. Users will see the failure.

Fault
The result of an error residing in the code or document. Fault is the view from inside the system. Fault is the state where mistake or error exists. Developers will see the fault.

Function point analysis (FPA)
A method aiming to measure the size of the functionality of an automated system. The measurement is independent of the technology. This measurement may be used as a base for the measurement of productivity, the estimation of the needed resources, and project control.

Initial level
The first level of maturity in the TPI model. It can be described as "ad hoc activities".

Improvement suggestion
A practice-based and adaptable description of how Checkpoints can be met. Also contains useful hints and tips related to the Key area.

Inspection
A formal evaluation technique, with products being read thoroughly by a group of experts. In addition to determining whether the solution is adequately processed, an inspection focuses primarily on achieving consensus on the quality of a product. The aim of the inspection is to help the author find as many deviations as possible in the available time. This quality improvement process for written material consists of two dominant components; product (document itself) improvement and process improvement (of both document production and Inspection).

Integration test
A test, aimed at proper functioning and interaction of two or more identifiable components.

Key area
Part of the test process that is considered as a combination of coherent aspects.
In order to measure and improve the test process in a more detailed way and step by step, the Business Driven TPI model consists of a set of 16 Key areas. For each Key area, the maturity can be measured separately. The Key areas together cover all aspects of the test process.

Known errors
Defects that have been found but have not been solved (yet).

Logical test case
Describes, in logical terms, the circumstances in which the system behavior is examined by indicating which test situations are covered by the test case.

Master test plan
Test plan by which the various test levels are geared to one another.

Maturity
A software engineering term indicating to which extent it is planned how to do things when testing software.

Maturity category
The extent of maturity indicated by Initial, Controlled, Efficient and Optimizing.

Maturity level
For a specific Key area, the maturity category that has been determined by an assesment or that serves as a goal for future improvement actions. The maturity level of the combination of Key areas defines the maturity of the test process as a whole.

Maturity Matrix
See: Test maturity matrix.

Maturity stage
See: Tool-specific maturity stage.

Metrics
Quantified observations of the characteristics of a product or process used to estimate and manage the test process, to give justification for the test process, to substantiate test advice and to compare systems or processes. Metrics are also important for improving the test process.

Optimizing level
The fourth (and highest) level of maturity in the TPI Model, after Initial, Controlled and Efficient. It can be expressed as; "Continuously adapting to ever-changing circumstances".

Outsourcing
Subcontracting a process, such as product design or manufacturing, to a third-party company. More specific for testing: An organization's test process can be (partly) outsourced to a supplier.

Glossary

Physical test case
The concrete elaboration of a logical test case, with choices having been made for the values of all required inputs and settings of the environmental factors.

Pre-test
Testing the delivered product in such a way that it is determined whether or not the product is of sufficient quality to execute a complete test of this product.

Principal stakeholder
The person responsible for the test assignment and the first in line for test reports.

Product risk
The chance that the product fails in relation to the expected damage if this occurs:
Product risk = Chance of failure * Damage
where Chance of failure = Chance of defects * Frequency of use
A product risk can obstruct the proper functioning of a product (especially an information system). Usually product risks are part of the Test strategy.

Product risk analysis
Analyzing the product to be tested with the aim of achieving a joint view, for the test manager and other stakeholders, of the more or less risky characteristics and parts of the product to be tested so that the thoroughness of testing can be related to this view.

Project risk
A risk that can obstruct the execution of a project in accordance with the plan.
Project risks can apply to the entire project or more specific to the test project.

Quality
The totality of features and characteristics of a product or service that bear on its ability to satisfy stated or implied needs.

Quality assurance
All the planned and systematic activities necessary to provide adequate confidence that a product or service meets the requirements for quality.

Quality characteristic
A property of an information system.

Regression
Regression is the phenomenon that the quality of a system deteriorates as a whole as a result of individual amendments.

Regression test
A regression test is aimed at verifying that all the unchanged parts of a system still function correctly after the implementation of a change.

Return On Investment (ROI)
The ratio of money gained or lost (whether realized or unrealized) on an investment relative to the amount of money invested.

Reliability
The degree to which the information system remains free from interruptions.

Reusability
The degree to which parts of the information system, or the design, can be reused for the development of different applications.

Review
An evaluation technique where a product (60-80% complete) is submitted to a number of reviewers with the question to assess it from a certain perspective (depending on the review type). A review focuses primarily on finding courses for a solution on the basis of the knowledge and competencies of the reviewers, and on finding and correcting defects. There are various review types, such as: technical review (e.g. selecting solution direction/alternative), management review (e.g. determining project status), peer review (review by colleagues), and expert review (review by experts).

Risk reporting
A description of the extent to which the system meets the specified quality requirements and the risks associated, as defined in the product risk, with bringing a particular version into production, including any available alternatives.

Role
Describes one or more tasks and the knowledge and skills required to carry them out.

SDLC
See: Software Development Life Cycle.

Software Development Life Cycle
The Software Development Life Cycle (SDLC), or Systems Development Life Cycle in systems engineering and software engineering, is the process of creating or altering systems, and the models and methodologies that people use to develop these systems. The concept generally refers to computer or information systems.

In software engineering the SDLC concept underpins many kinds of software development methodologies. These methodologies form the framework for planning and controlling the creation of an information system.

SPI
Software Process Improvement, a generic term for models that aim at improving the quality of software and the related processes. Examples are CMMI® and SPICE®.

SPICE®
Software Process Improvement and Capability Determination is based on the international standard ISO/IEC 15504 and is a specific framework for a software process improvement.

Stakeholder
A person who affects and/or can be affected by and/or has an interest in the test process and/or the improvement of the test process.

Static testing
Testing by examining end-products (such as manuals or source code) without any programs being executed.

System integration test
A test carried out by or on behalf of the future user(s) in an optimally simulated production environment, with the aim of demonstrating that (sub)system interface agreements have been met, correctly interpreted and correctly implemented.

System test
A test carried out by the supplier in a (manageable) laboratory environment, with the aim of demonstrating that the developed system, or parts of it, meet with the functional and non-functional specifications and the technical design.

Test basis
The test basis is the information that defines the required system behavior.

Test case
Used to examine whether the system displays the desired behavior under specific circumstances.

Test design technique
A standardized method of deriving test cases from a particular test basis that will achieve a certain coverage.

Test environment
A composition of parts, such as hardware and software, connections, environment data, maintenance tools and management processes in which a test is carried out.

Test goal
A test goal is a success criterion for the test assignment formulated in the language of the client or stakeholder.

Test infrastructure
Consists of the facilities and resources necessary to facilitate the satisfactory execution of the test. A distinction is made between test environments, test tools and workplaces.

Test level
A group of test activities that are managed and executed collectively.

Test line
The operational organization to provide test services to one or more clients. A test line has a fixed team of testers, infrastructure, test tools and standardized work procedures.

Test maturity matrix
A matrix that visualizes the combination of Key areas, Checkpoints and Maturity levels.

Test object
The information system (or part thereof) to be tested.

Test organization
A test organization is the whole of test functions, facilities, procedures, activities, responsibilities and authorities including their relationships.

Test plan
In a test plan the general structure and the strategic choices with respect to the test to be executed are formulated. The test plan forms the scope of reference during the execution of the test and also serves as an instrument to communicate with the client of the test. The test plan is a description of the test project, including a description of the activities and the planning; therefore it is not a description of the tests themselves.

Test point
Unit of measurement for the size of the high-level test to be executed.

Test point analysis (TPA)
A method with the possibility to perform a technology-independent measurement of the test depth level of an information system, on the basis of a function point analysis, and to use this measurement as a basis for a productivity measurement, an estimate of the required resources, and project management.

Test policy
Describes how an organization deals with the people, resources and methods involved with the test process in the various situations.

Test process
The collection of working methods, techniques and tools used to perform a test.

Test Process Improvement
Optimizing quality, costs and lead time of the test process, in relation to the total information services.

Test script
Combines multiple physical test cases to be able to execute them in an efficient and simple manner.

Test situation
An isolated condition under which the test object displays a specific behavior that needs to be tested.

Test strategy
The distribution of the test effort and coverage over the parts to be tested or aspects of the test object aimed at finding the most important defects as early and cheaply as possible.

Test team
A group of people who, led by a test manager, undertake test activities.

Test technique
A set of actions aimed at creating a test deliverable by a universal method.

Test tool
An automated instrument that supports one or more test activities, such as planning, control, specification and execution.

Glossary

Test tool policy
Describes how an organization handles the acquisition, implementation and use of test tools in the various situations.

Test type
A group of test activities with the intention of checking the information system in respect of a number of correlated (part aspects of) quality characteristics.

Test unit
A collection of processes, transactions and/or functions that are tested collectively.

Testability
The ease and speed with which characteristics of the system can be tested (following each adjustment).

Testing
A process that provides insight into, and advice on, quality and the related risks.

Testware
All artifacts that are produced in test activities, such as a test plan, test cases and test report. In TPI NEXT artifacts that are used as input to the test process, like the test basis and the test object, are considered as testware as well. The authorship and ownership of these artifacts lies outside the test team, but as these artifacts are essential to the test process, they are within scope of testware management.

Tool-specific maturity stage
These maturity stages allow for a more specific assesment of the maturity in the use of test tools and provide particular guidance for improving the way a tool is used. Tool-specific maturity stages take into account both the objectives of a tool and how the use of a tool should be incorporated in the testing process. Tool-specific maturity stages have no one-on-one relationship with the Maturity levels.

TPI NEXT
A frame of reference for determining the maturity of an organization's test process and for setting up and implementing specific and realistic measures, based on the business-drivers, for the improvement of this test process.

Glossary

Unit integration test
A test carried out by the developer in the development environment, with the aim of demonstrating that a logical group of units meets the requirements defined in the technical specifications.

Unit test
A test carried out in the development environment by the developer, with the aim of demonstrating that a unit meets the requirements defined in the technical specifications.

Users acceptance test
A test carried out by the future user(s) in an optimally simulated production environment, with the aim of demonstrating that the developed system meets the requirements of the users.

Walkthrough
An evaluation technique by which the author explains the contents of a product during a meeting. Several different objectives are possible: bringing all participants to the same starting point, transfer of information, asking the participants for additional information or letting the participants choose from the alternatives proposed by the author.

Bibliography

[1] Aalst, 2008, TMap NEXT BDTM
Aalst, L van der, Baarda, R., Roodenrijs, E., Vink, J., Visser, B., (2008), TMap NEXT® Business Driven Test Management, Tutein Nolthenius, 's-Hertogenbosch, ISBN 90-72194-92-6

[2] ASL
A Framework relating Application Management Processes and categorizing best practices, maintained by the ASL BiSL Foundation

[3] Beizer, 1990
Beizer, B. (1990), Software Testing Techniques, International Thomson Computer Press

[4] [BiSL]
A process model relating ICT and Business Processes and their mutual relations, maintained by the ASL BiSL Foundation

[5] Boehm, 1981
Boehm, B.W., Software Engineering Economics, Prentice-Hall Inc., Englewood Cliffs, ISBN 0-13-822122-7

[6] CMMI
Capability Maturity Model Integration (CMMI®) in software engineering and organizational development is a process improvement approach that provides organizations with the essential elements for effective process improvement. CMMI is owned by the Software Engineering Institute at the Carnegy Mellon Univerity.

[7] Crispin, 2009
Crispin, L., Gregory, J. (2009), Agile Testing, a Practical Guide for Testers and Agile Teams, Addison Wesley, ISBN 978-0-321-53446-0

[8] Deming, 1992
Deming, W. Edwards (1992), Out of the crisis, University of Cambridge, ISBN 0-521-30553-5

[9] DSDM
Dynamic Systems Development Method (DSDM®) is a rapid developing method, based on time boxing and active participation of users.

[10] ISO/IEC Guide 2, 1991
(Testing ISO), Definition of testing: Technical operation that consists of the determination of one or more characteristics of a given product, process or service according to a specified procedure.

[11] ISTQB
The International Software Testing Qualifications Board (ISTQB): It is the ISTQB's role to support a single, universally accepted, international qualification scheme, aimed at software and system testing professionals, by providing the core syllabi and by setting guidelines for accreditation and examination for national boards.

[12] ITGI
The IT Governance Institute (ITGI): Identifying and aligning business goals and IT-goals.

[13] ITIL
Information Technology Infrastructure Library (ITIL), A set of concepts and policies for managing information technology, (IT) infrastructure, development and operations, owned by OGC (Office of Government Commerce) in Great Britain.

Bibliography

[14] Kaner, 1999
Kaner, C., Falk, J., Nguyen, H.Q. (1999), Testing Computer Software, 2nd edition, Wiley, ISNB 0-471-35846-0

[15] Kit, 1995
Kit, E. (1995), Software Testing in the Real World, Addison Wesley, ISBN 0-201-87756-2

[16] Koomen, 1999, TPI
Koomen, T., Pol, M. (1999), Test Process Improvement (TPI®): a practical, step-by-step guide to structured testing, Addison Wesley, London, ISBN 0-210-59624 5

[17] Koomen, 2006, TMap NEXT
Koomen, T., Aalst van der, L., Broekman, B., Vroon, M. (2006), TMap® NEXT for result-driven testing, Tutein Nolthenius, 's-Hertogenbosch, ISBN 90-72194-79-4

[18] Moerman, 2006
Moerman, R., (2006), InFraMe®, Structuur en voorspelbaarheid in IT-infrastructuur projecten (Structure and Predictability in IT Infrastructure Projects) Sdu Uitgevers, Den Haag, ISBN 90-12-11770-4

[19] Pettichord, 2000
Pettichord, B., (2000), Testers and Developers Think Differently, Article in Software Testing and Quality Engineering Magazine

[20] Pettichord, 2002
Pettichord, B., Bach, J., Kaner, C. (2002), Lessons Learned in Software Testing, John Wiley & Sons Inc.

[21] RUP
The Rational Unified Process (RUP) is an iterative software development process framework, created by the Rational Software Corporation (currently part of IBM).

[22] SCRUM
Scrum is an iterative incremental framework for managing complex work commonly used with Agile software development.

[23] Smit, 2009
Smit, R., Baarda, R., End-to-end testing with TMap NEXT® (2009), UTN Publishers, ISBN 90-89072-194-961

[24] SPICE
ISO/IEC 15504, also known as SPICE (Software Process Improvement and Capability Determination), is a "framework for the assessment of processes"

[25] Watts, 2000
Watts S. Humphrey, Introduction to the Team Software Process, Addison Wesley, ISBN 0-201-47719-X

About Sogeti

Sogeti Group
Sogeti is a leading provider of professional technology services, specializing in Application Management, Infrastructure Management, High-Tech Engineering and Testing. Working closely with its clients, Sogeti enables them to leverage technological innovation and achieve maximum results. Sogeti brings together more than 20,000 professionals in 14 countries and is present in over 200 locations in Europe, the US and India. Sogeti is a wholly-owned subsidiary of Cap Gemini S.A., listed on the Paris Stock Exchange.

Quality assurance and testing services
Sogeti is a world leader in innovative, business-driven quality assurance and testing services. As independent and objective testing specialists, our clients benefit from the identifiable results from our onshore and offshore cost-effective testing solutions: Managed Testing Services, TMap®-based project and program testing, and TPI® - test process improvement. As the largest testing service provider in Europe and USA, with over 2,800 test professionals and a further 5,000 application specialists with test experience, in 14 countries worldwide, we help organizations achieve their testing and QA goals.

For more information, please visit: www.sogeti.com

Index

A
acceptance test 70, 142
ad hoc testing 33
agile development 191, 193, 195, 197, 199
agile testing 122
ASL 135, 205
automated test execution 251
automated test execution tool 256 - 257
awareness 140

B
backwards compatibility 269 - 270, 272, 274
balancing clusters 266
base cluster 52, 151, 203, 262
BDTPI 235
BDTPI model 269
benchmark 51
benefits of evaluation 229
best-case picture 242
BiSL 135, 205
Boehm 226
BOOTSTRAP 207
bottom-up approach 141
boundary value analysis 124
budget 59, 92, 100
business case 66
business continuity 159
Business Driven TPI 36, 41, 52, 235
Business Driven TPI model 273
business driver 32, 53, 140, 142, 159 - 160, 163, 243
business value 29
business-driven cluster 53

C
capability level 213
capability model 212
change management 61, 134, 168, 172
change process 139
change request 60, 65
checklist 228
checkpoint 42, 49, 148
client environment 132
cluster 24, 42, 52
CMMI 62, 207 - 208, 212, 215
CMMI maturity level 214
communication 44, 78, 155, 164, 190
completion 87
configuration management 111, 172
continuous 213
continuous model 52
controlled 37, 42, 47, 49

conversion table 272 - 273
cost reduction 159
coverage 164
creating new clusters 261 - 262, 264, 266
critical path 47, 169 - 170, 248
current situation 36, 41, 51, 53

D
data driven 256
defect detection percentage 102
defect detection ratio 184
defect introduction rate 102
defect life cycle 105
defect lifecycle 104
defect management 45, 103, 167, 174, 178
defect management tool 105
defect meeting 104
degree of involvement 43, 63, 167, 170, 174, 194
Deming's cycle 48
dependency 264
design process 123 - 124
design technique 121
development method 114
development test 34
development testing 70, 223, 225
disaster recovery test 164
document study 240
driver 232
DTAP model 133

E
effectiveness increase 159
efficient 37, 42, 47, 49
enabler 24, 55, 150, 211
end product 227
end-to-end test 190, 231
end-to-end testing 73
equivalence class 124
estimating and planning 45, 92, 170, 178
evaluation 166, 227, 229
evaluation strategy 230
evaluation technique 230
execution 87
exploratory testing 121, 188, 190 - 191

F
function point analysis 94
functional design 65
functional maintenance 206
functional regression test tool 168

291

Index

G
generic master test plan 222
generic test agreement 222
grouping of key areas 270
guideline 113

H
HRM 118
human resource management 118

I
IEC 15504 210
impact analysis 65
implementation 153
improvement suggestion 42, 54
incident management 104, 125
indicator 183, 185
initial 42, 47
initial level 49, 203
inspection 125, 228
integration 230 - 231, 233
integration strategy 232
integration test 231 - 232
integrator 233
interdependency between checkpoints 264
intermediary product 227
interview 239
ISO 210
ISTQB 13, 28
IT goal 160 - 161, 163
iterative software development 187
ITIL 135, 205

K
key area 42, 148, 213
keyword driven 257

L
logical test case 122
low level test 66

M
maintenance 41
managed test services 220 - 221
mandate 89
maturity level 37, 47, 213
maturity model 212
measurement and analysis 71, 97
methodology practice 45, 113, 115, 202
metrics 45, 88, 96, 178 - 179, 183, 202
mindset 192, 224
model based testing 124
moment of involvement 63

O
offshoring 217, 219
optimizing 37, 42, 48 - 49
original TPI model 273
outsourcing 217, 219

overall test strategy 222

P
peer review 228
performance test tool 127, 258 - 259
permanent test organization 220
planning 87
precondition 58
preparation 87
principal stakeholder 29, 58, 64, 68
problem management 104
process area 213
process management 66, 71
process quality 103
product quality 78, 103
product risk 29, 67, 83, 85
product risk analysis 59, 67 - 69, 73, 170, 195
progress 83
project closure report 90
project management 59, 64 - 65, 70, 79, 84, 88, 93, 95, 104, 168, 172
project planning 64
project risk 67, 83, 87, 90

Q
quality assurance 59, 88, 119
quality management 120
quality measure 29, 119
query tool 127

R
ratio 92
re-clustering 262 - 263, 265, 267
record & playback 127, 129, 256
record & playback test tool 256
regression test 68 - 69, 110, 129, 188, 195, 233
release advice 83
release management 134, 176
reporting 44, 83, 164, 177, 185, 202, 204
requirement 29, 65
requirements lifecycle management 168
requirements management 111
resources 59
review 228
risk management 68

S
sandbox environment 227
scope 142
SDLC 55, 61
self-assessment 237
service catalogue 136
service level agreement 135
short checkpoint notation 264
software development life cycle 30, 55, 72
software maintenance 205
software process improvement 35, 62, 86, 207
specification 87

Index

SPI 35, 207
SPICE 207, 210, 212
stakeholder 43, 58, 68, 78, 140, 194
stakeholder commitment 164, 189, 202
stakeholder management 81
stakeholder relations 43
static analysis 228
static testing 227
stepwise improvement 24
structured approach 33
stub 127, 232
subject matter expertise 122
SWOT analysis 150
system test 70, 142

T
target situation 53
technical review 228
template 113
test assignment 64
test automation 73
test basis 34, 100, 109
test case design 46, 121, 167, 170, 190
test coverage 68, 121, 123, 129, 188
test data 132, 173
test depth 67 - 68
test design technique 70, 118, 123, 125, 167, 188
test driven development 122
test effectiveness 125
test engineering skills 117
test environment 34, 46, 132, 165, 170, 173, 197
test execution tool 251, 256
test function 72
test goal 69, 85
test level 31, 68, 143, 200, 225
test management 43
Test Management Approach (TMap) 24
test management skills 117
test management tool 127, 251, 253, 255
test maturity matrix 37
Test maturity matrix 50
test method 113
test modeling tool 127
test object 34
test organization 44, 72, 174
test outsourcing 217
test plan 87 - 88
test point analysis 94
test policy 76, 130
test process management 44, 87, 92, 177, 202
test profession 43
test strategy 44, 59, 67, 121, 167, 170, 173, 177, 189, 195, 202, 204
test tools 46, 127, 129, 170, 173 - 175, 251
test type 68
testability review 63, 94, 229
test-driven development 191

tester professionalism 46, 117, 167, 196
testing 28
testware management 45, 108, 121, 165, 190, 196, 223
time to market 159, 168
TMap 24
TMap NEXT 28
tool policy 130
tool-specific maturity stage 251
TPI NEXT website 273
traceability 110
transparency 176
transparency improvement 159
trend analysis 105
Trillium 207
types of tool 253

U
unit integration test 225
unit test 225

V
version management 109
V-model 30

W
walkthrough 125, 228
waterfall development 187
working agreements 133
worst-case picture 242

293